Seventies Spotting Days Around Yorkshire & the North East

Strathwood

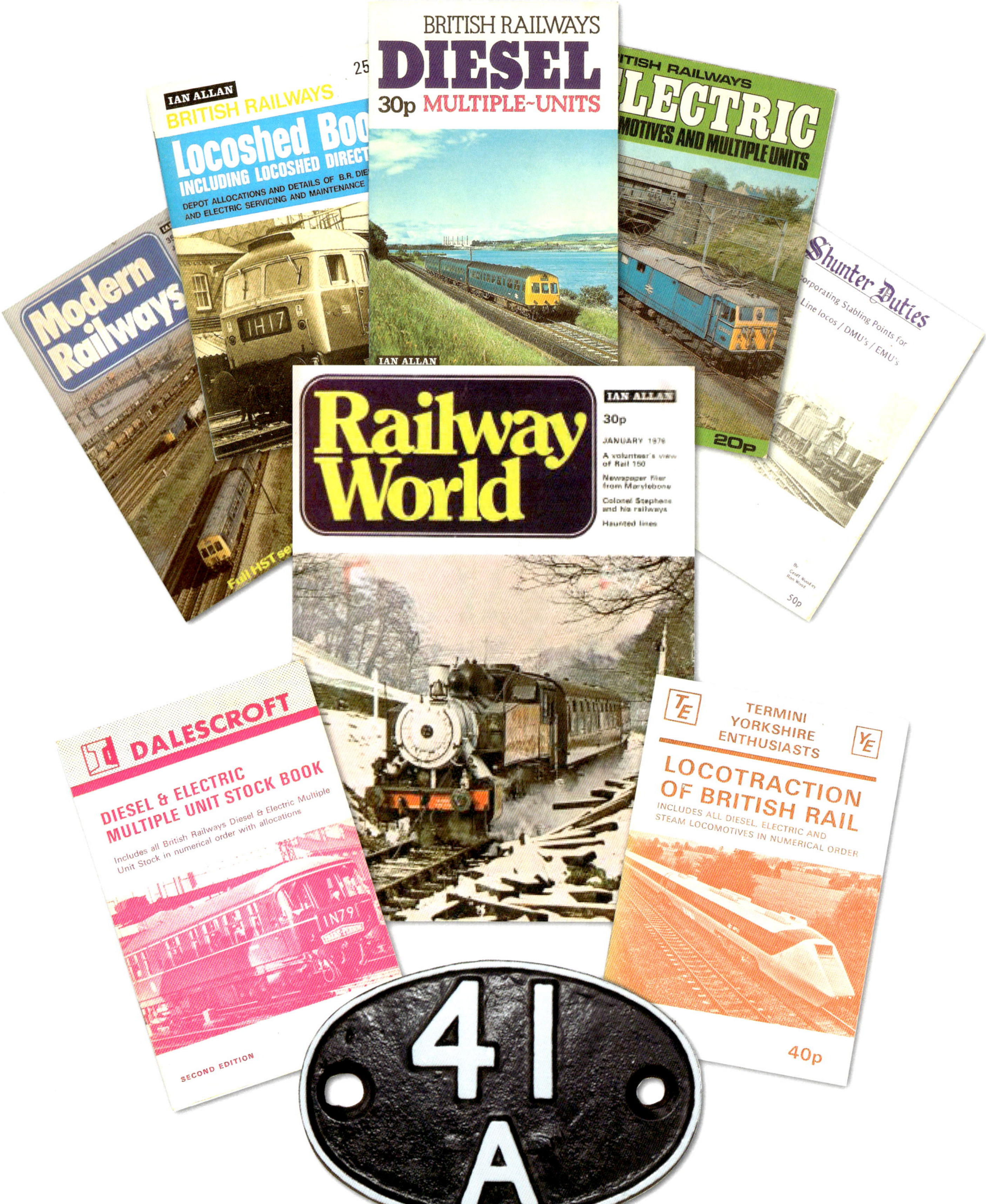
Modern Railways
IAN ALLAN
BRITISH RAILWAYS
Locoshed Boo
INCLUDING LOCOSHED DIRECT
DEPOT ALLOCATIONS AND DETAILS OF B.R. DIE
AND ELECTRIC SERVICING AND MAINTENANCE
BRITISH RAILWAYS
DIESEL
30p MULTIPLE-UNITS
IAN ALLAN
ELECTRIC
MOTIVES AND MULTIPLE UNITS
20p
Shunter Duties
50p
Railway World
IAN ALLAN
30p
JANUARY 1976
A volunteer's view of Rail 150
Newspaper flier from Marylebone
Colonel Stephens and his railways
Haunted lines
DALESCROFT
DIESEL & ELECTRIC MULTIPLE UNIT STOCK BOOK
Includes all British Railways Diesel & Electric Multiple Unit Stock in numerical order with allocations
SECOND EDITION
TERMINI YORKSHIRE ENTHUSIASTS
LOCOTRACTION OF BRITISH RAIL
INCLUDES ALL DIESEL, ELECTRIC AND STEAM LOCOMOTIVES IN NUMERICAL ORDER
40p
41 A

Seventies Spotting Days Around Yorkshire & the North East

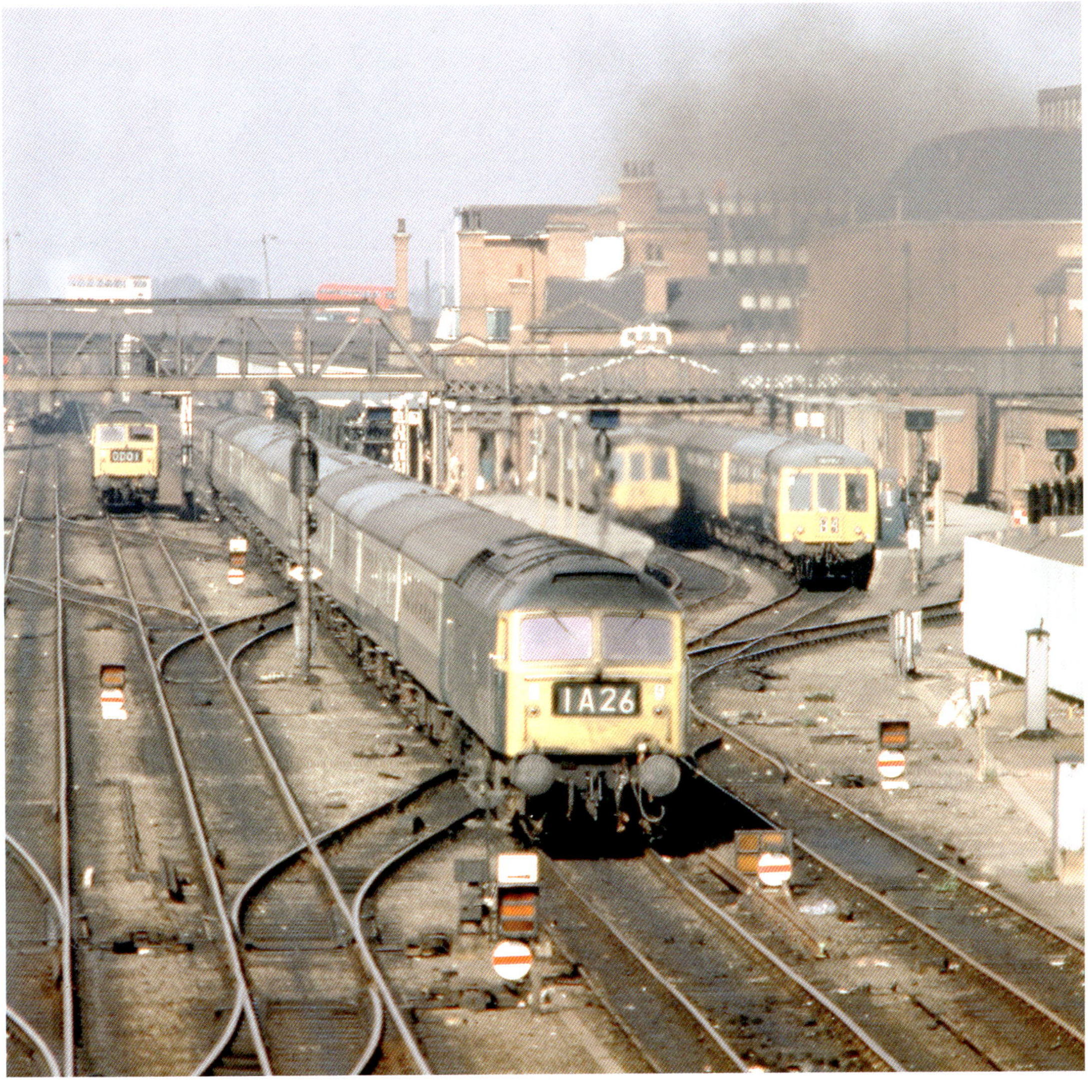

Cover: It is a busy station as 47458 departs Doncaster with the 13.25 Leeds to Kings Cross on 16 September 1975. ***Barrie Watkins/Strathwood Library Collection***

Kevin Derrick

Strathwood

Seventies Spotting Days Around Yorkshire & the North East

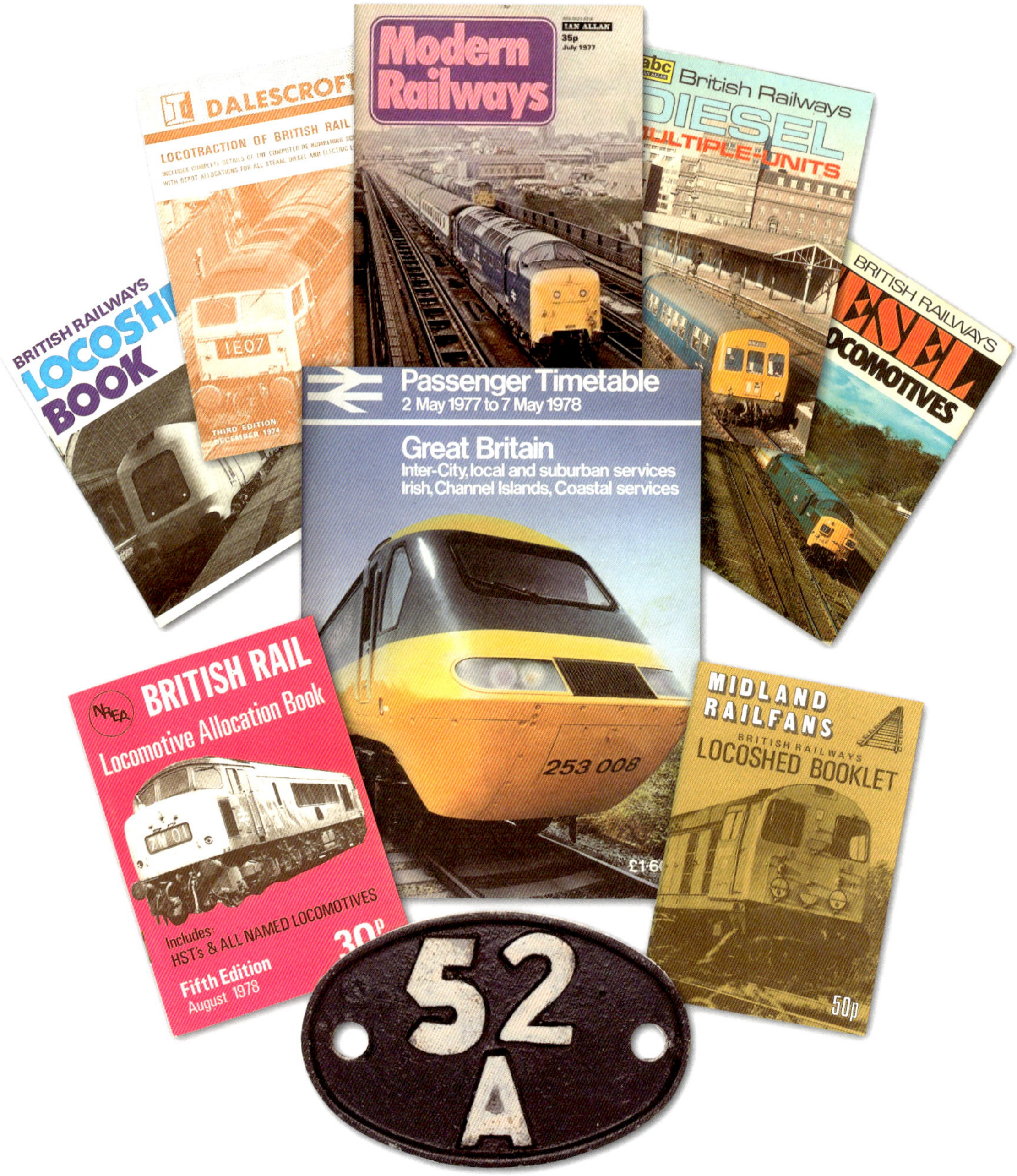

First published 2012

ISBN 1-905276-58-3
ISBN 978-1-905276-58-5

Published by Strathwood Ltd, Glenavon House, Kinchurdy Road,
Boat of Garten, Inverness-shire, PH24 3BP. Tel 01479 831139
Proudly printed in Great Britain

Contents

Page

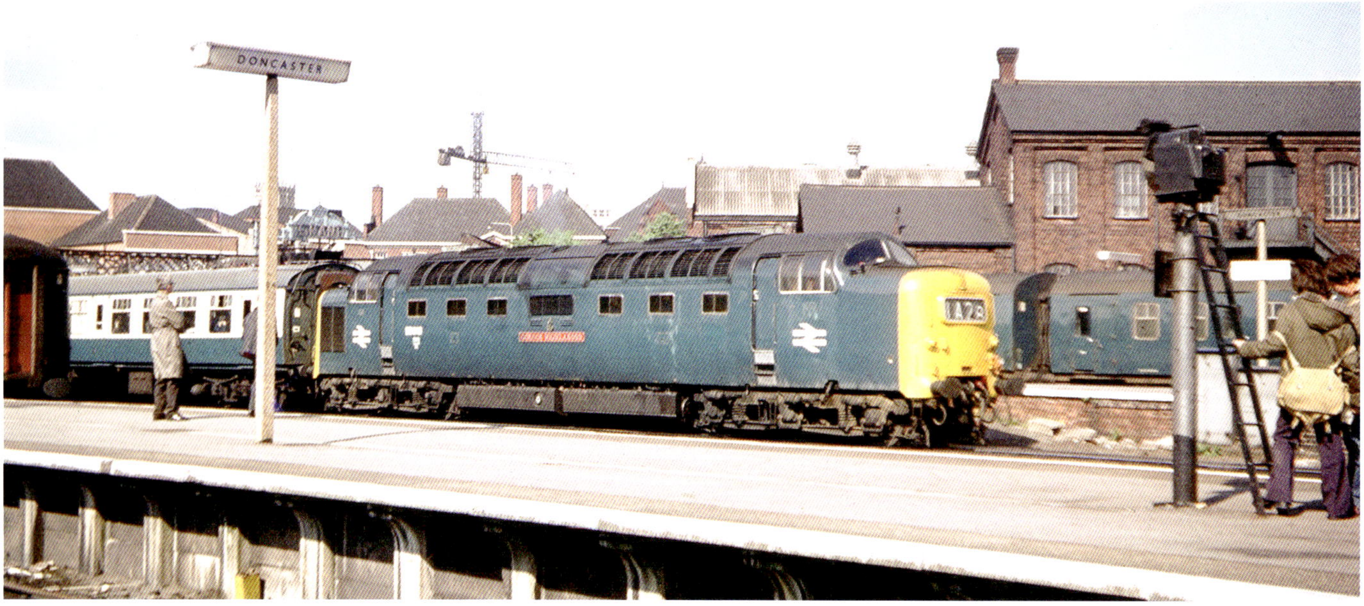

On 29 May 1974 Sugar Baby Love from The Rubettes was at number one and 55016 Gordon Highlander was making it's own music from the twin Napier Deltic engines as it awaited departure south from Doncaster. ***Strathwood Library Collection***

Introduction

The extensive rail network of Yorkshire and North East had been born out the optimism of the pre-grouping companies moving large quantities of coal and goods, supplemented by passenger revenues. It was also the cradle of the railways with the Stockton & Darlington Railway leading the world. By the start of the 1970s it was a very different affair as already many routes had lost their passenger services, this was in spite of many locations not being served with an adequate bus service. The main east coast route from London to Newcastle and Scotland by road was although a major road was far from the A1 we enjoy today. Thus it was that many would still rely on the train for any longer journeys. The heavy industry on Tyneside and Teeside would continue to contract whilst the following decade of the eighties would see the coal mines decimated.

As a spotter active during the 1970s we enjoyed a wide variety of locomotive types maintained by a large workforce based out of a huge number of depots, stabling points and works. Maybe we took it for granted that it would always be there, but the changing traffic patterns and combined with contemporary government policy soon put paid to the railway network we once knew.

Today the East Coast Main Line is fit for bursting once again with a large increase in passenger numbers attracted by the much faster journey times since the arrival of HSTs and electrification where line speeds mean the paths for freight have to be carefully worked out and even preserved steam and diesels with excursions have to get a sprint on to keep out of their way.

So thanks to the kindness of our picture contributors we can go back in time once more to the seventies and as elsewhere in this collectable series cast our minds back to news and events of the time.

Kevin Derrick
Boat of Garten 2012

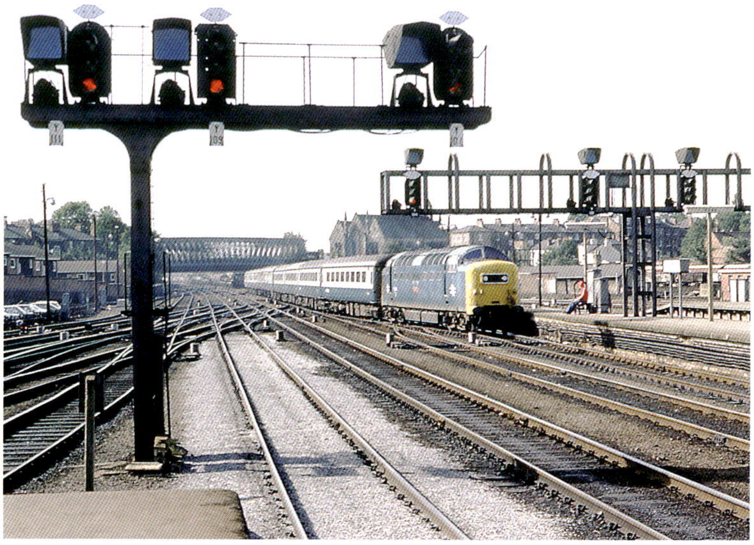

Drawing gently into York with a semi-fast from the south in September 1978 was 55009 Alycidon. ***David T Williams***

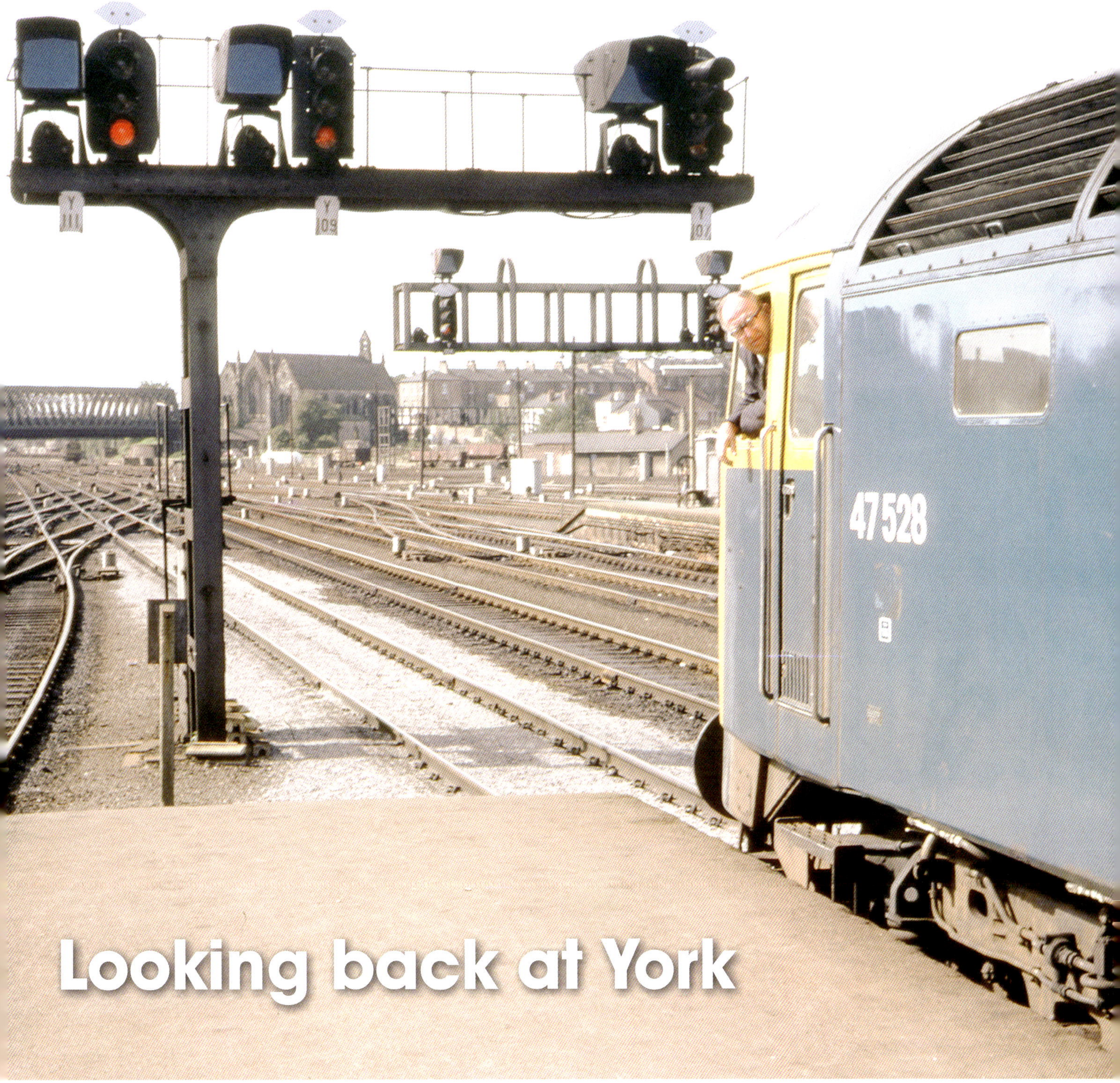

Looking back at York

The driver of this southbound departure from York looks back for some signals from the platform staff having backed his steed 47528 onto the coaching stock in September 1978. The first York railway station was a temporary wooden building on Queen Street outside the walls of the city, opened in 1839 by the York and North Midland Railway. It was succeeded in 1841, inside the walls, by what is now York old railway station. In due course, the irksome requirement that through trains between London and Newcastle needed to reverse out of the old York station in order to continue their journey necessitated the construction this new through station outside the walls. It was designed by the North Eastern Railway architects Thomas Prosser and William Peachey, and opened in 1877. It had 13 platforms and was at that time the largest station in the world. As part of the new station project, the Royal Station Hotel (now The Royal York Hotel), designed by Peachey, opened in 1878.

In 1909 new platforms were added, and in 1938 the current footbridge was built and the station resignalled. The building was damaged during the Second World War and extensively repaired in 1947. The track layout seen here through and around the station was remodelled again in 1988 as part of the resignalling scheme that was carried out prior to the electrification of the ECML shortly afterwards. ***David T Williams***

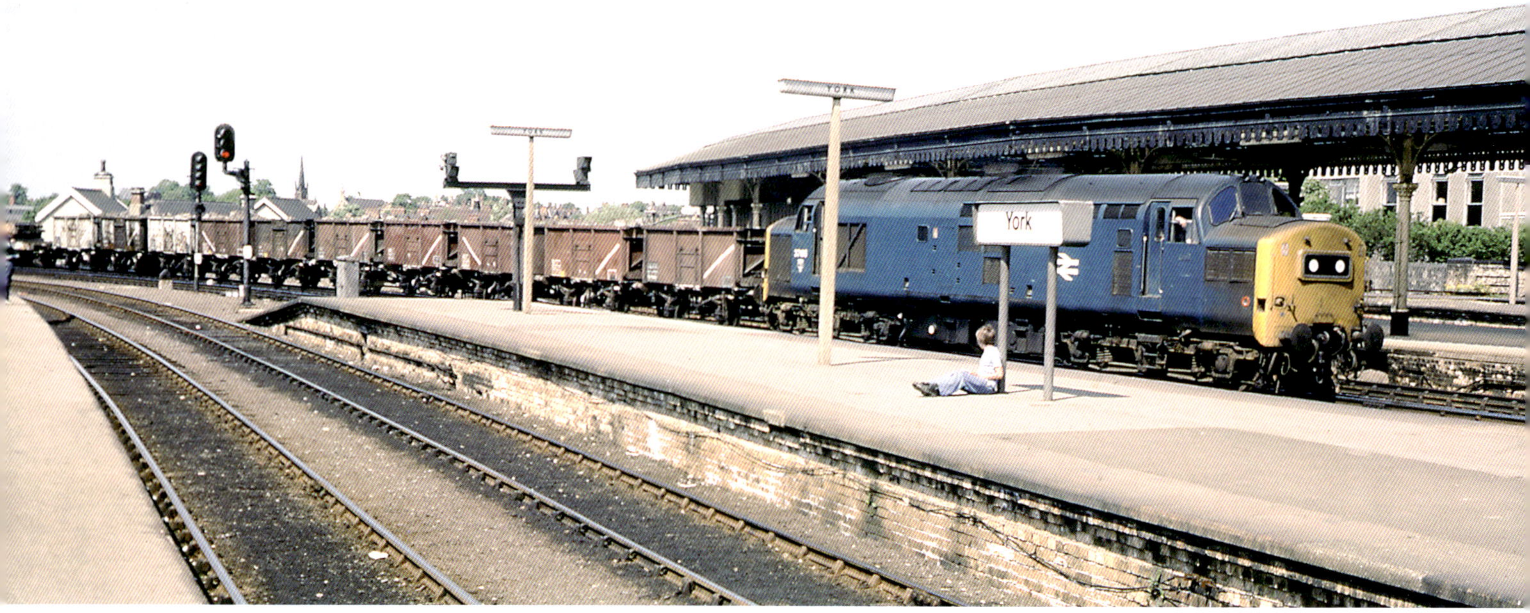

Two spotters are on hand in the summer sunshine of July 1978 as 37165 from Thornaby wanders through with a rake of empty mineral wagons from the north. ***David T Williams***

Ready for departure with a semi fast service on 17 June 1978 was 55013 The Black Watch which was still based at Haymarket at the time, although a transfer to York would come the foolowing May. Born on this day was James Corden, who would go on and find fame as one of the writers and stars of Gavin & Stacey on television twenty nine years later. ***Phil Bidwell***

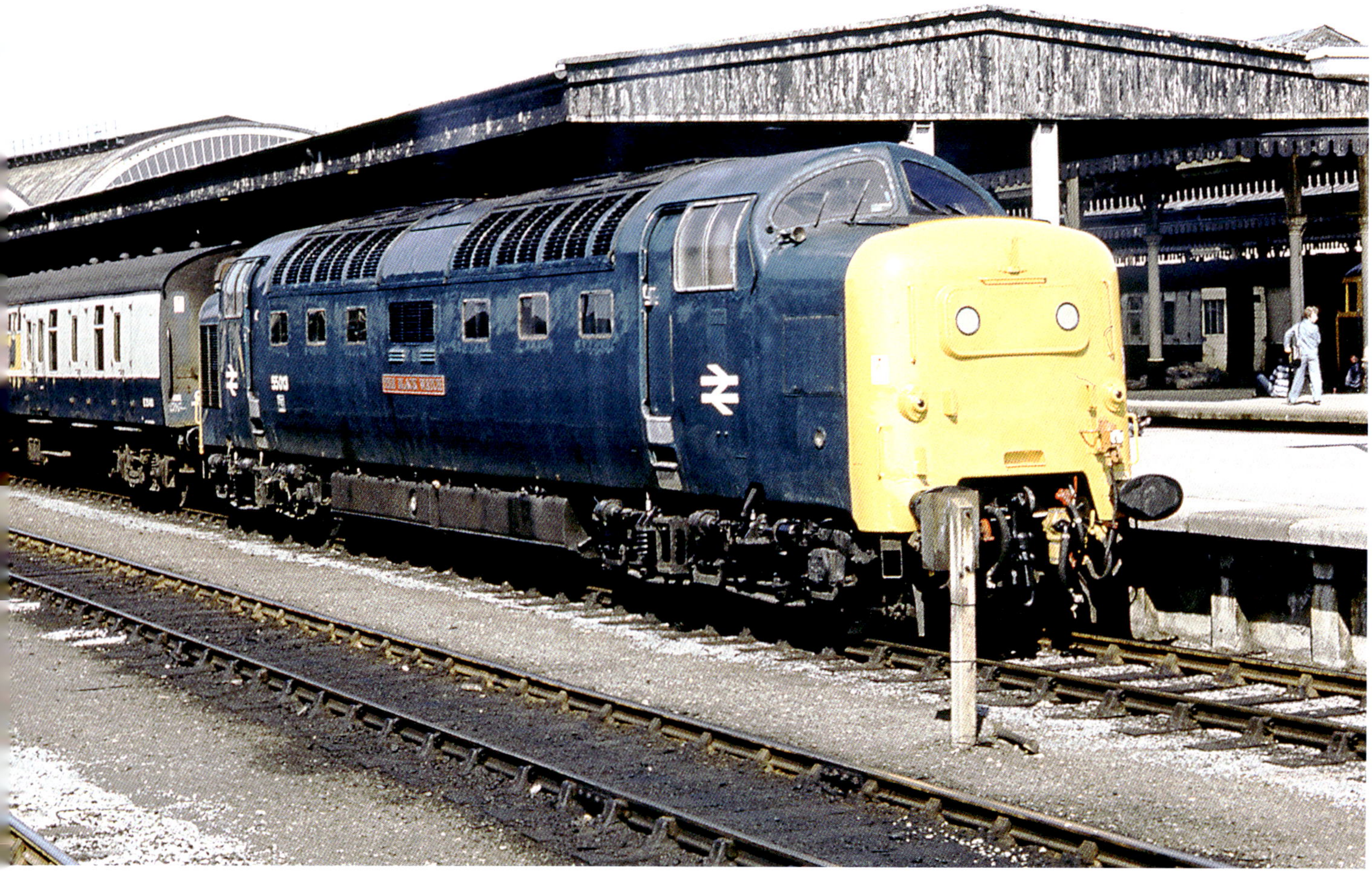

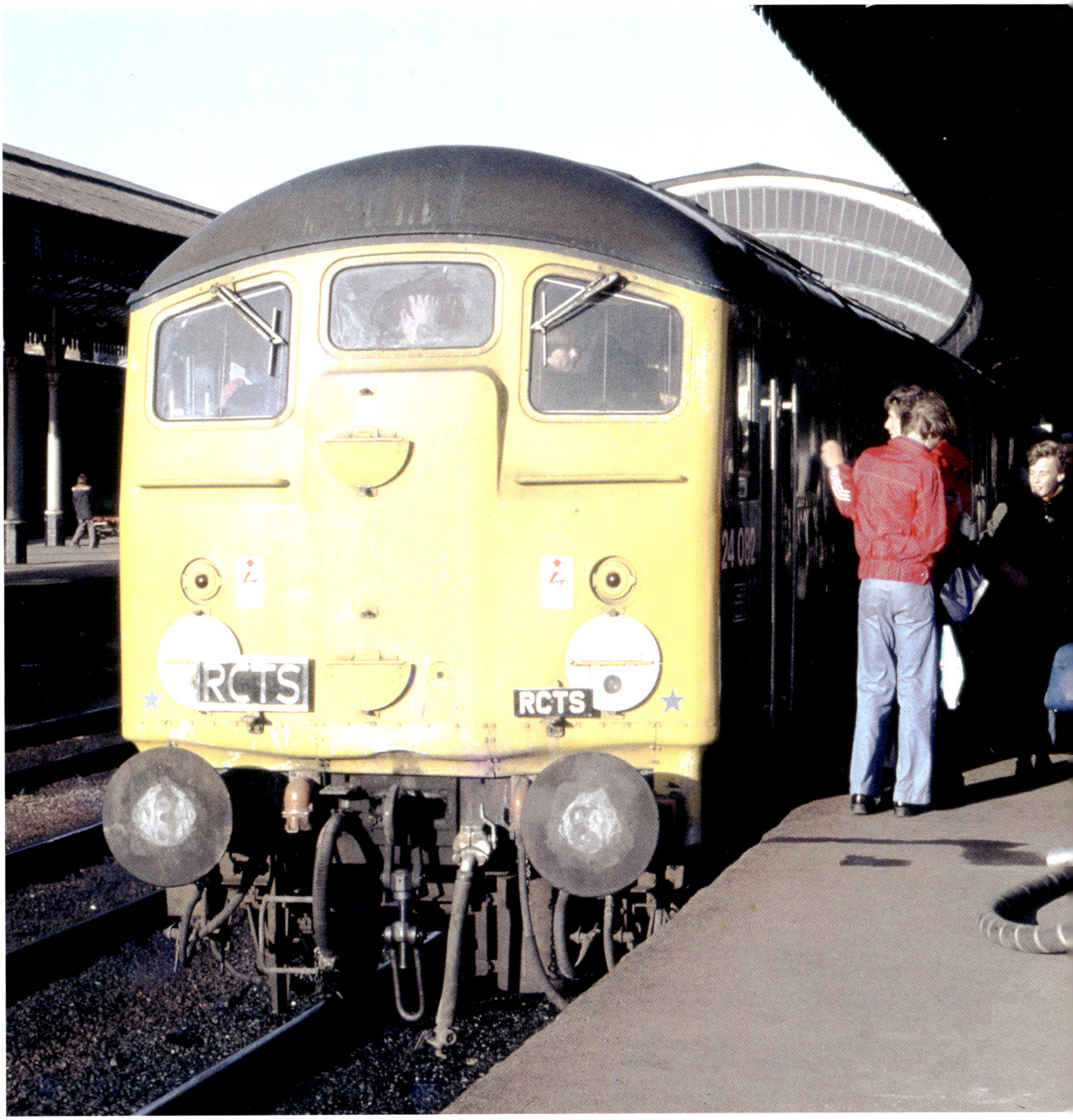

On 1 October 1977 the RCTS ran their Roses No. 2 from Crewe using the pairing of two of the last serviceable Class 24s, 24133 and 24082. Travelling outwards via Stockport, Guide Bridge, Woodhead, Sheffield Victoria, Tinsley, Rotherham, Doncaster, and Knottingley to arrive here at York where a three hour plus stop was made to allow participants to visit the museum, bunk the shed or linger around the station platforms. The return journey departed at teatime via Wakefield, Blackburn, Manchester Victroia and Stockport arriving back at Crewe at 20.44, after a fascinating round trip of almost 262 miles behind doubleheaded Class 24s. Anyone fancy it today if it were possible passing all of those stabling points and depots? ***Bruce Smetham***

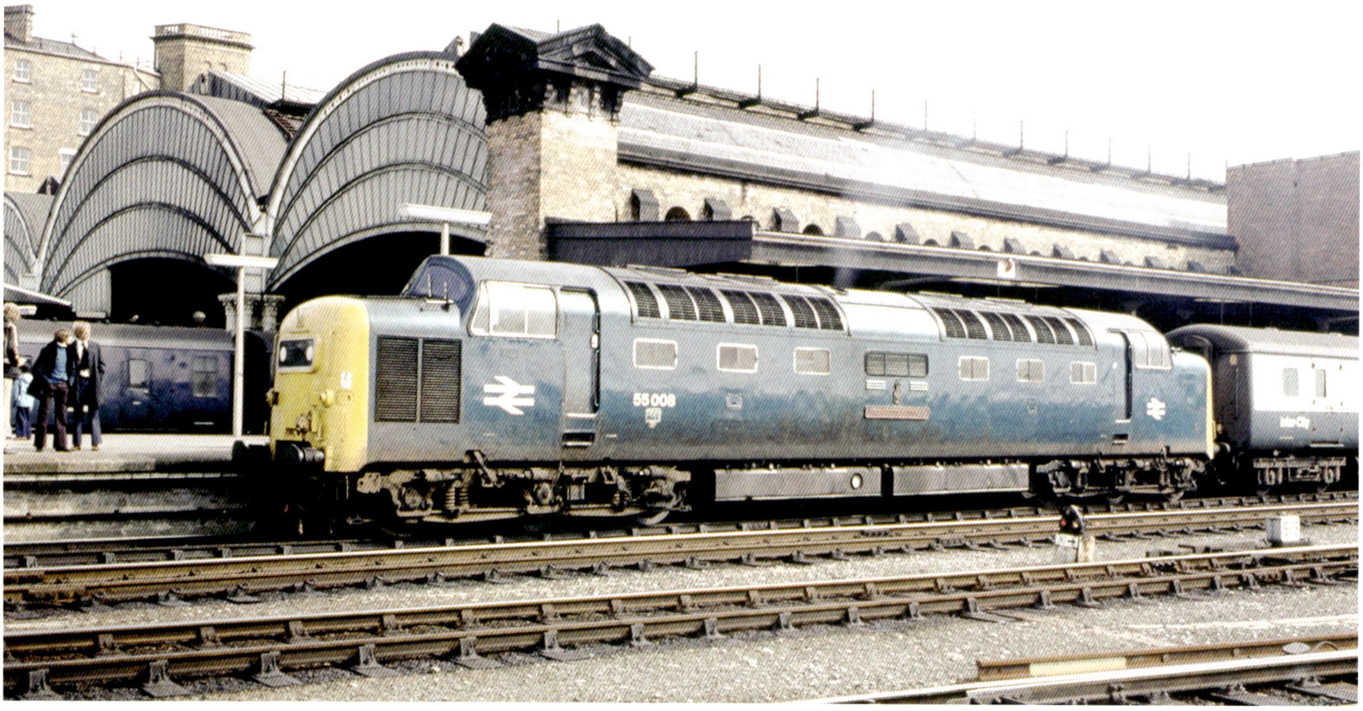

Spotters are on hand as usual back then on York's platforms to greet 55008 The Green Howards as it works a Kings Cross to Aberdeen service on 9 April 1977. ***John Arthur Bennett/Strathwood Library Collection***

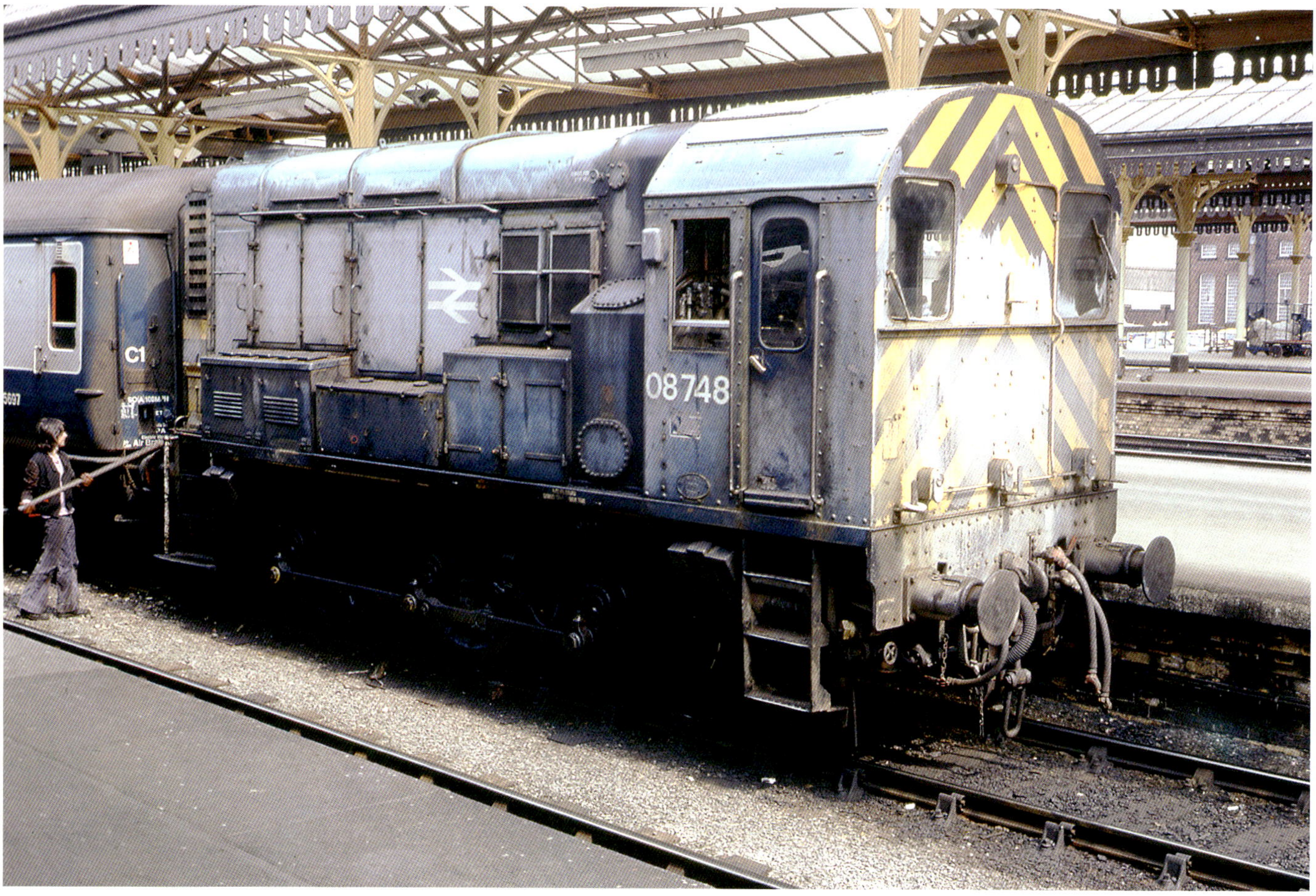

A somewhat bleached 08748 acts as station pilot in August 1979, no doubt the faded paintwork was attributable to this shunters time based at the Leeds depot of Neville Hill and working coaching stock through the washer there. ***David T Williams***

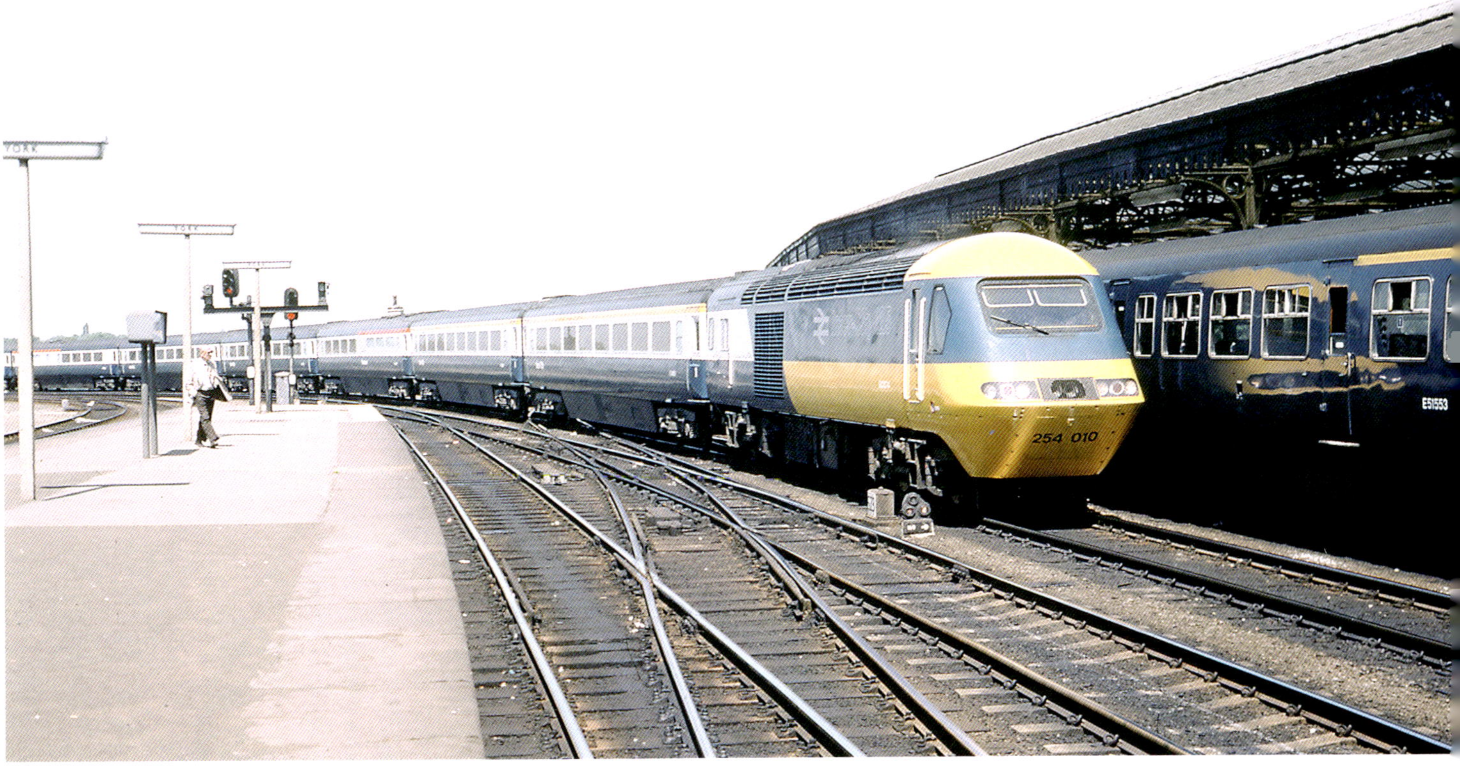

A Metropolitan Cammell DMU sits in the adjacent road as 254010 led by E43074 draws in from the north during July 1978.

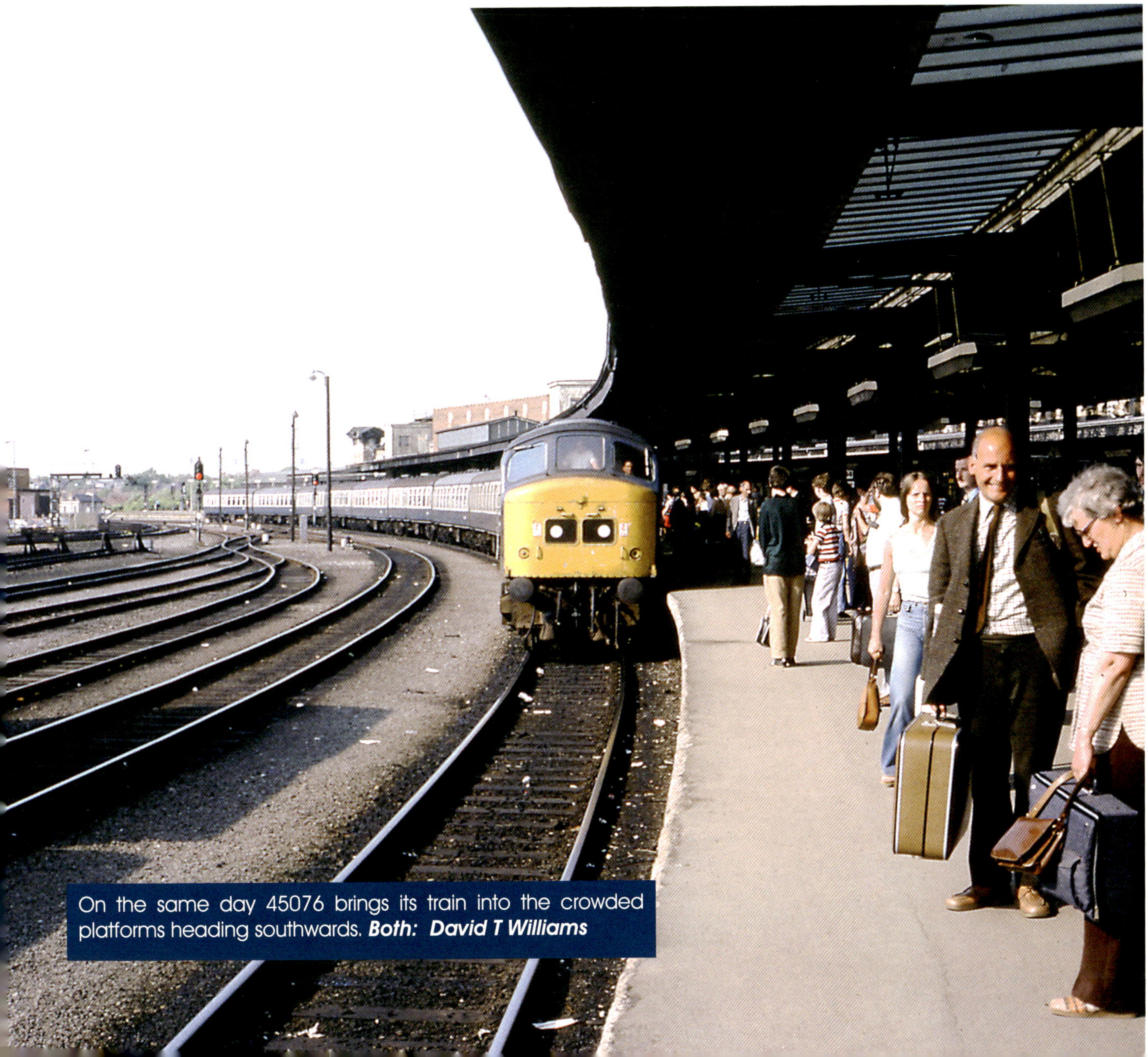

On the same day 45076 brings its train into the crowded platforms heading southwards. ***Both: David T Williams***

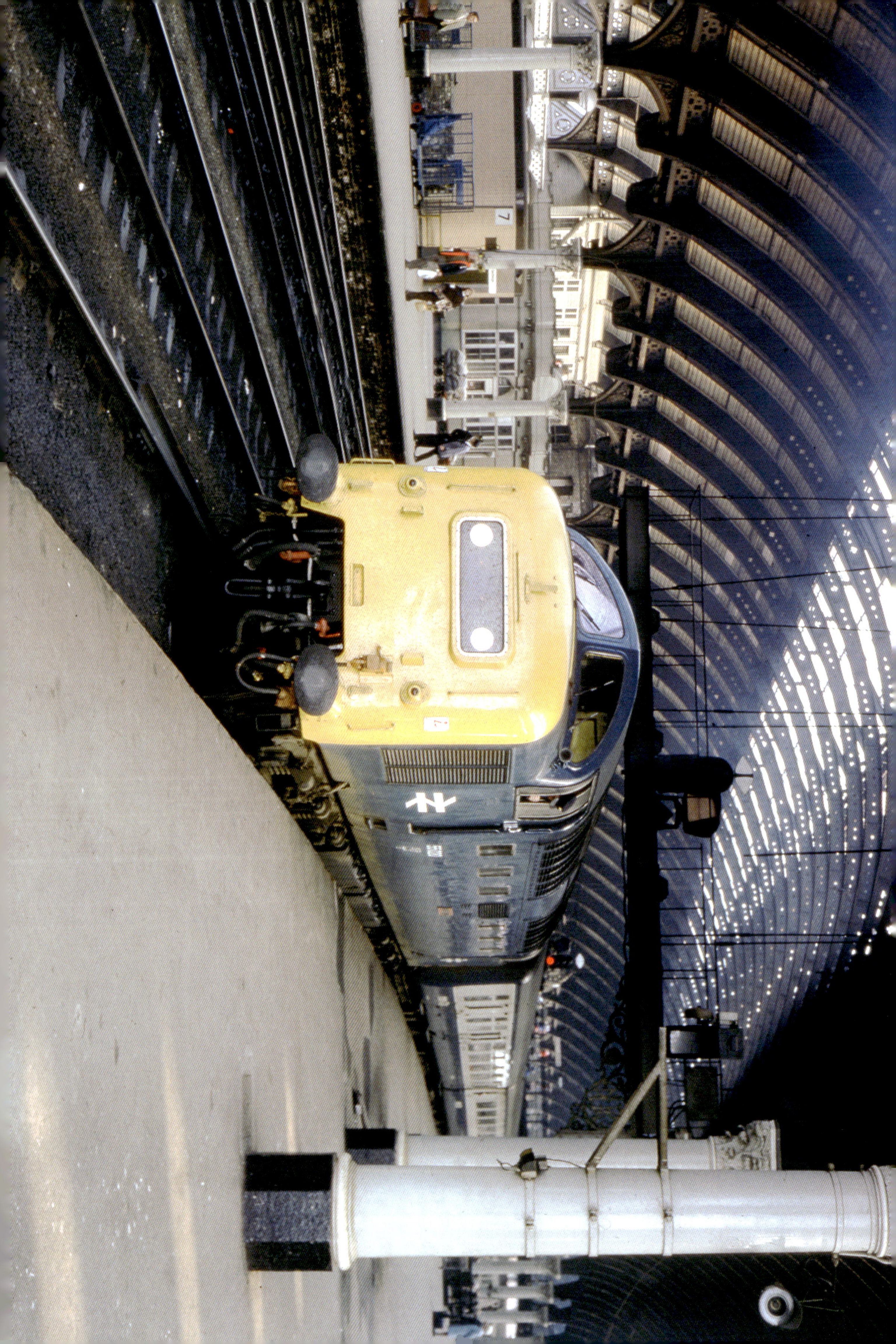

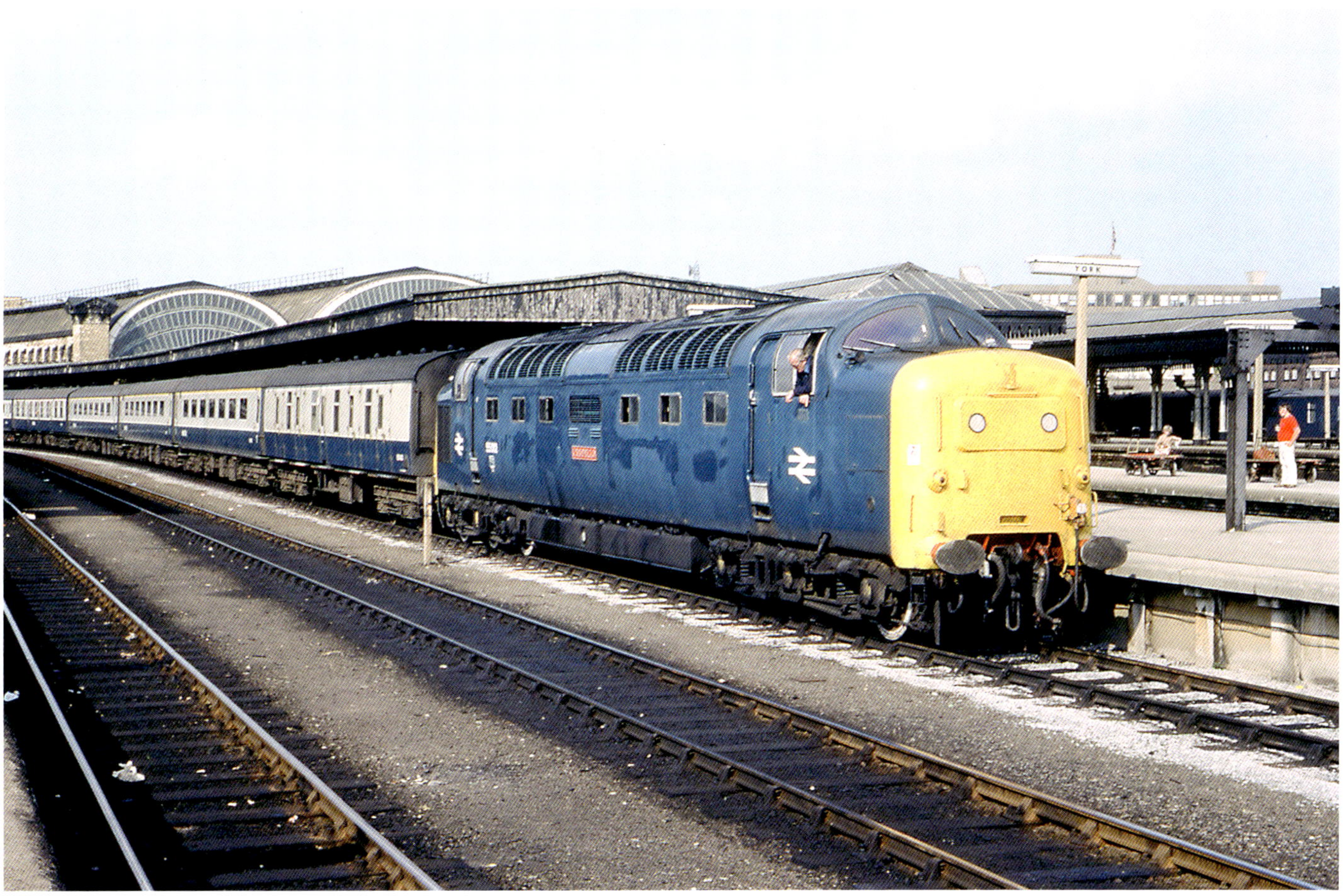

The driver on board 55012 Crepello leans out of his hot cab for a breath of a breeze in the summer of 1978. The crude patch repainting of this magnificent locomotive's flanks lets its appearance down considerably.

The high level former four digit headcode has been plated over on E51559 as the lead car in this rake sending up exhaust fumes into the glass panelled roof in July 1978.

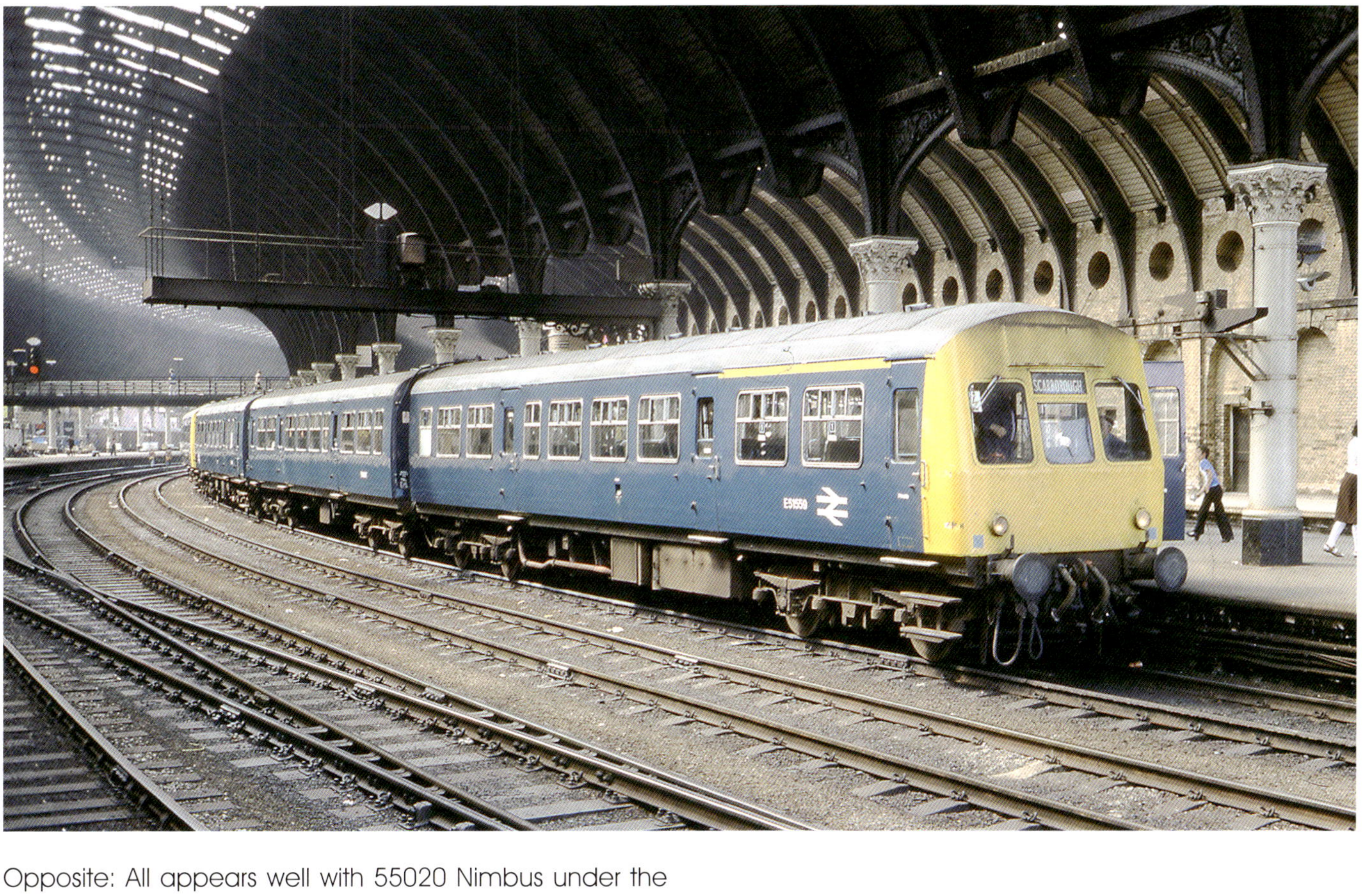

Opposite: All appears well with 55020 Nimbus under the superb curved overall roof with a northbound working in October 1977. ***All: David T Williams***

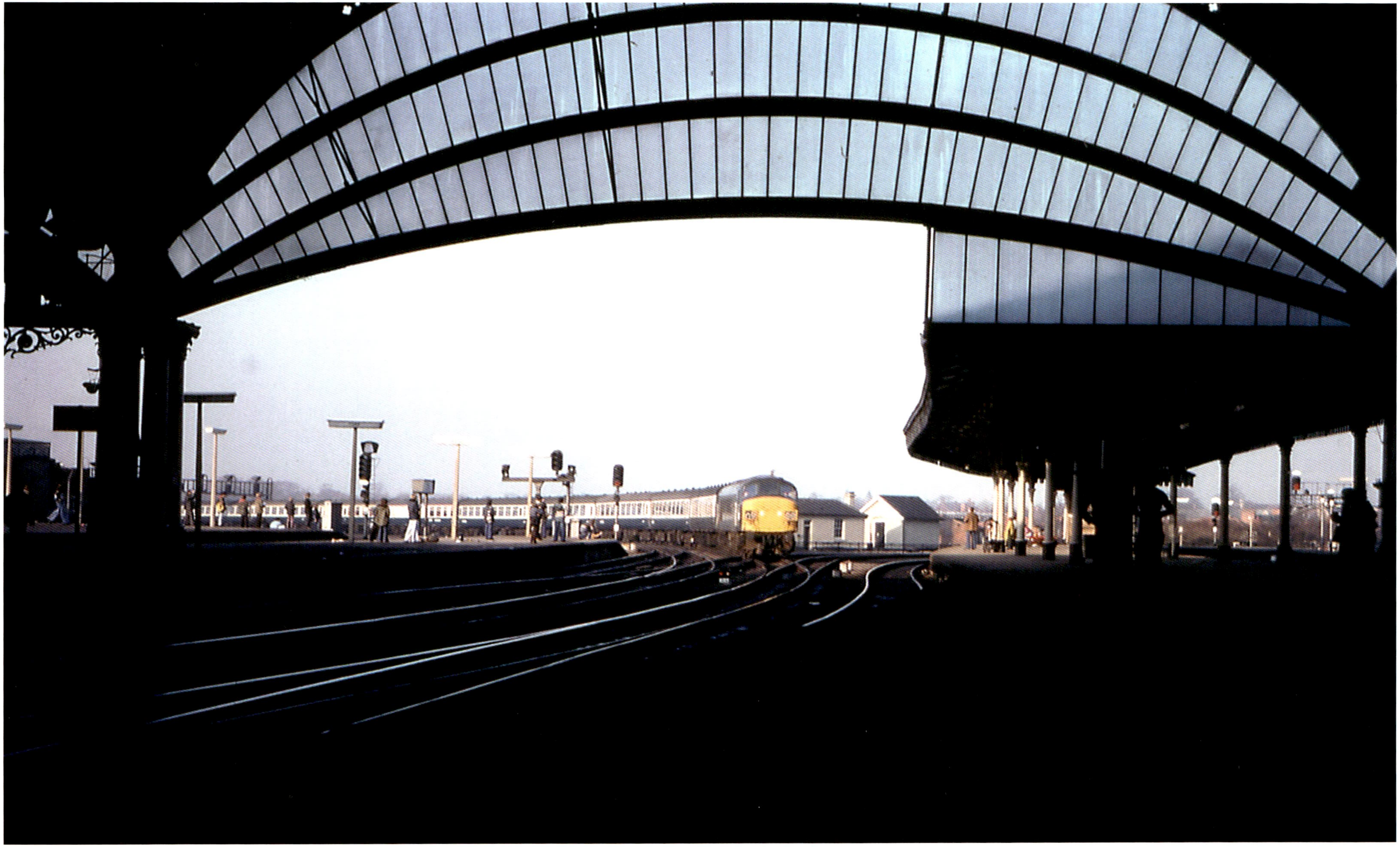

Turning around to look northwards from under the roof spans we see 45052 arriving and negotiating the crossovers for the Scarborough lines radiating from the right under the gaze of a good number of spotters on the platforms. ***Paul Dalton***

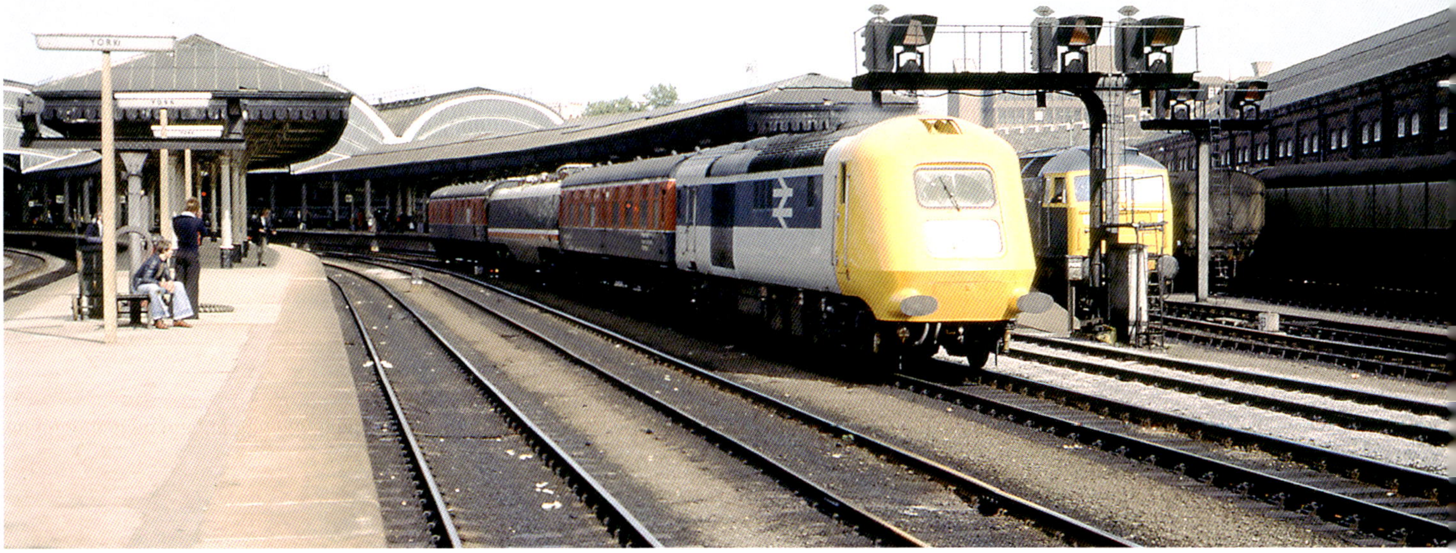

The prototype HST power car W43000 has an APT power car in this test train ready to depart south in October 1978.

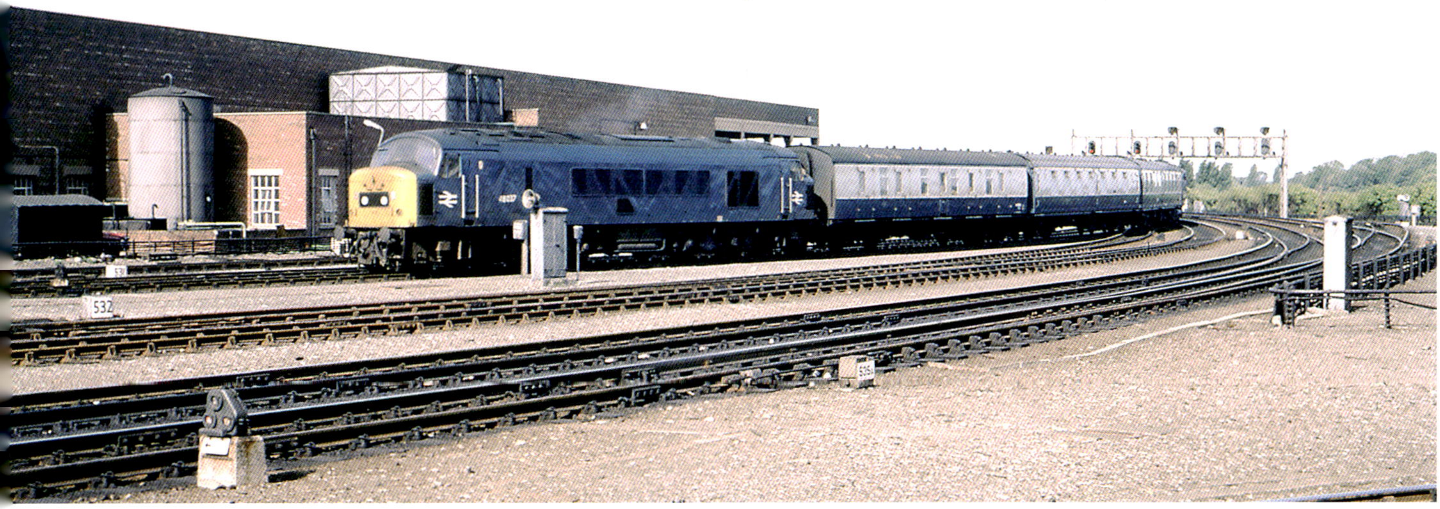

The building behind 46037 still housed an active diesel depot when seen in September 1978 before the NRM took it over. ***Both: David T Williams***

Crowds flock the depot yard on 20 November 1976 to catch a glimpse of D1023 Western Fusilier. ***Tony Shaw***

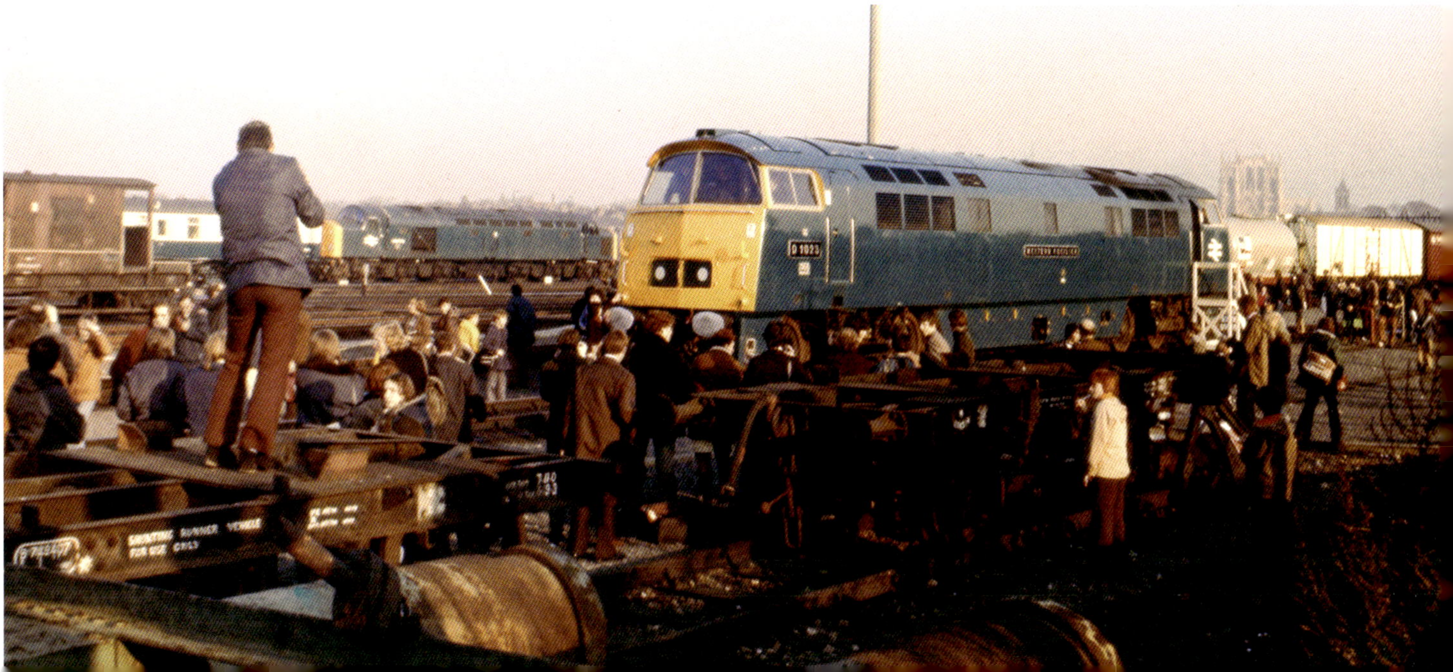

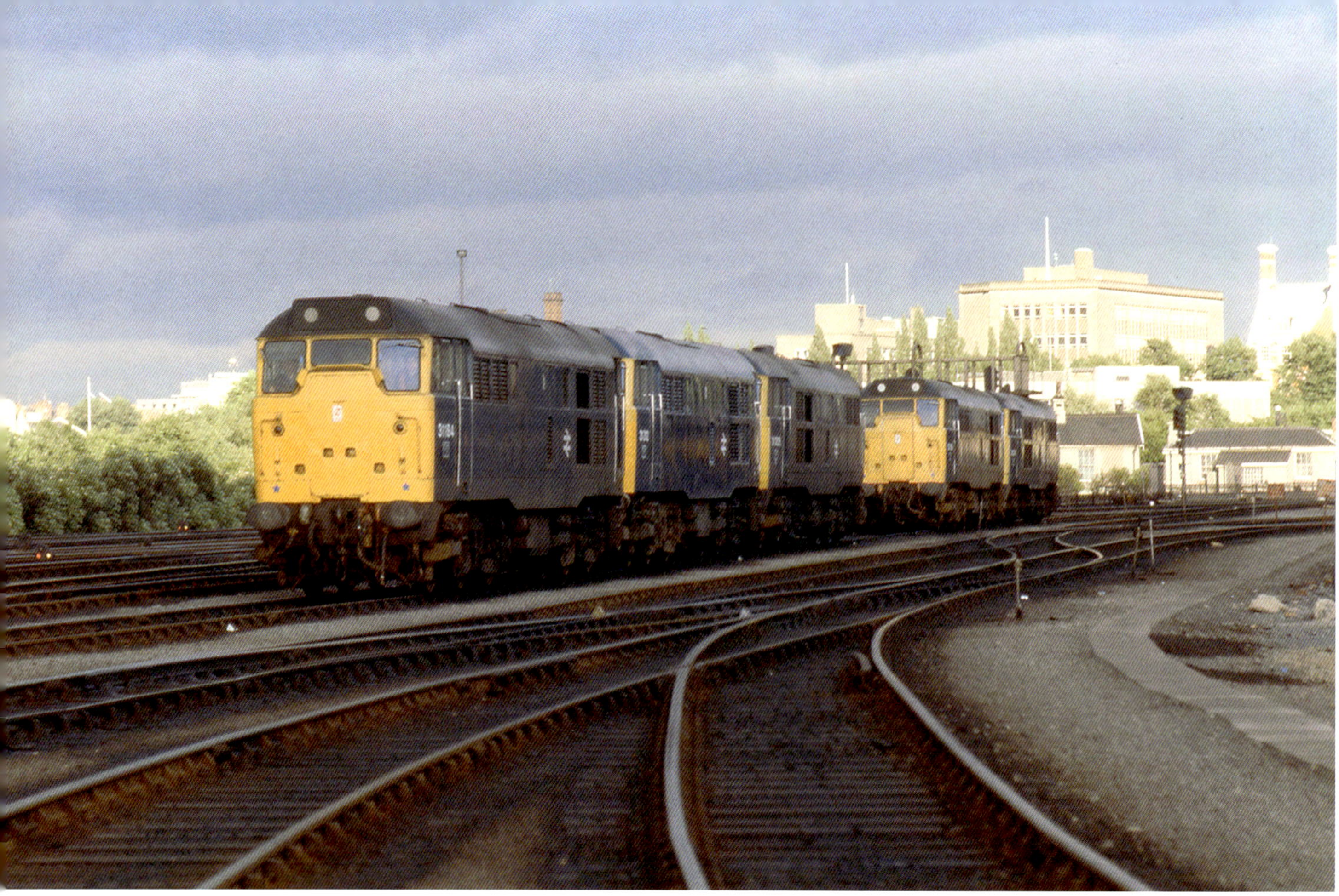

A visit on 18 July 1979 found the depot yard with a fine display of Class 31s on hand. In the country's cinemas we could enjoy Steve Martin bumbling around as The Jerk, or maybe Mel Gibson as Mad Max or perhaps you fancied Sigourney Weaver leading the challenge to slay The Alien. ***Brian Daniels***

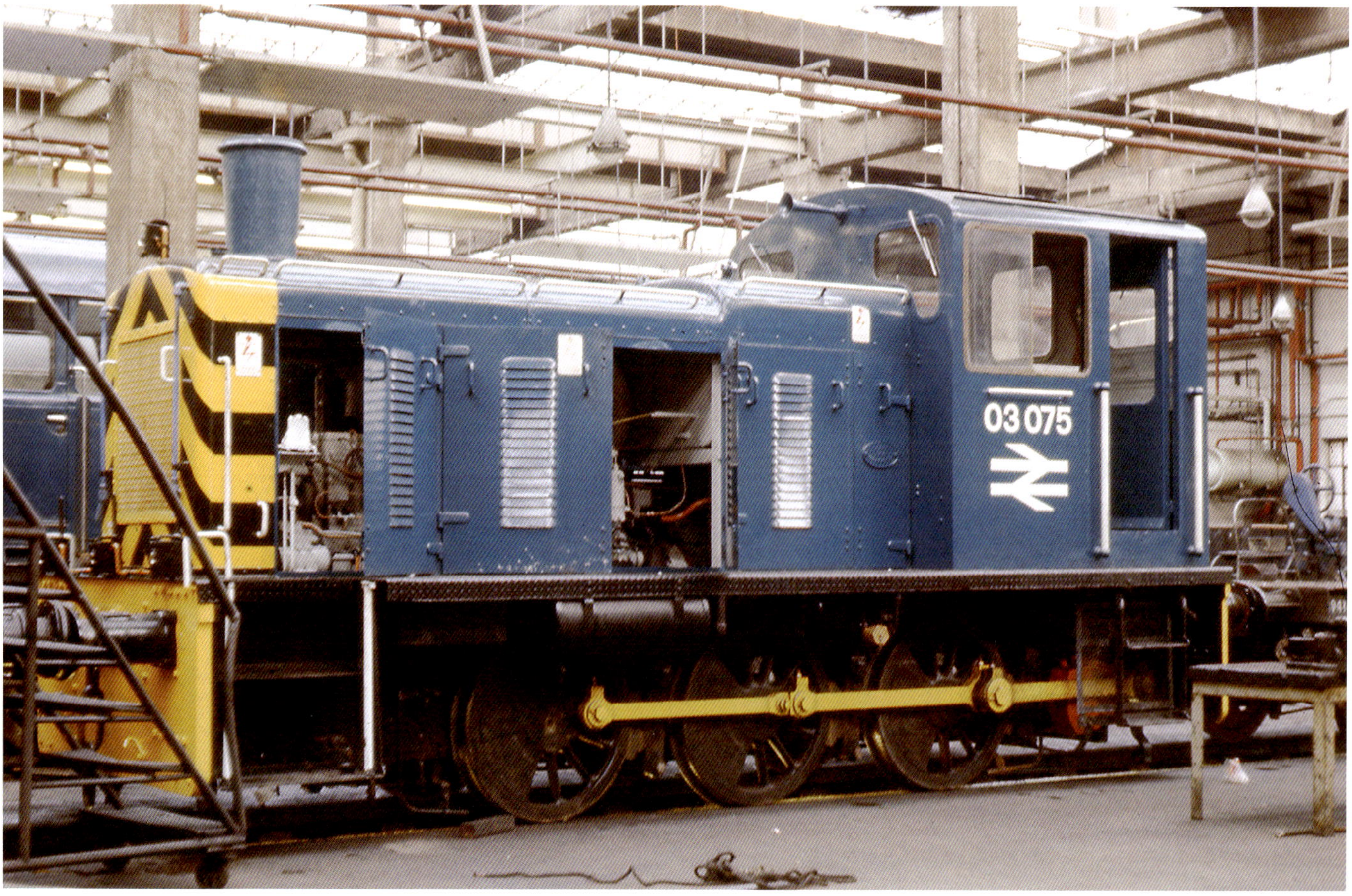

This smart looking Class 03 in March 1974 had arrived at York when new in November 1959 and would stay here until transferred to Thornaby in April 1976 who very quickly withdrew it three months later. It returned to Yorkshire and Doncaster Works that December and was swiftly broken up within weeks of arriving at the Plant. ***Steve Carter Collection***

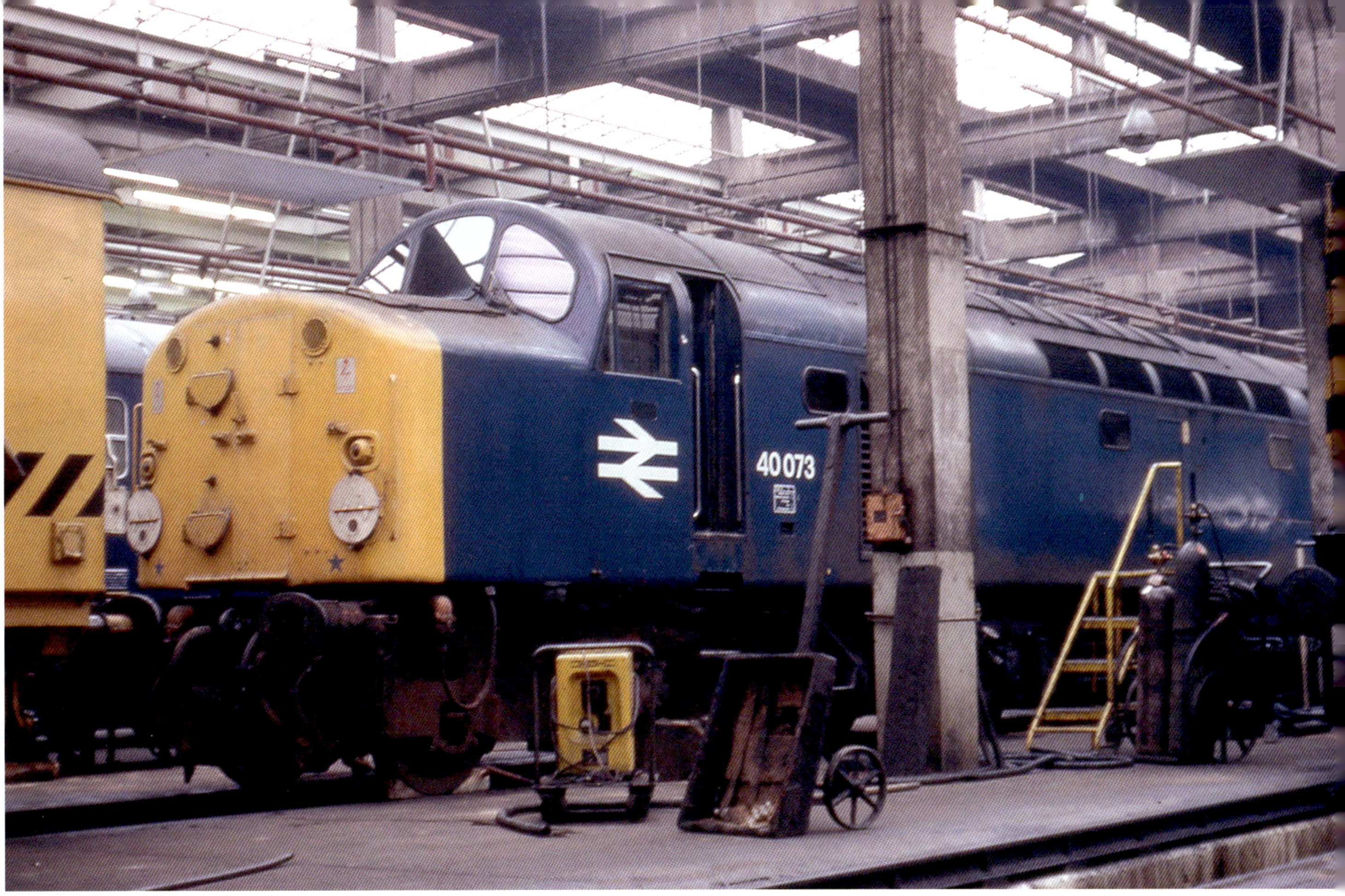

Staying inside this bright and clean maintenance shed we next find Thornaby's 40073 under going minor repairs on 17 January 1978, this locomotive had long been a regular for spotters in Yorkshire and the North East with multiple stints based at Gateshead, York and Healey Mills previously. ***Brian Daniels***

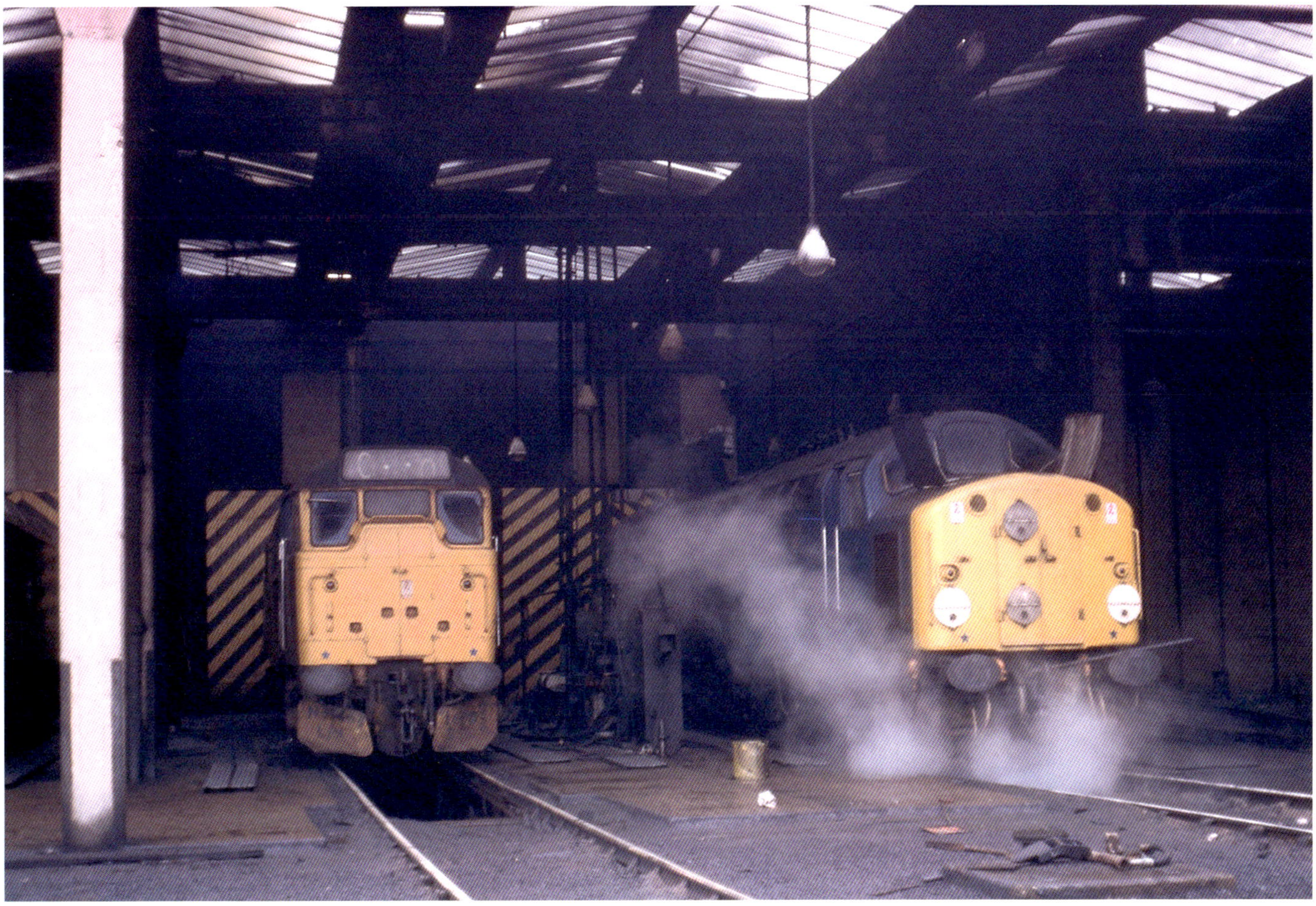

It appears the steam heating boiler onboard 40075 is working well for the fitters on 17 January 1978 whilst 31142 has a three piece snowplough fitted in preparation for any light clearing duties that may be required this winter. ***Brian Daniels***

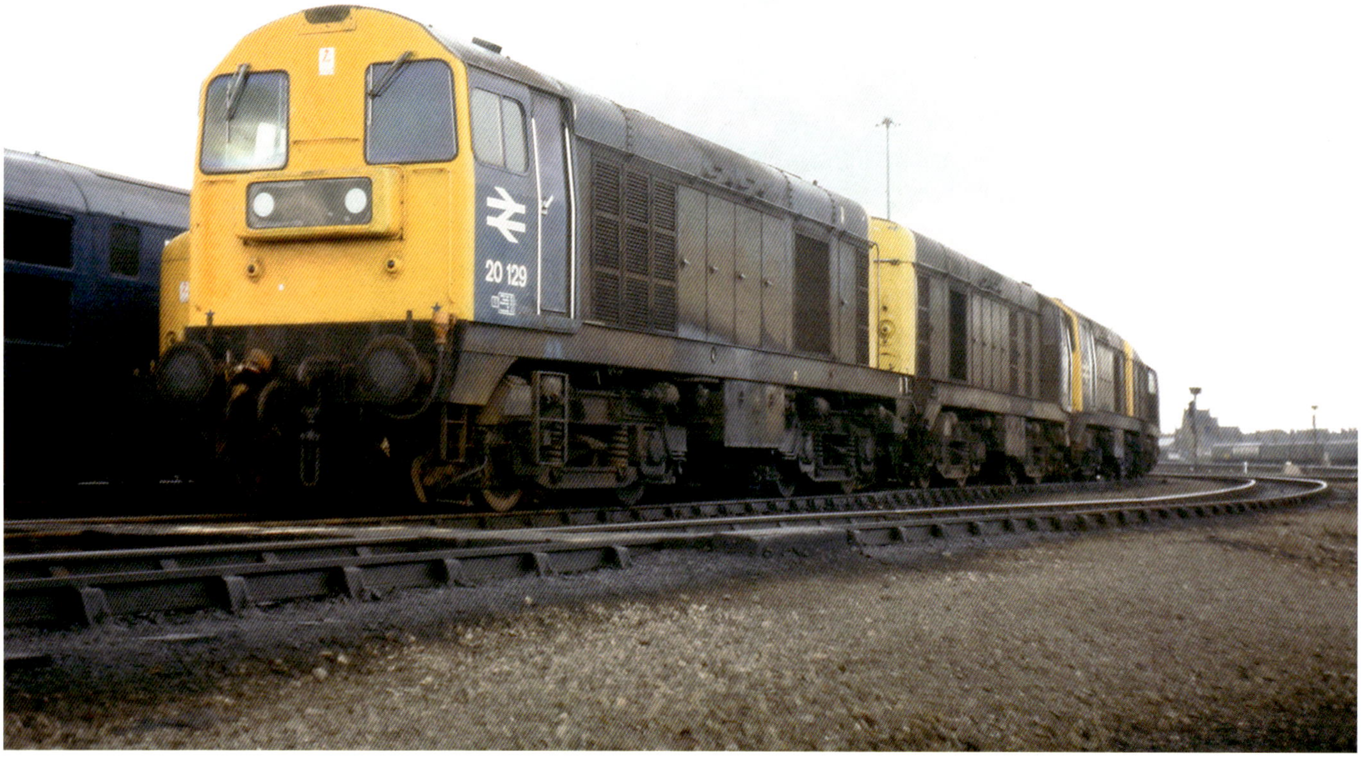

Our next visit on the last day of September 1978 rewards us with two pairs of Class 20s led by 20129 between duties from the city. In the news that month were reports that Iranian Army troops opened fire on rioters in Teheran, killing 122, wounding 4,000 people. Whilst two days before this photograpgh was taken Pope John Paul I died after only thirty three days of papacy. ***Brian Daniels***

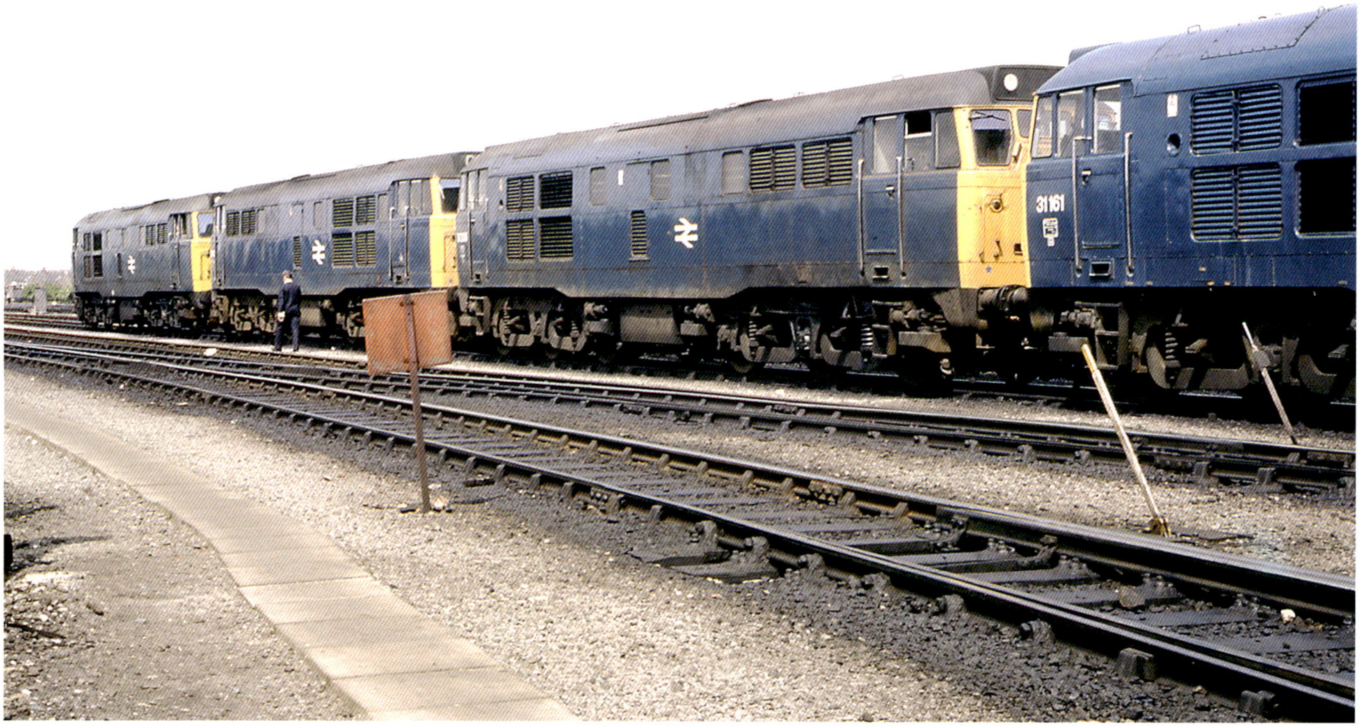

A driver walks along a line of stabled Class 31s including 31163, 31142 and 31308 in August 1979, the same month saw Michael Jackson release his first breakthrough solo album Off the Wall. It quickly sold seven million copies in the United States alone. ***David T Williams***

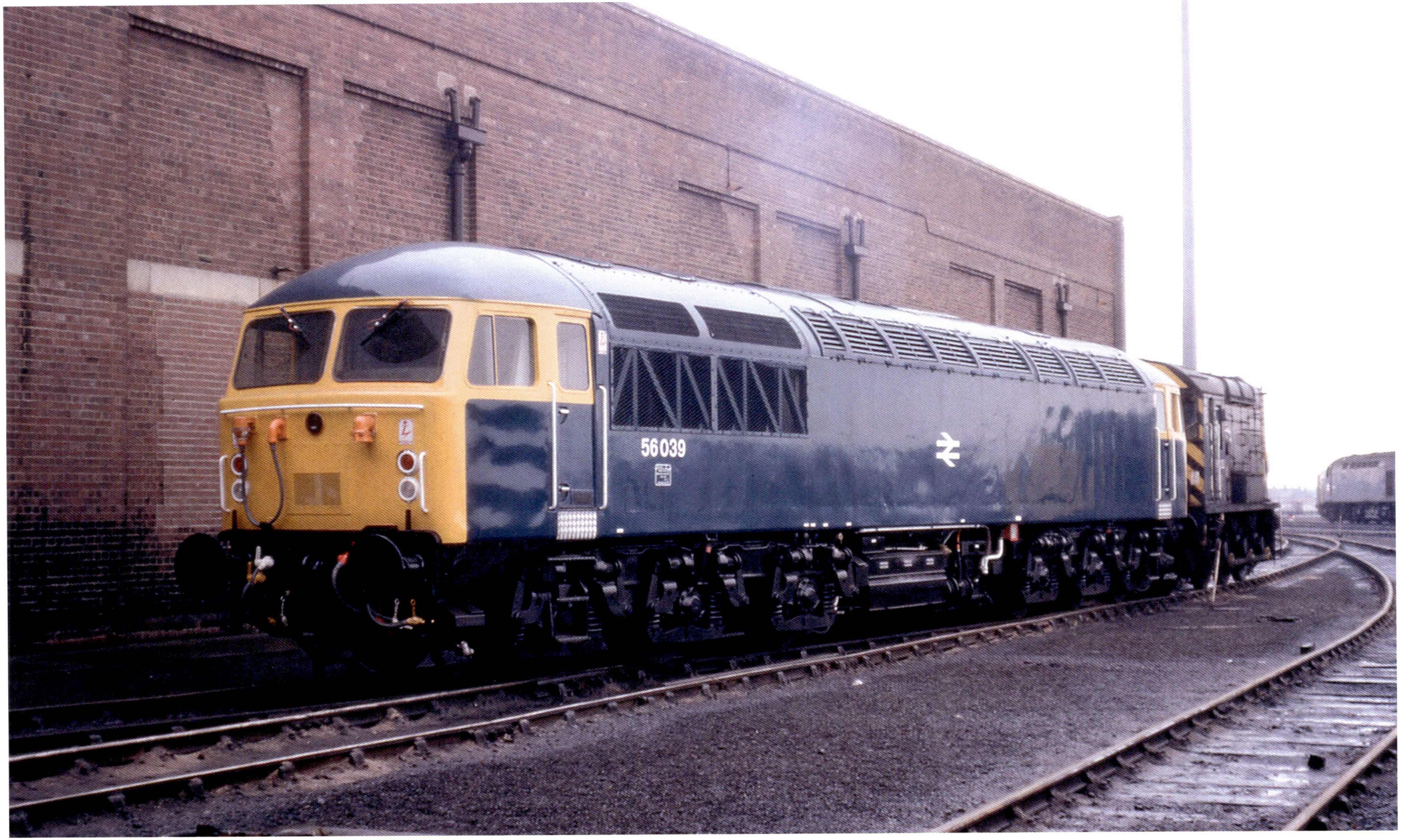

A brand new British built 56039 has arrived at York on 17 January 1978 on test from Doncaster Works, it would not enter service until 7 February when it was allocated to Toton. On 31 January an 18-year-old prostitute Helen Rytka is murdered in Huddersfield; she is believed to be the eighth victim of the Yorkshire Ripper as fear grips women across Yorkshire and northern England. ***Brian Daniels.***

Preserving the Past

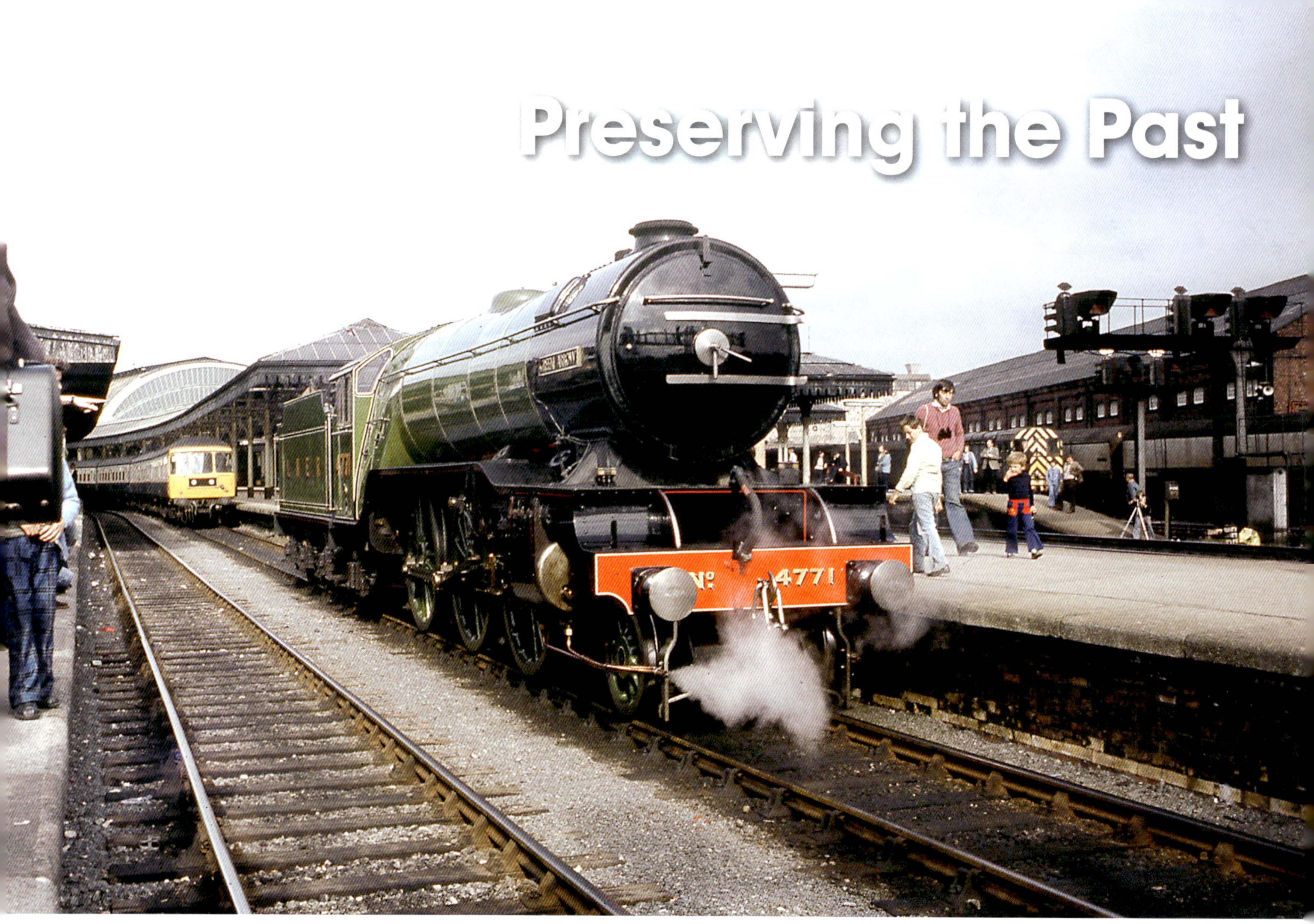

A shunting manouver takes 4771 Green Arrow into the same platform road as a Trans-Pennine DMU as the Gresley designed V2 is all prepared and set to work the 14.15 Yorkshire Circular on 3 September 1978. ***John Arthur Bennett/Strathwood Library Collection***

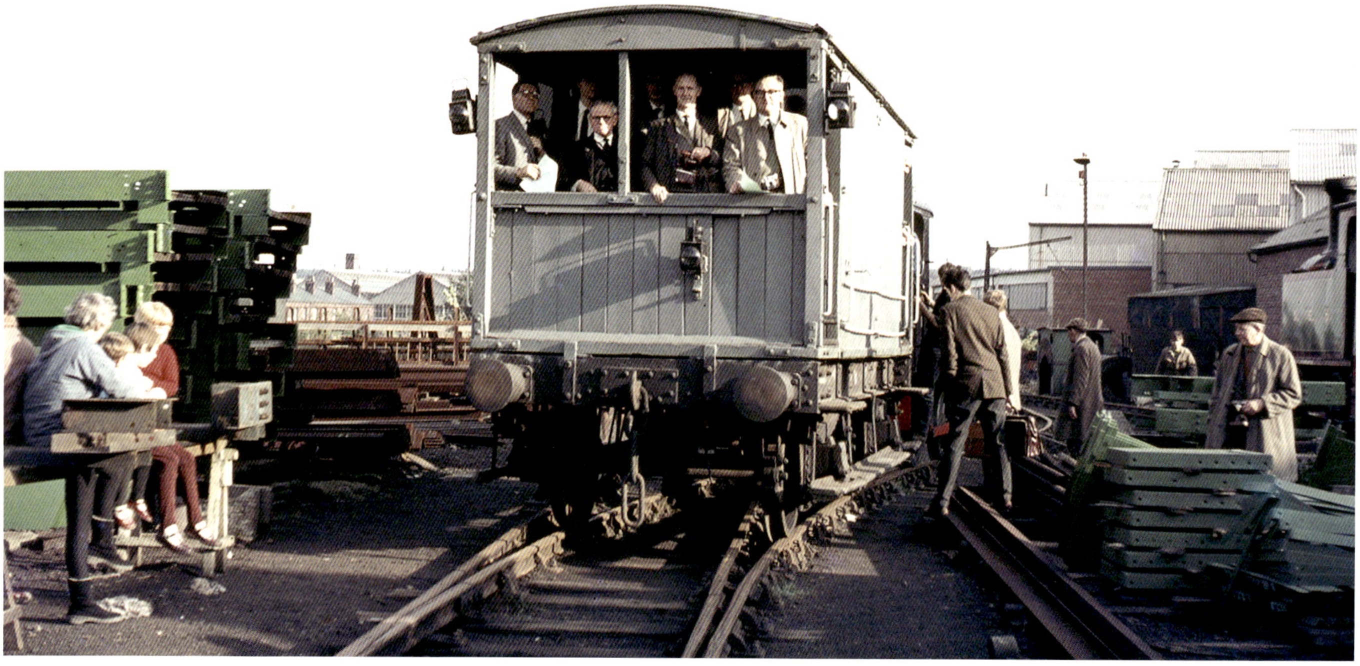

Brake van rides were a popular atraction for the fledgling preservation movement as here on the Middleton Railway near Leeds in 1970 when health and safety considerations were based upon common sense and looking out for yourself, we all made it through though. ***Late Derek Whitnell/Strathwood Library Collection***

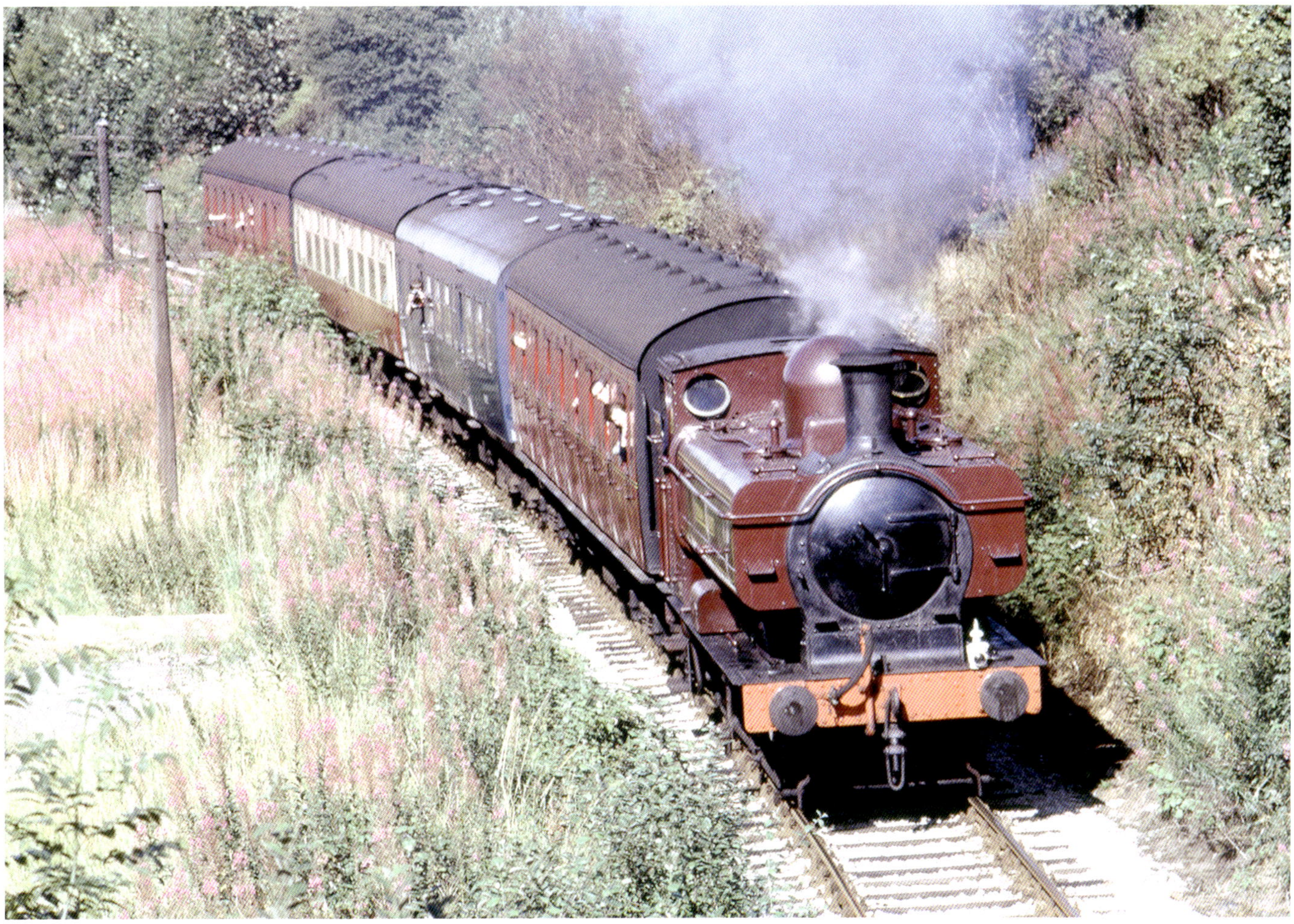

The second coach in this service headed by the ex-London Transport liveried Pannier Tank L89 which had been numbered as 5775 in British Railways days was one of the shortlived Buffet Cars once to be found in a few of the Metropolitan Cammell DMUs. This shot was taken approaching Ingrow on 17 August 1974, sadly this historic DMU coach was later broken up. ***Aldo Delicata***

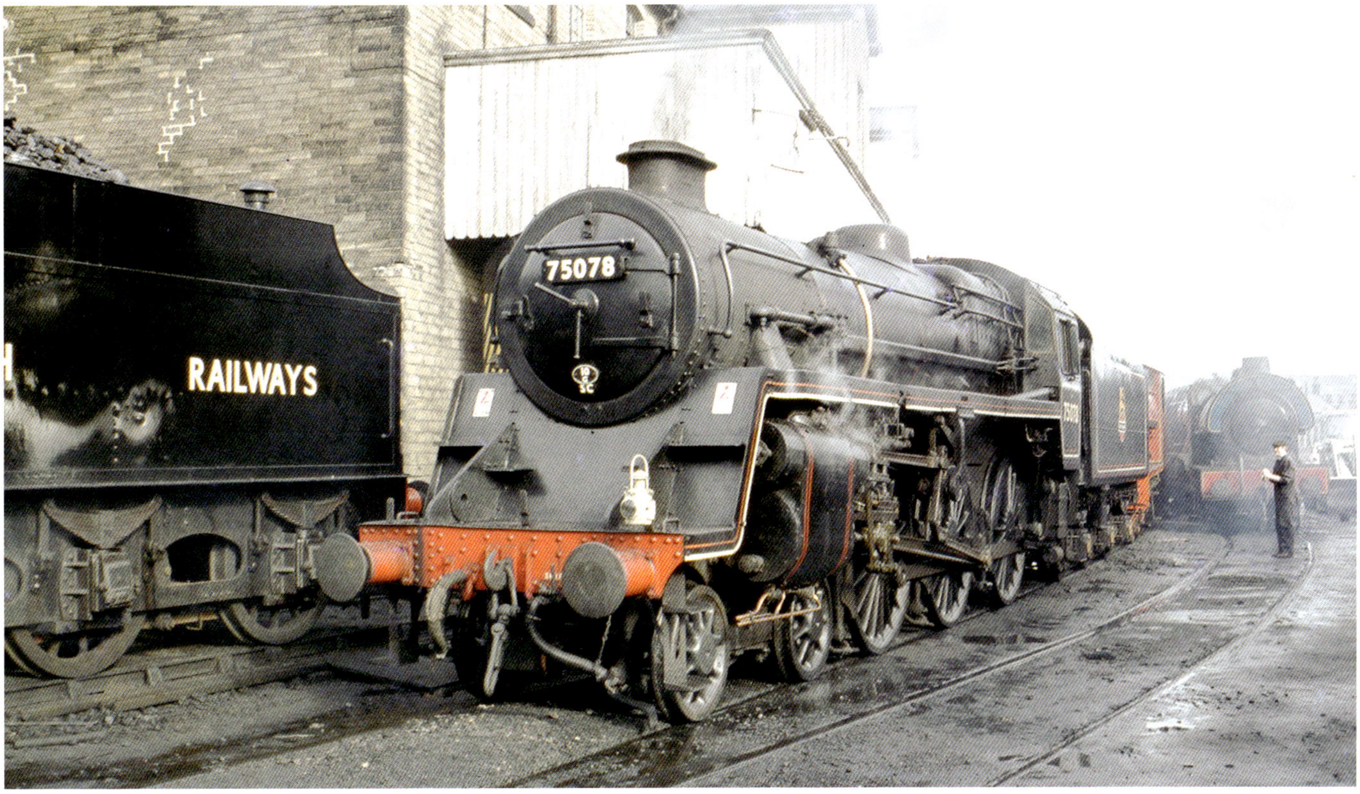

Staying on the Keighley & Worth Valley Railway we find Standard Class 4MT 75078 back in steam after being rescued from from Barry Scrapyard, it would be one of the locomotives used for filming the movie Yanks released in 1979 staring Richard Gere. ***Late Derek Whitnell/Strathwood Library Collection***

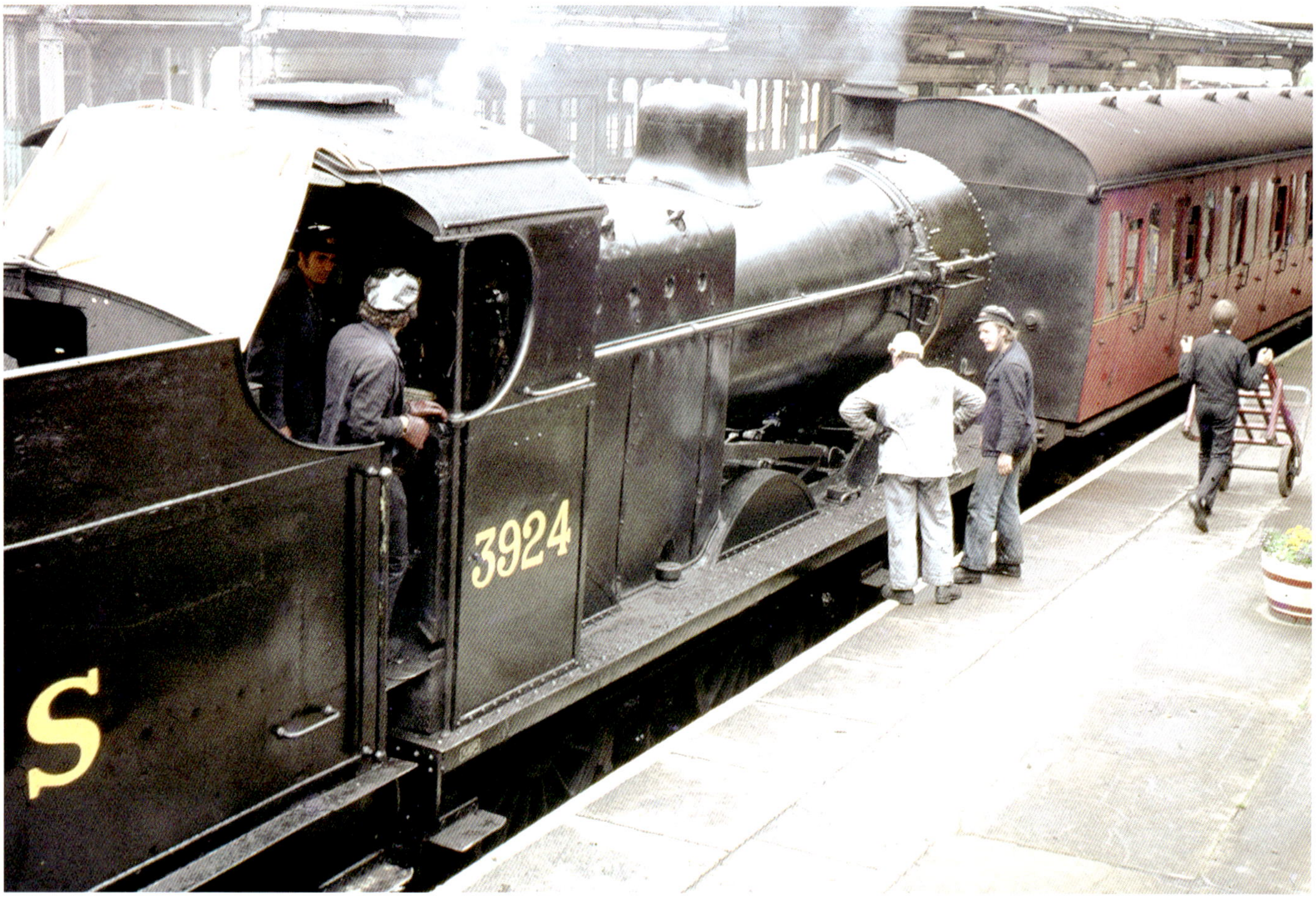

The first steam locomotive to be liberated from Woodham's famous scrapyard was 43924 which left Barry in September 1968, sixteen months would elapse before the next escapee in the shape of 31618, this shot shows the 4F back in back in action once more at Keighley at the head of one of the ex Kings Cross suburban coaches. ***Strathwood Library Collection***

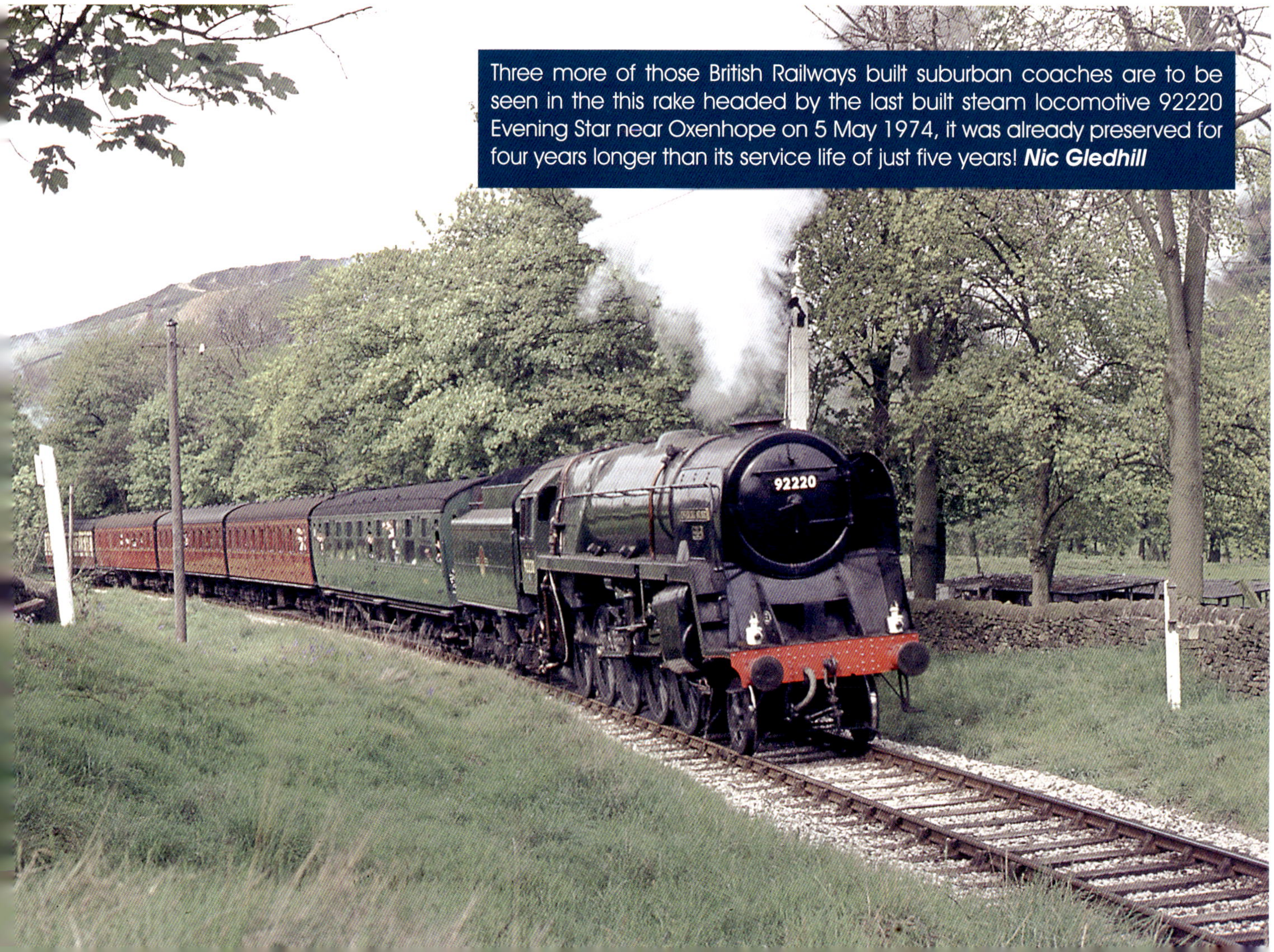

Three more of those British Railways built suburban coaches are to be seen in the this rake headed by the last built steam locomotive 92220 Evening Star near Oxenhope on 5 May 1974, it was already preserved for four years longer than its service life of just five years! ***Nic Gledhill***

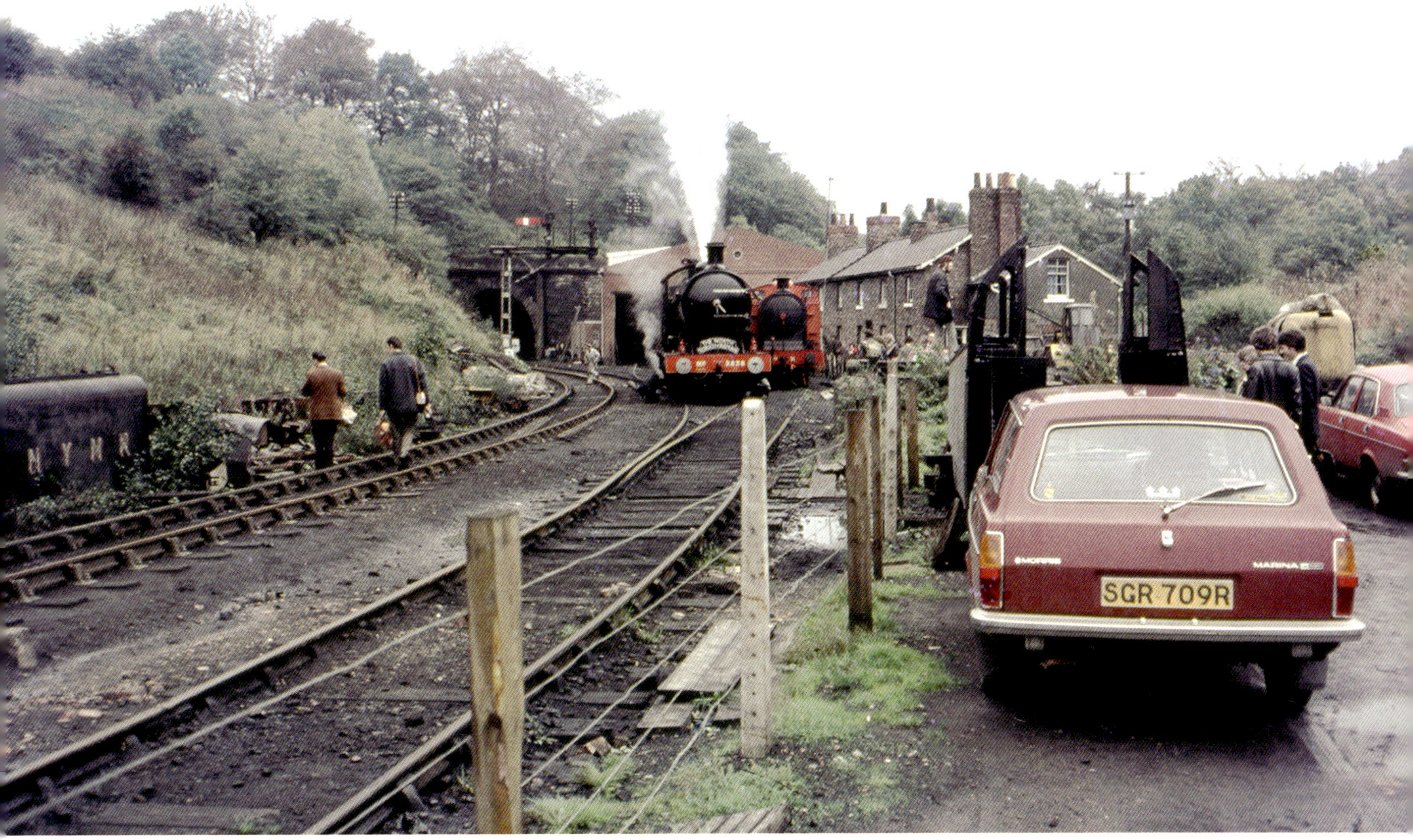

This was the scene one rainy day at the original running shed at Grosmont on 9 October 1976 on the North Yorkshire Moors Railway, the Morris Marina Estate in Damask Red gives this view a real seventies period feel. ***Late Derek Whitnell/Strathwood Library Collection***

The now preserved D1048 Western Lady waits at Goathland on 18 March 1979 whilst working a leg The Western Recall railtour and having pushed through a number of snow drifts along the route that day. ***Nev Sloper***

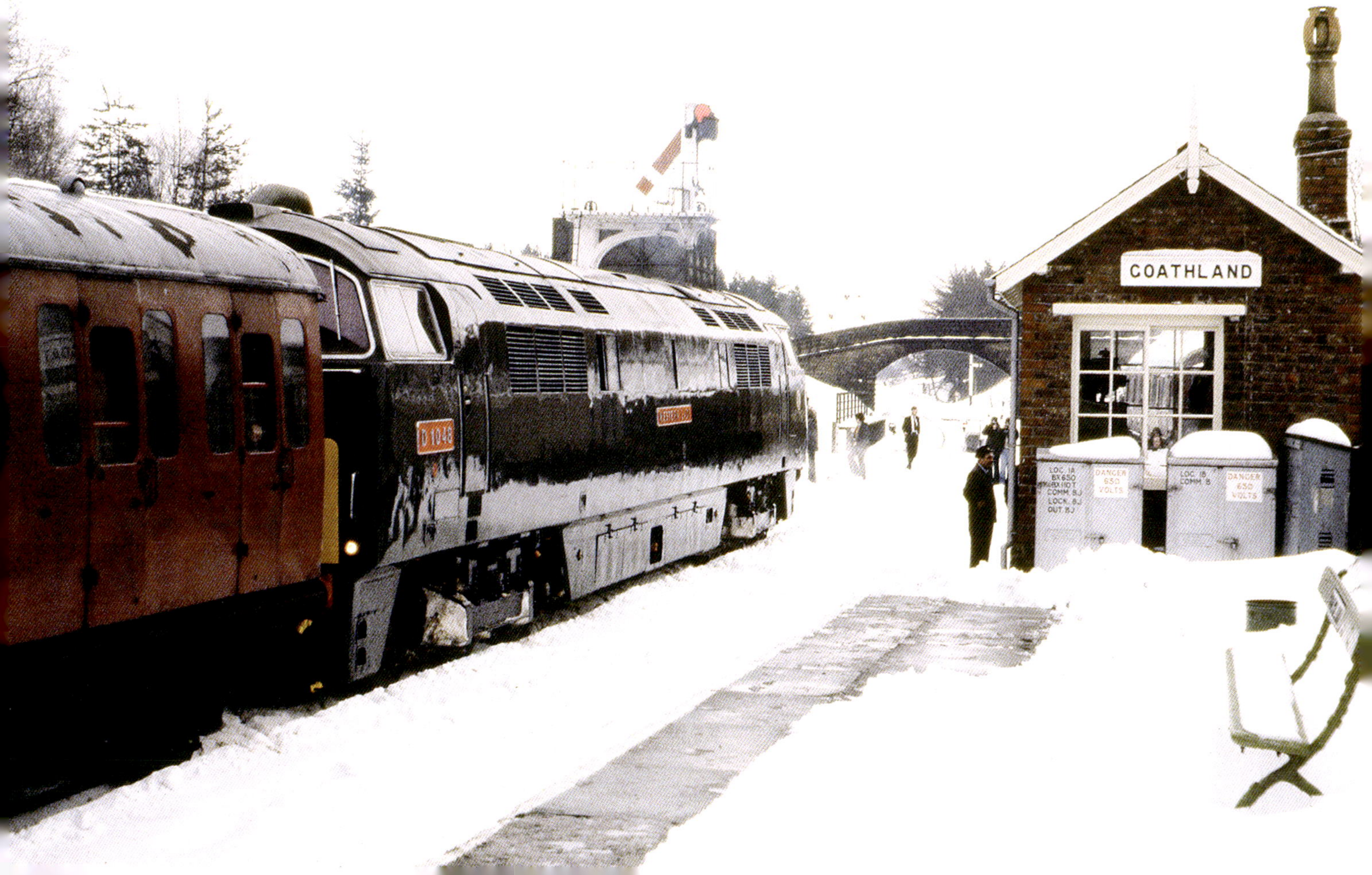

Open Day at the Plant

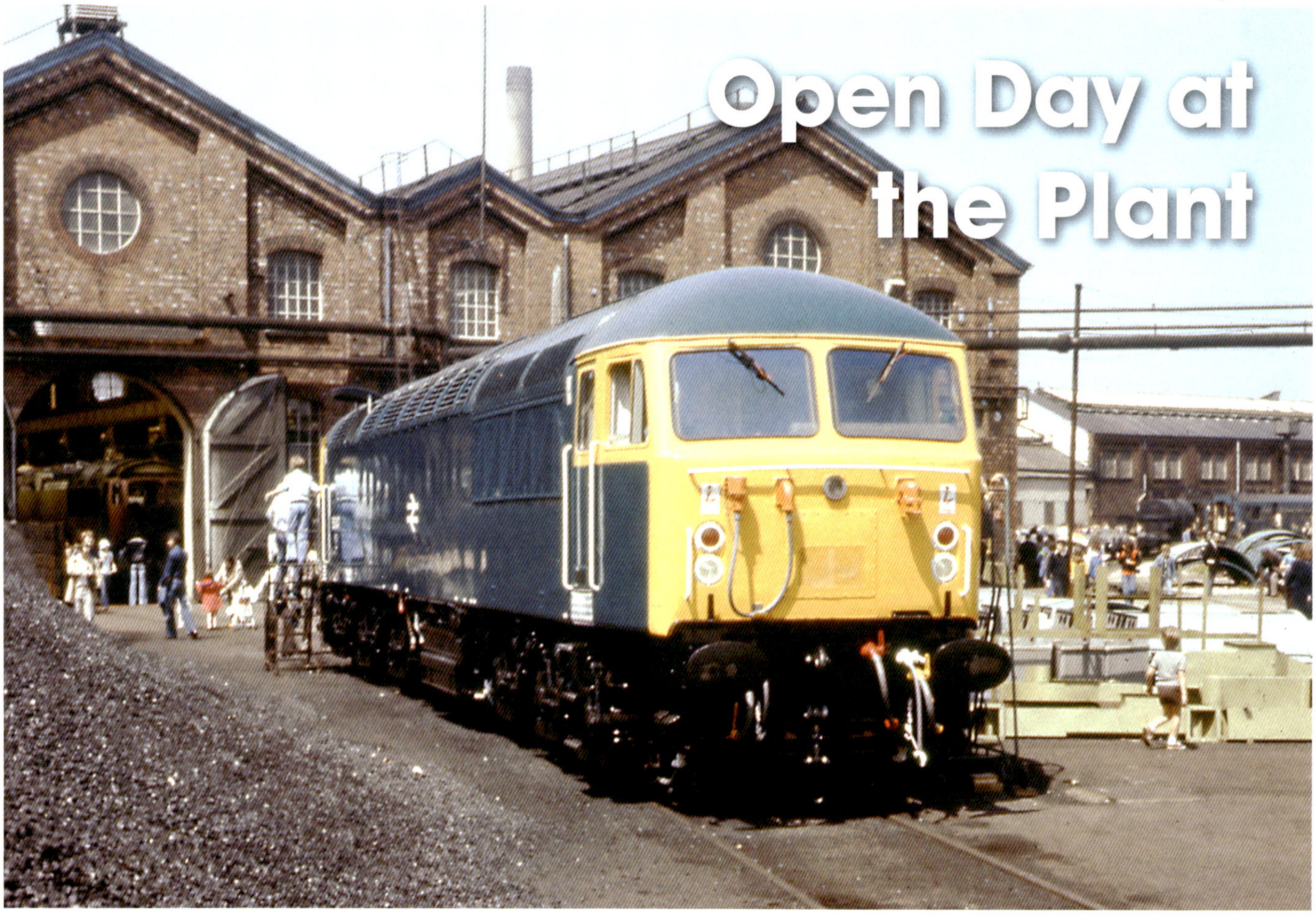

The smell of freshly dried paint in the sunshine would be on the noses of those lucky enough to cab the brand new 56047 displaying the latest built locomitve ready to leave Doncaster Works on 18 June 1978. ***Tim Hall***

Also ready to leave the works was the now eighteen year old Brush built 31208 which would return to traffic based out of March, the building in the background is the Test House. ***Nev Sloper***

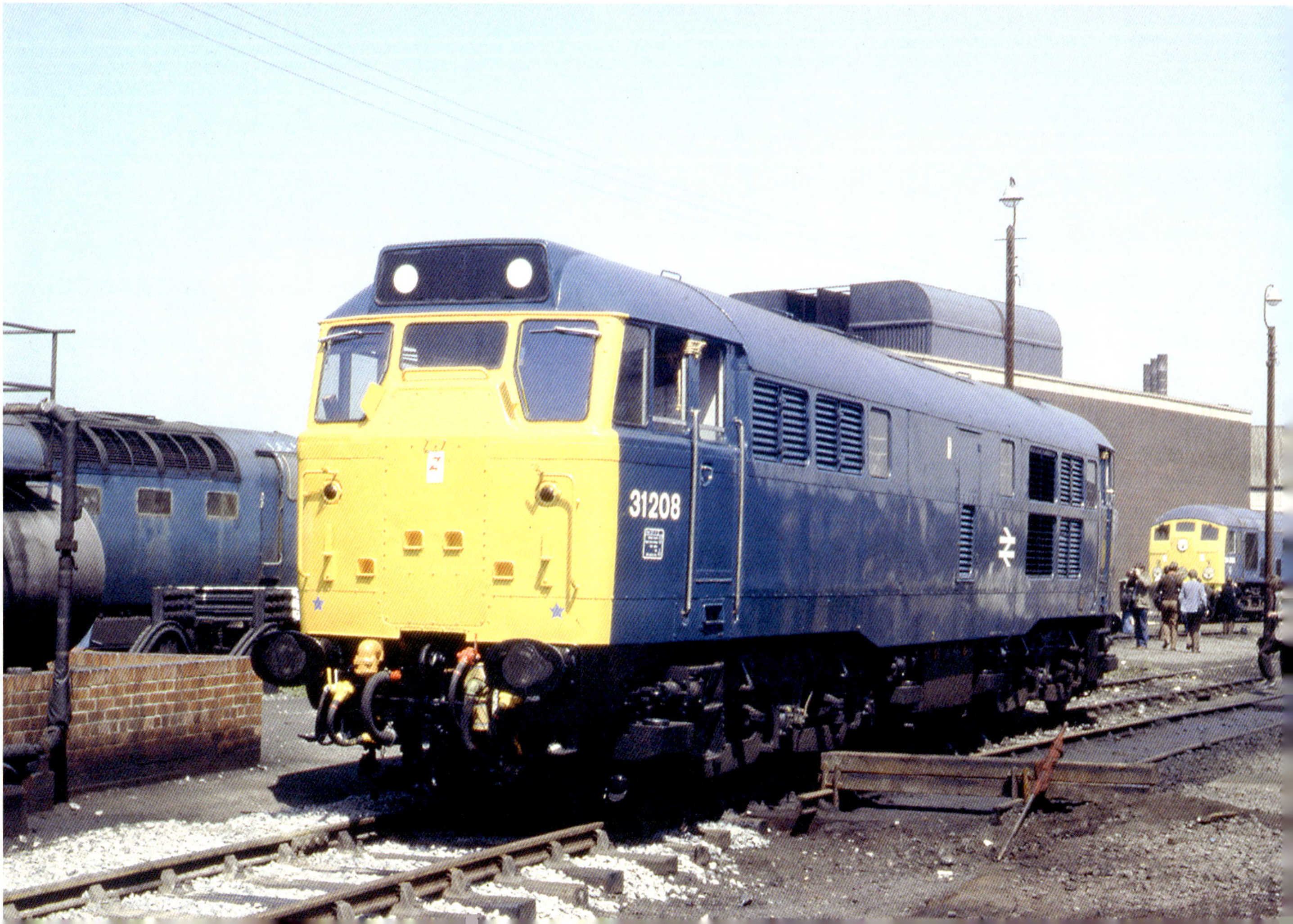

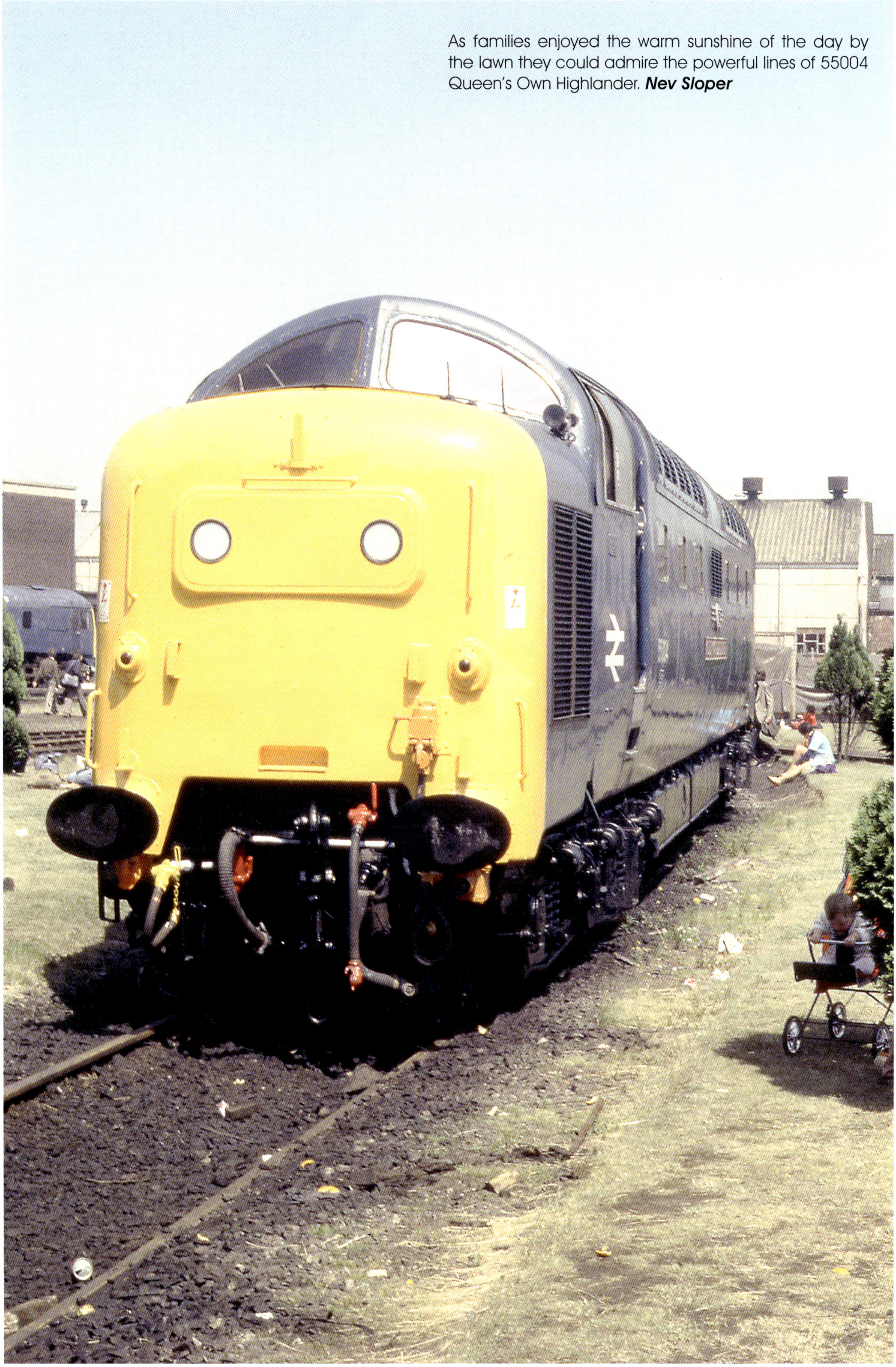

As families enjoyed the warm sunshine of the day by the lawn they could admire the powerful lines of 55004 Queen's Own Highlander. ***Nev Sloper***

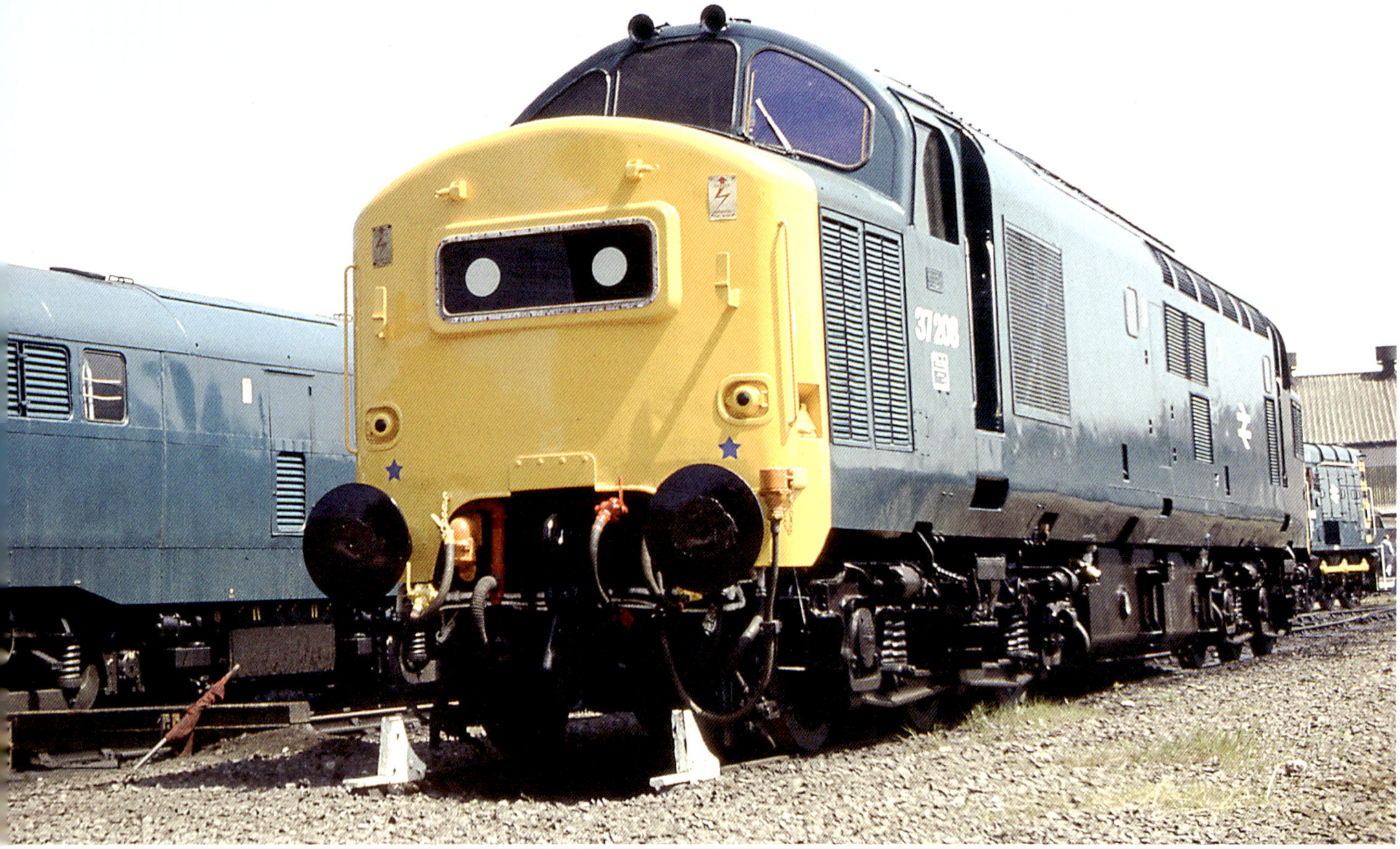

On the next road alongside 31208 was 37208 from faraway Landore also ex-works and ready for a return to use in South Wales shortly. ***Sid Steadman***

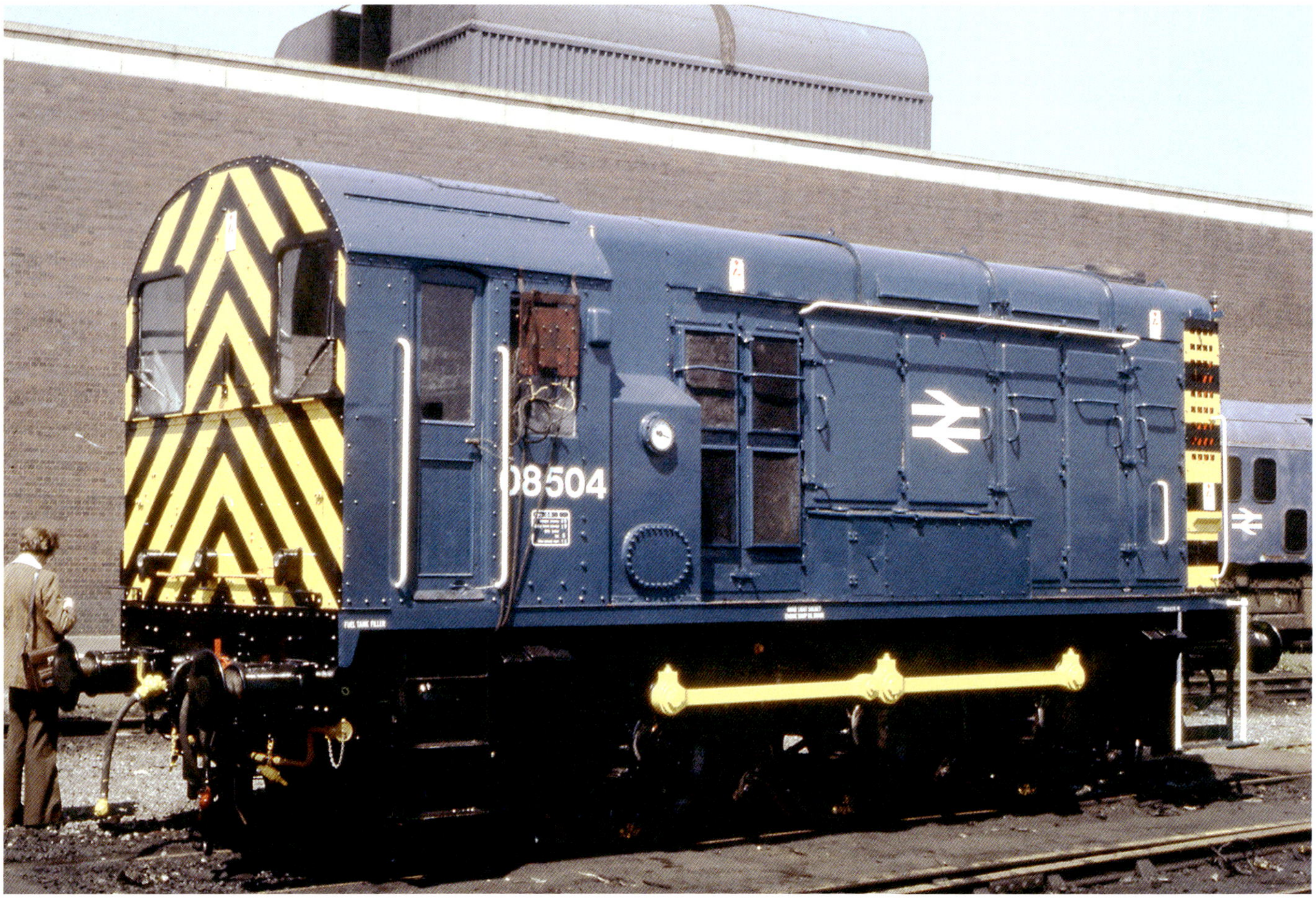

Whilst Immingham's 08504 was still awaiting final testing judging from the gauge board affixed to the cabside window. The prvious summer this shunter had spent some time in store at Barrow Hill pending a decision on its future. ***Nev sloper***

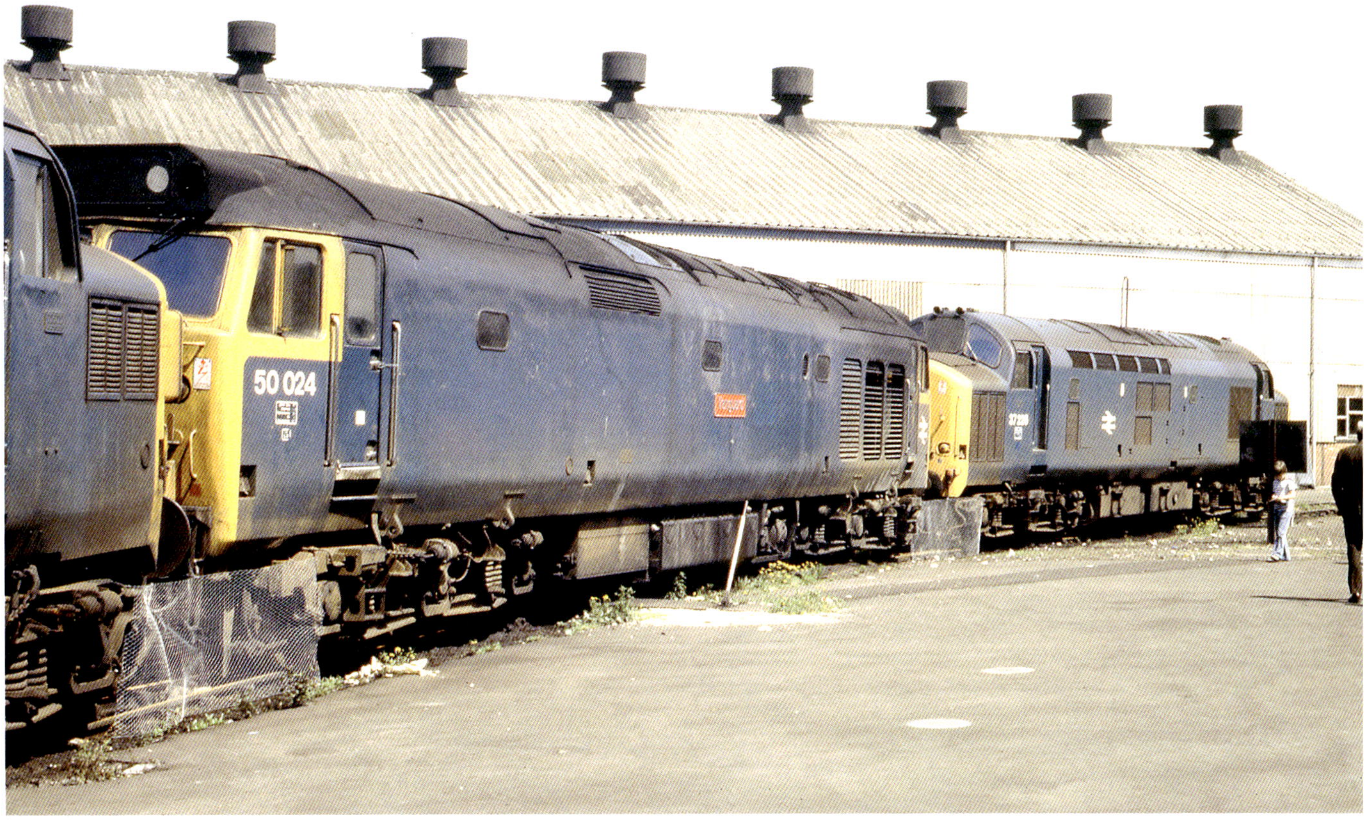

Wire mesh has crudely been affixed between the locomotives in this line up to deter visitors from ducking below their buffers to take a short cut, 50024 had only been given the name Vanguard a month beforehand. ***Nev Sloper***

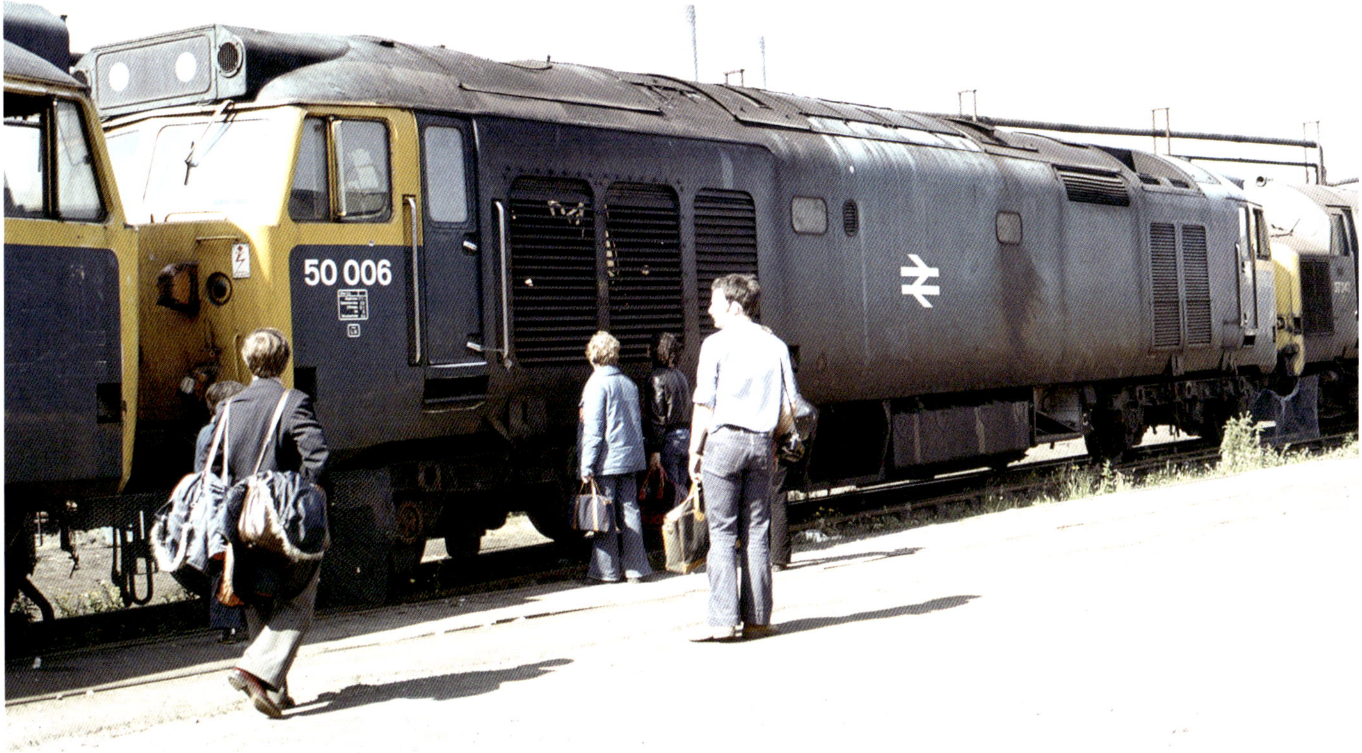

Whereas 50006 remained at Doncaster Works from July 1977 until November 1979, it certainly looked as though its future was grim sat on those accomodation bogies. ***Bob Dibley***

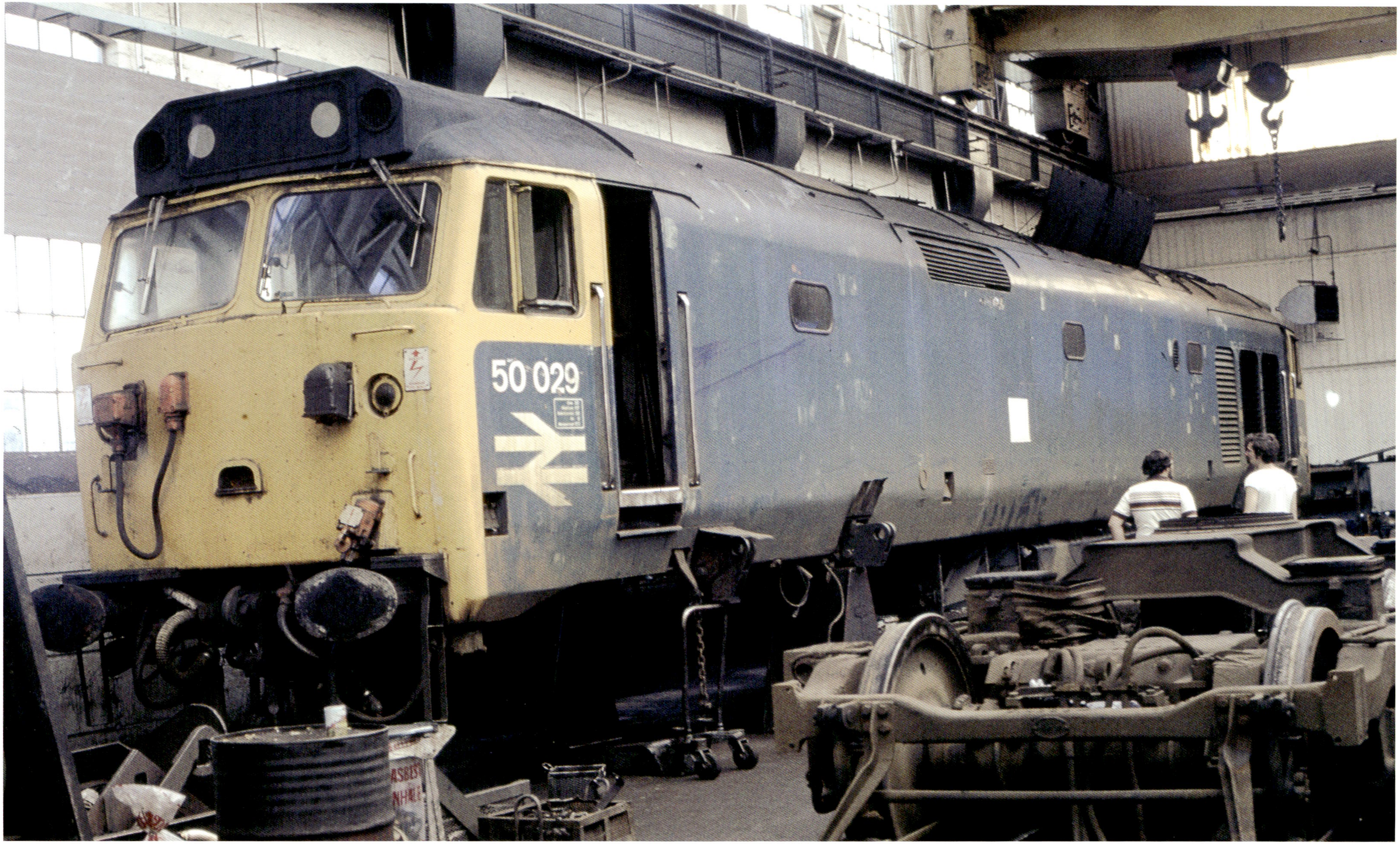

Refurbishment was underway however on 50029 which would be awarded the name Renown on 26 October a few months after this Open Day and it would take up duties from Laira on its return to the Western Region. ***Bob Dibley***

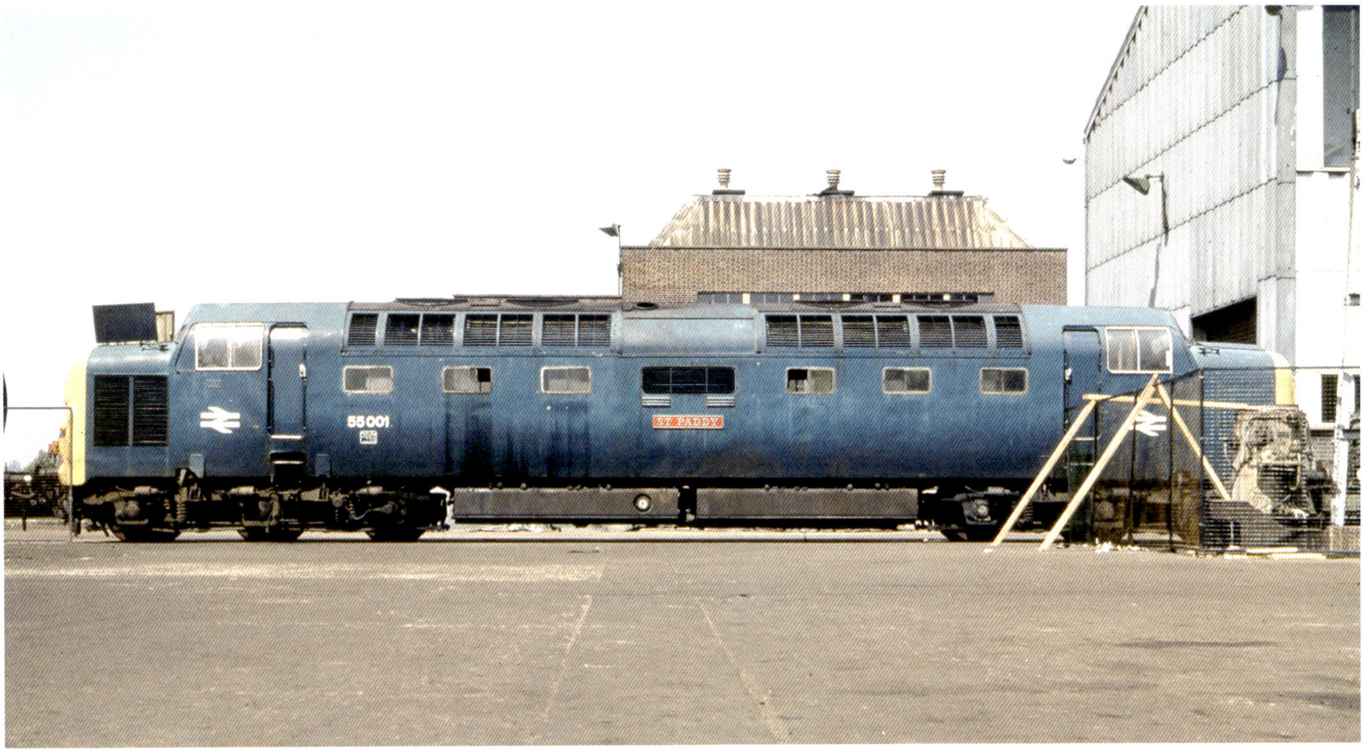

Hopes for a return to service for 55001 St. Paddy would be expected to be high when seen displayed outside the workshops, but this optimism would soon fade as we will see later. The day after this Open Day would give some cause for cheer though as Ian Botham became the first man in the history of cricket to score a century and take eight wickets in one inning of a Test match. ***Sid Steadman***

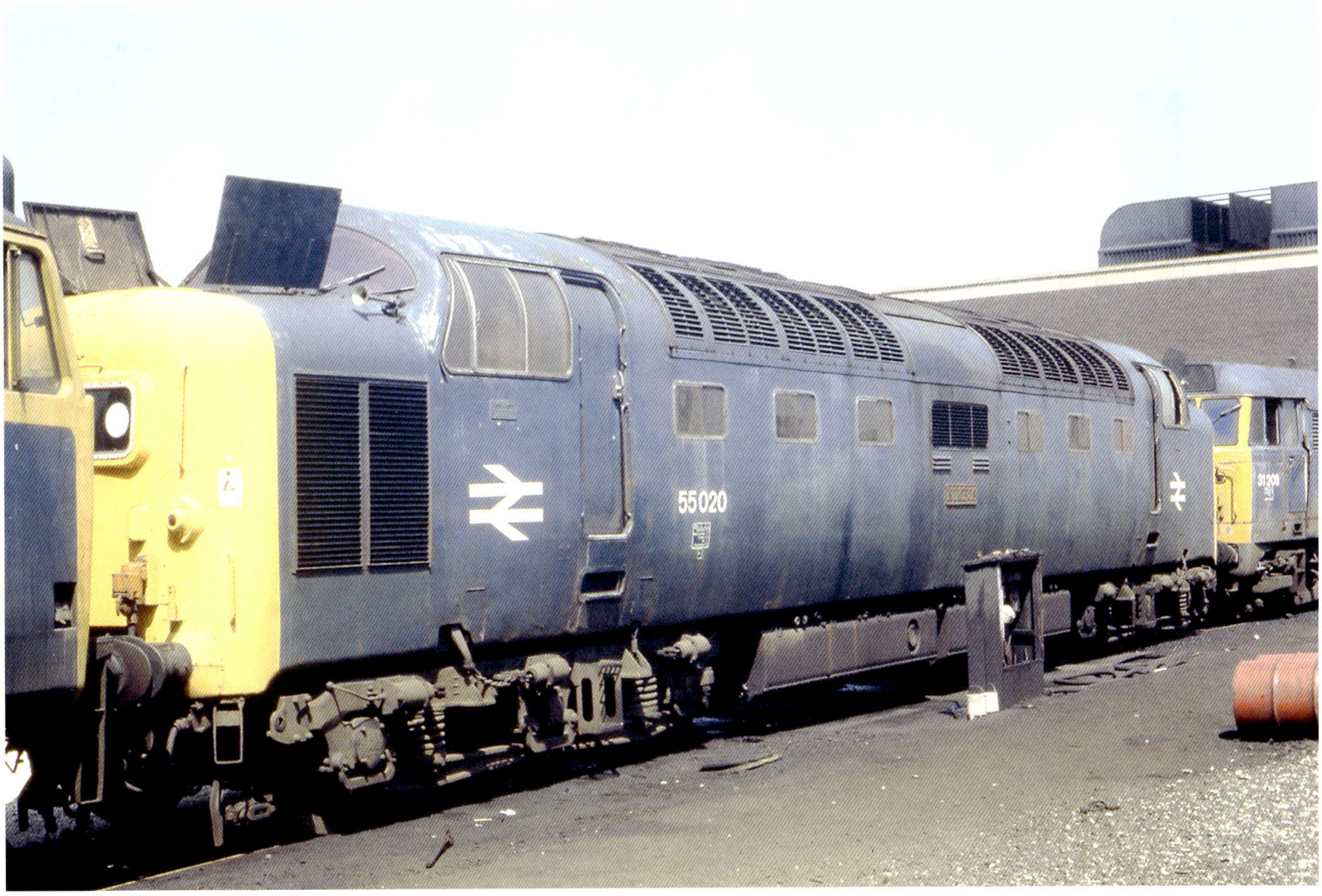

Likewise for sister Deltic 55020 Nimbus still with nameplates affixed we hoped she would be back in service again soon, this positive thinking would also be thwarted by Christmas of the following year. Although the Middlesborough born singer-songwriter Chris Rea brought the name Deltics to a wider audience in 1979 with his popular album of the same name. ***Nev Sloper***

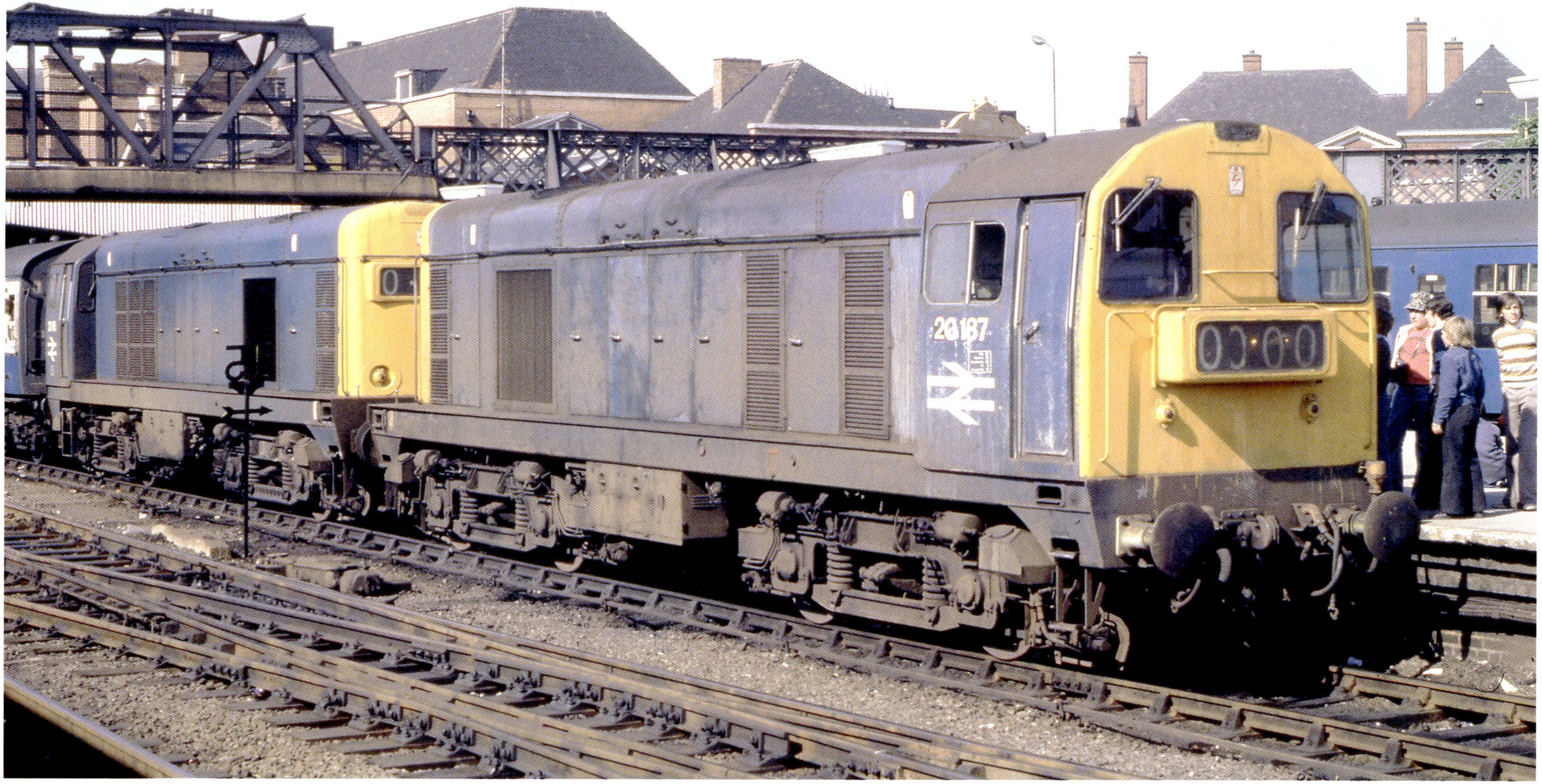

It was a busy day for enthusiasts on Doncaster's station as well on 18 June 1978 as two excursions brought in visitors from Paddington in connection with the Open Day, this one has arrived with 20186 and 20187 in charge having taken over from 50016 Barham at Birmingham New Street. The second tour would arrive behind 20064 and 20009 with this relief working taking over from 31123 and 31163. ***Aldo Delicata***

Focus on Freight Turns

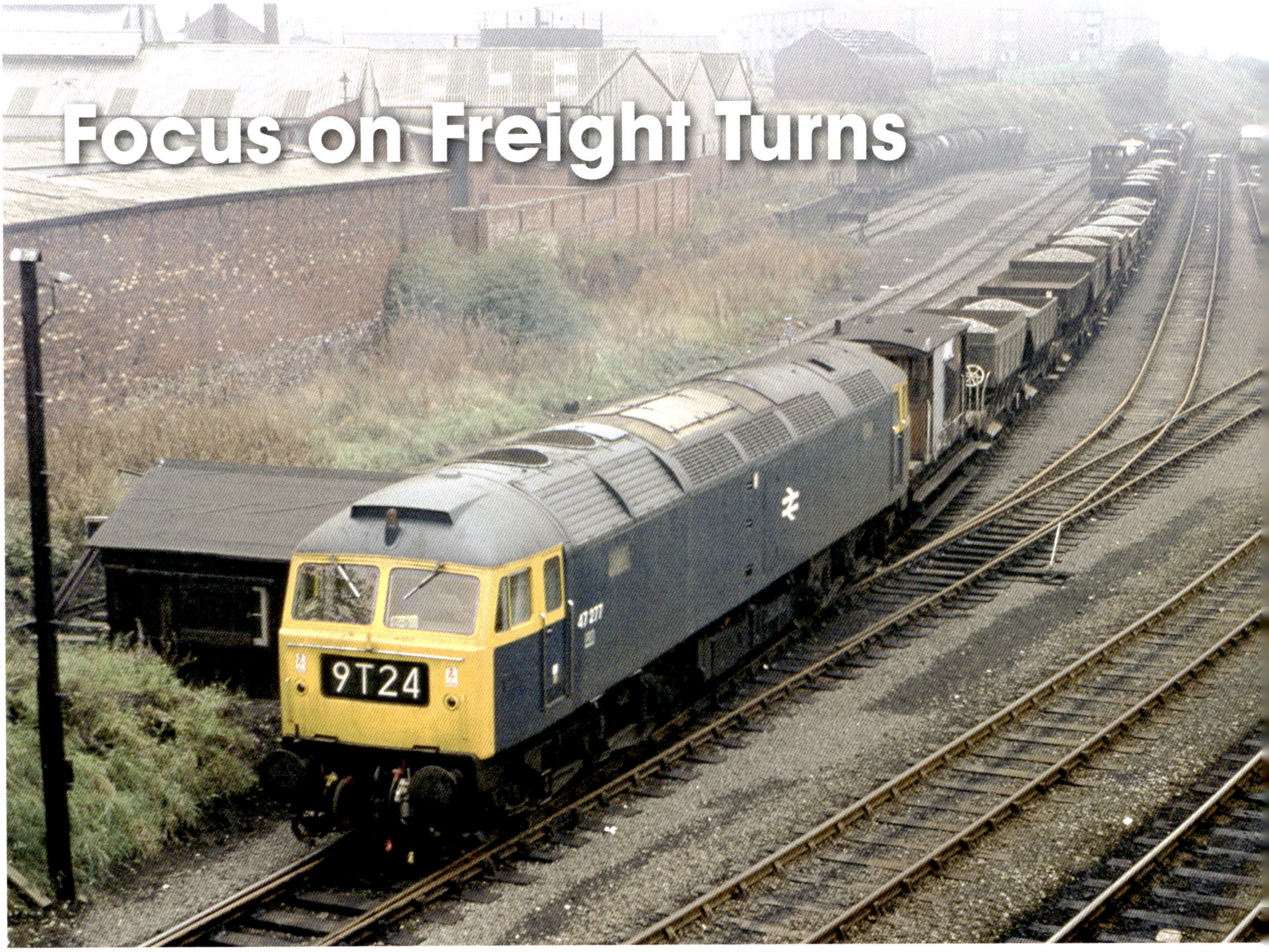

Flashing light fitted 47277 usually found employment on local merry go round workings gets an outing today at the head of a permanent way train from Knottingley on Sunday 20 October 1973. ***Roger Bradley***

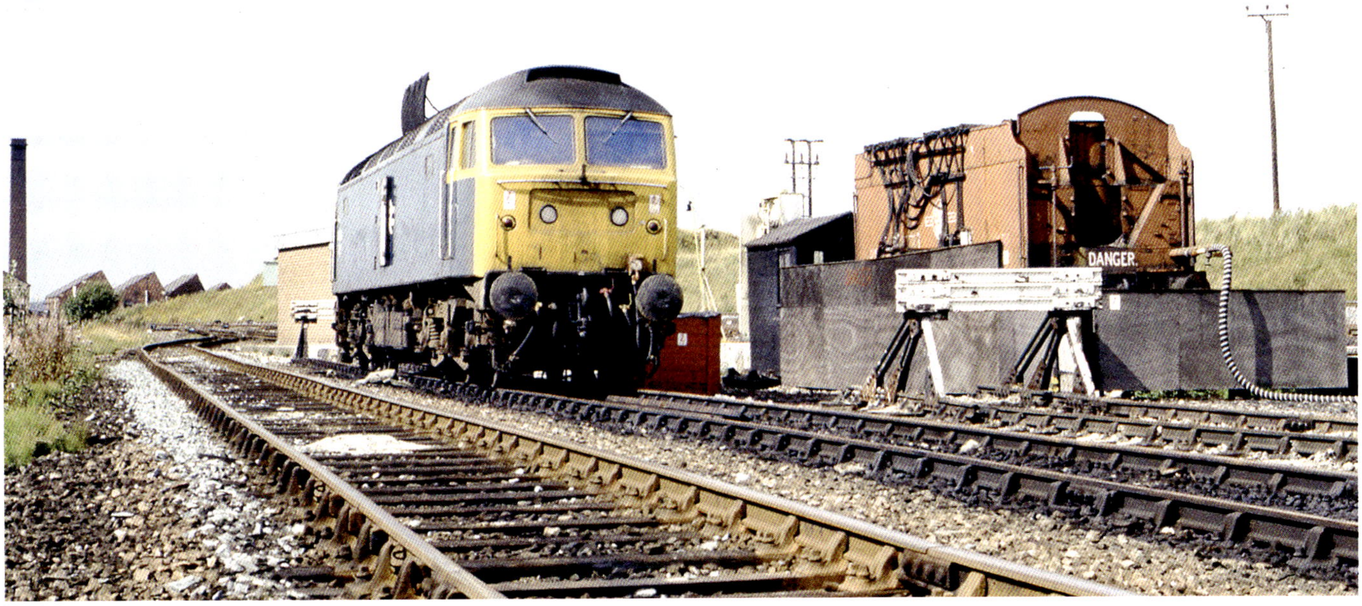

Being put on test connected up to an ex LNER tender as a load bank was 47551 at Healey Mills on 5 September 1977 this was another Yorkshire depot that once supplied a large range of freight duties. ***Nic Gledhill***

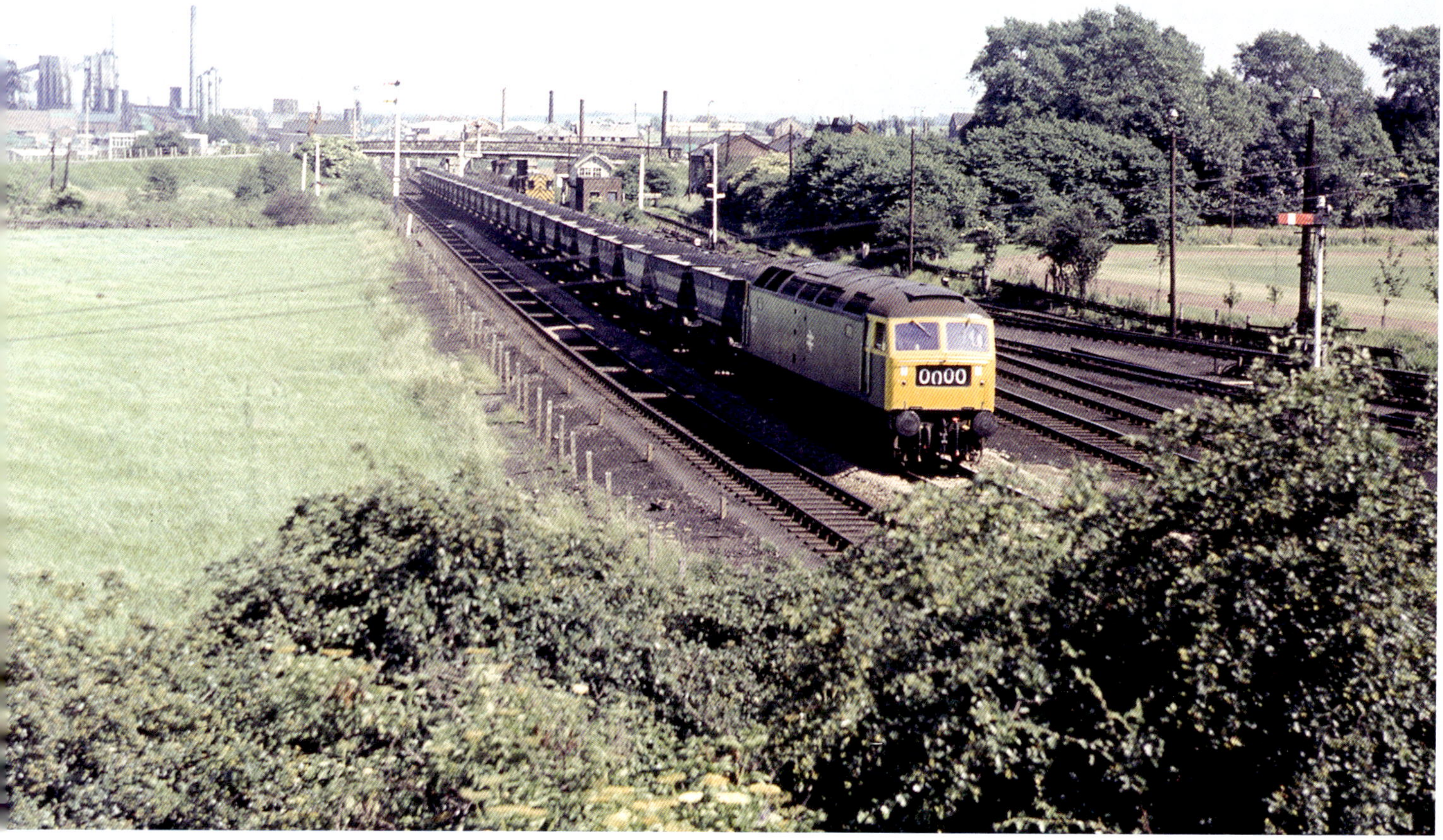

Part of the vast Manvers Main Coking Plant can be seen in the background to this view of Tinsley allocated 47368 with a loaded merry-go-round train near Wath on 24 June 1976. ***Phil Bidwell***

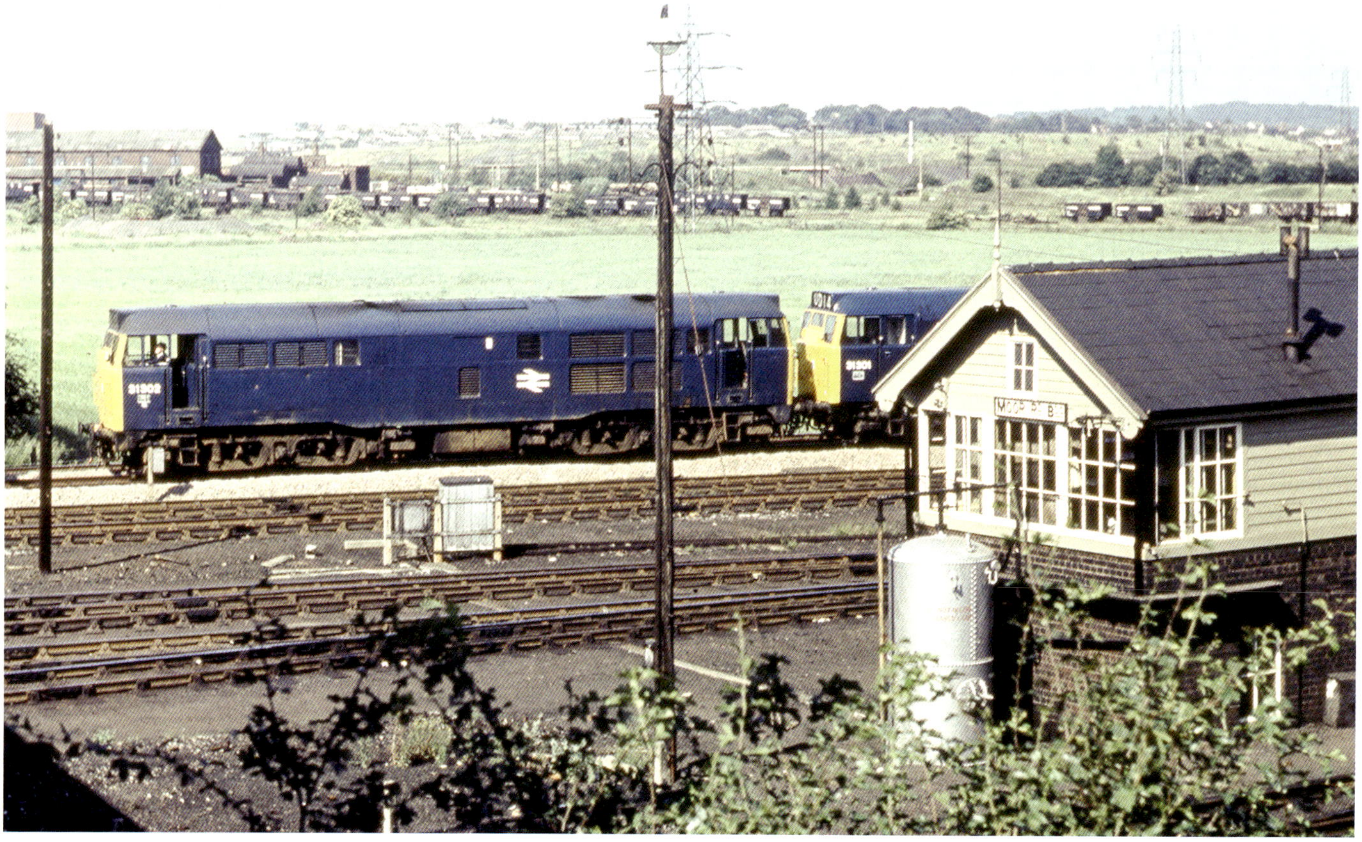

The Wath marshalling yards and depot complex can be seen across the fields in the background as 31302 and 31301 make their way light engine to pick up another freight working the same day. ***Phil Bidwell***

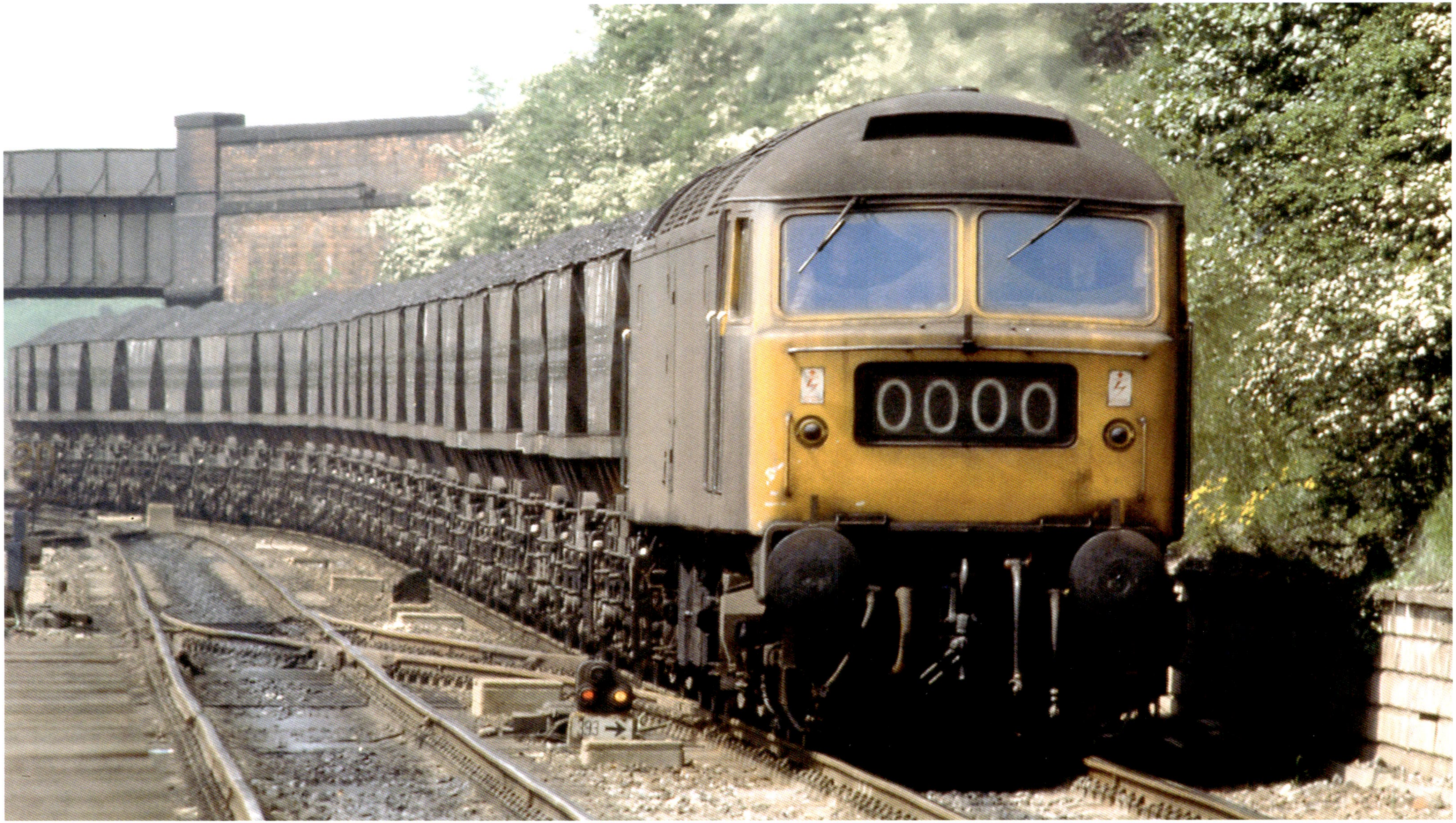

A powerful view of 47301 hard at work at Knottingley on 5 June 1979. This Class 47 had arrived at the depot here in the shadow of the huge power station at Drax. Today its generating capacity of 3,960 megawatts is the highest of any power station in the United Kingdom and Western Europe, providing about 7% of the United Kingdom's electricity supply. Opened in 1974 and extended in the mid-1980s, the power station was initially operated by the Central Electricity Generating Board. When first opened, the majority of the coal burned here was taken from various local collieries in Yorkshire including Kellingley, Prince of Wales, Ackton Hall, Sharlston, Fryston, Askern and Bentley. However, since the miners' strike in the mid-1980s, all but one of these mines have since shut. ***Brian Daniels***

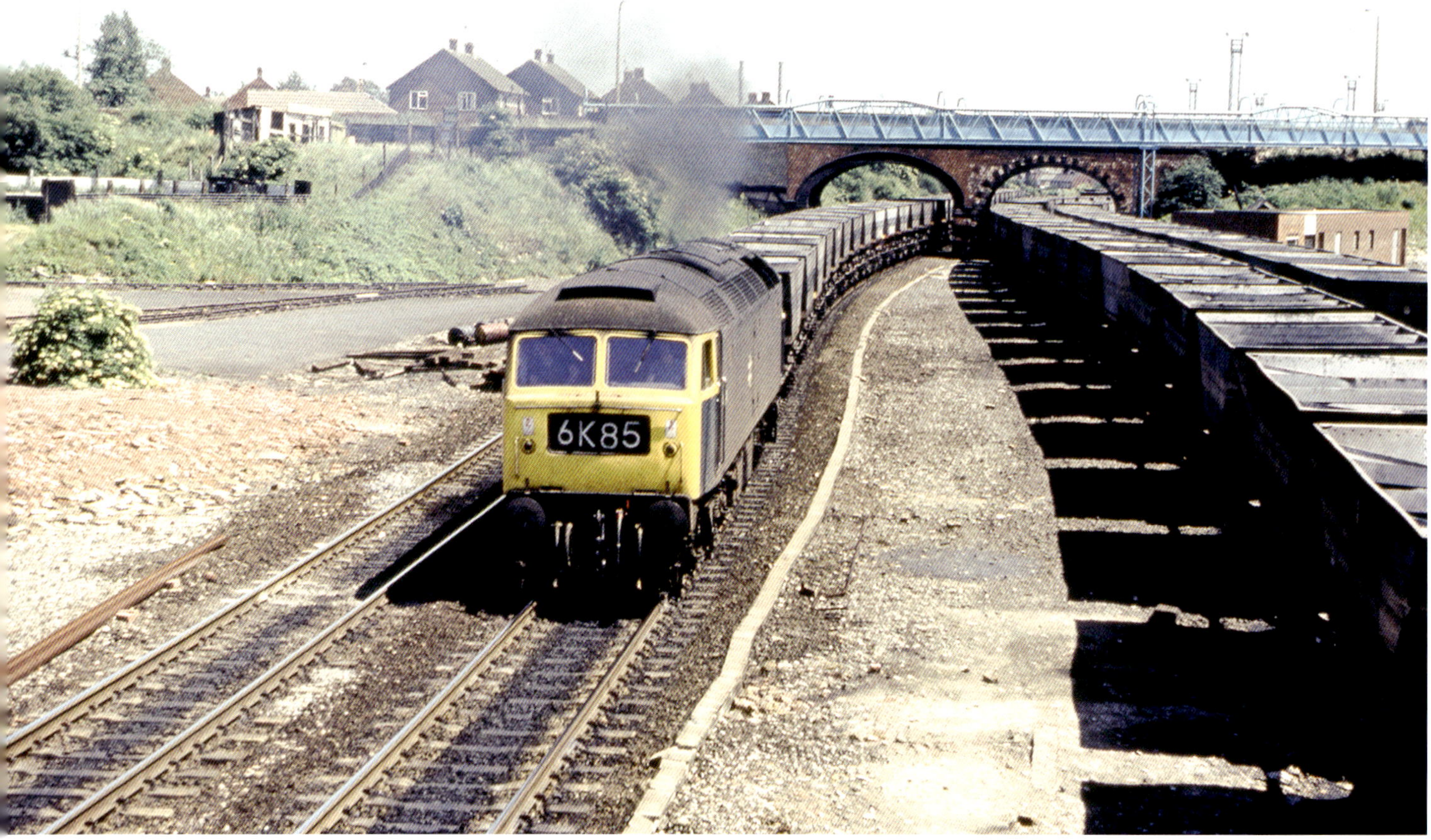

The exhaust shows that plenty of power is being applied here once again as 47374 passes through Knottingley on 24 June 1976. ***Phil Bidwell***

Below and Opposite: Two shots taken at Selby on 26 August 1978, firstly with 40074 with grain empties between Millerhill and Whitemoor. Then a light engine movement sends 20145 and 20144 back to York. ***Both: Len Ball***

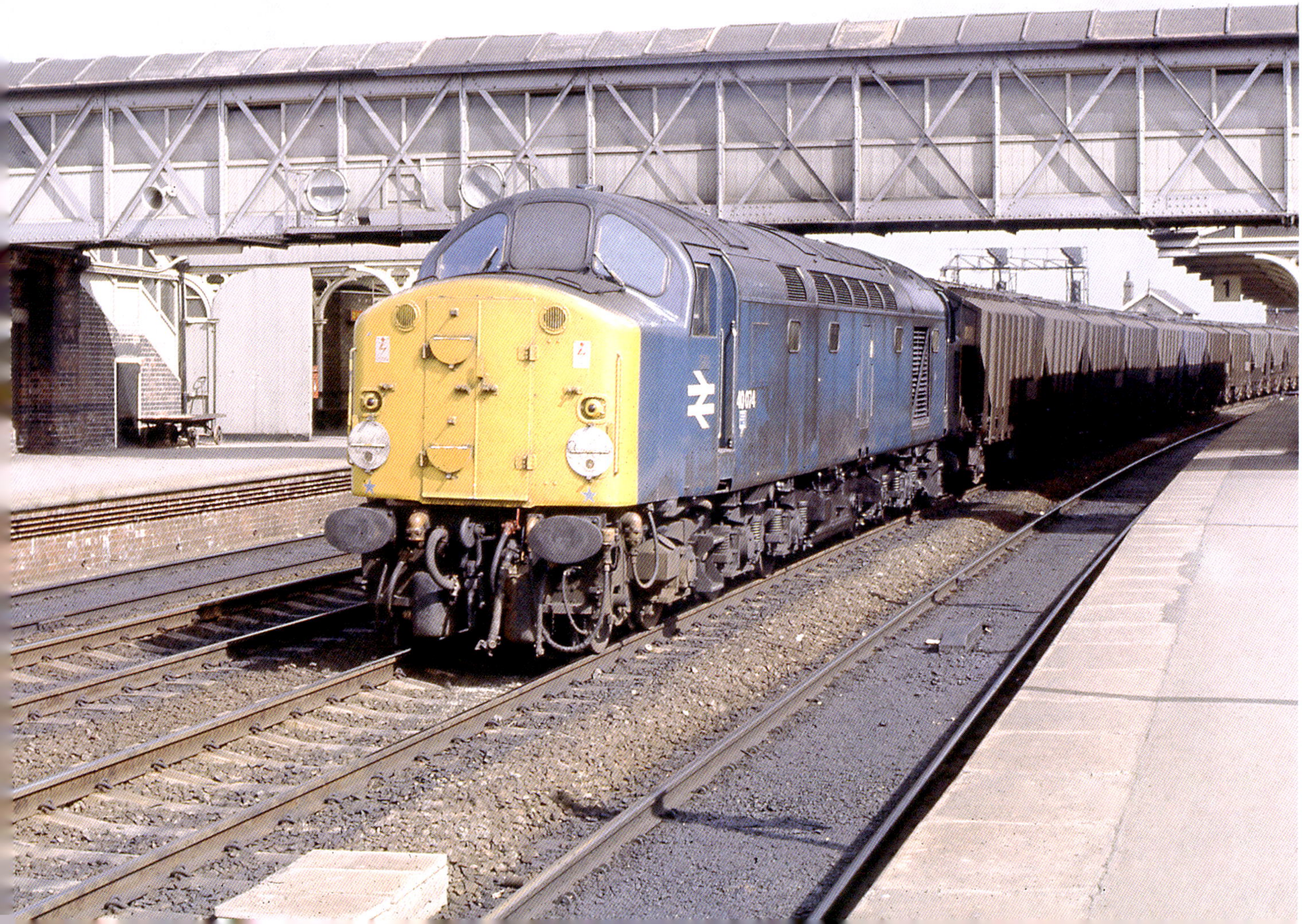

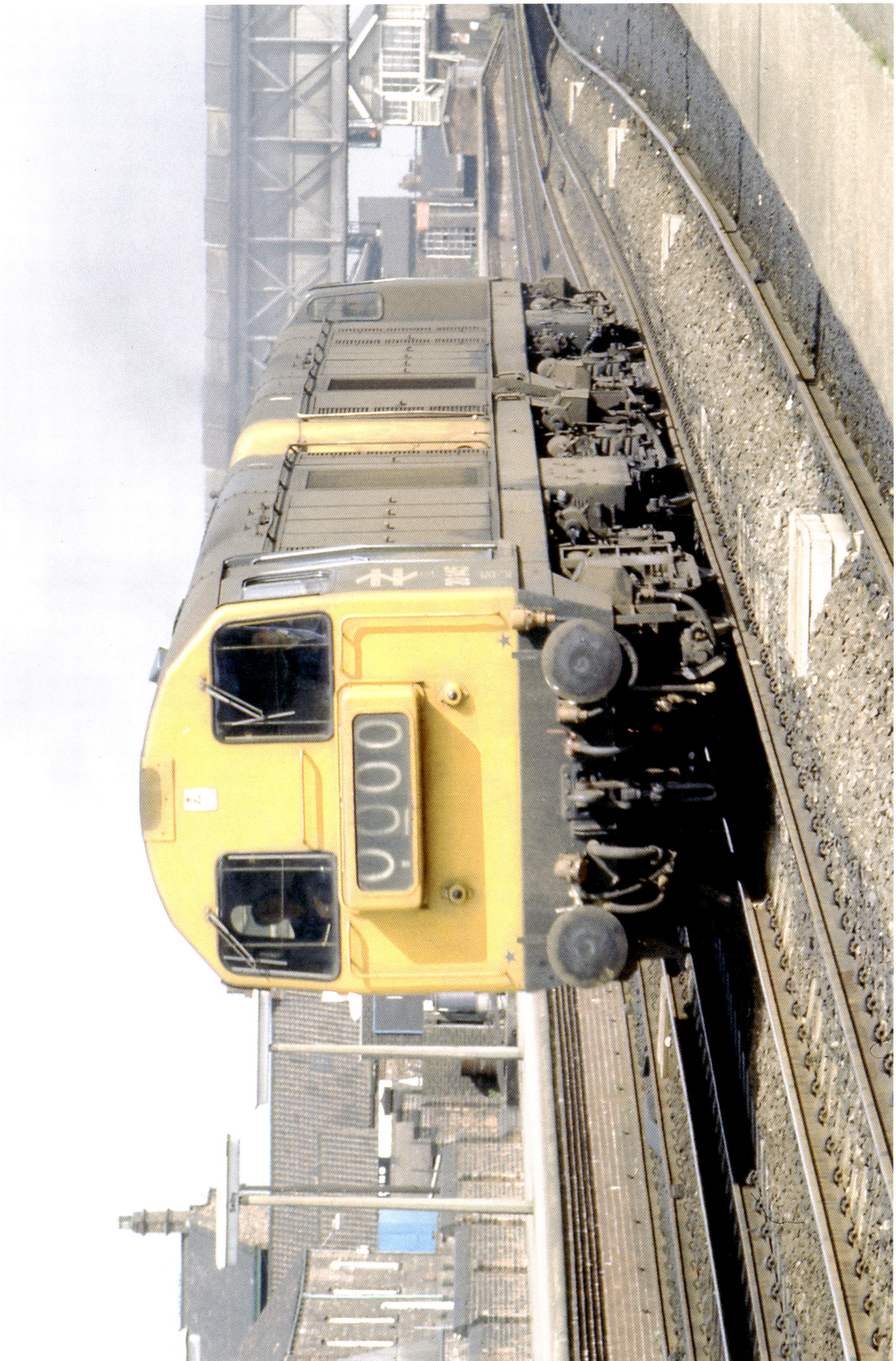

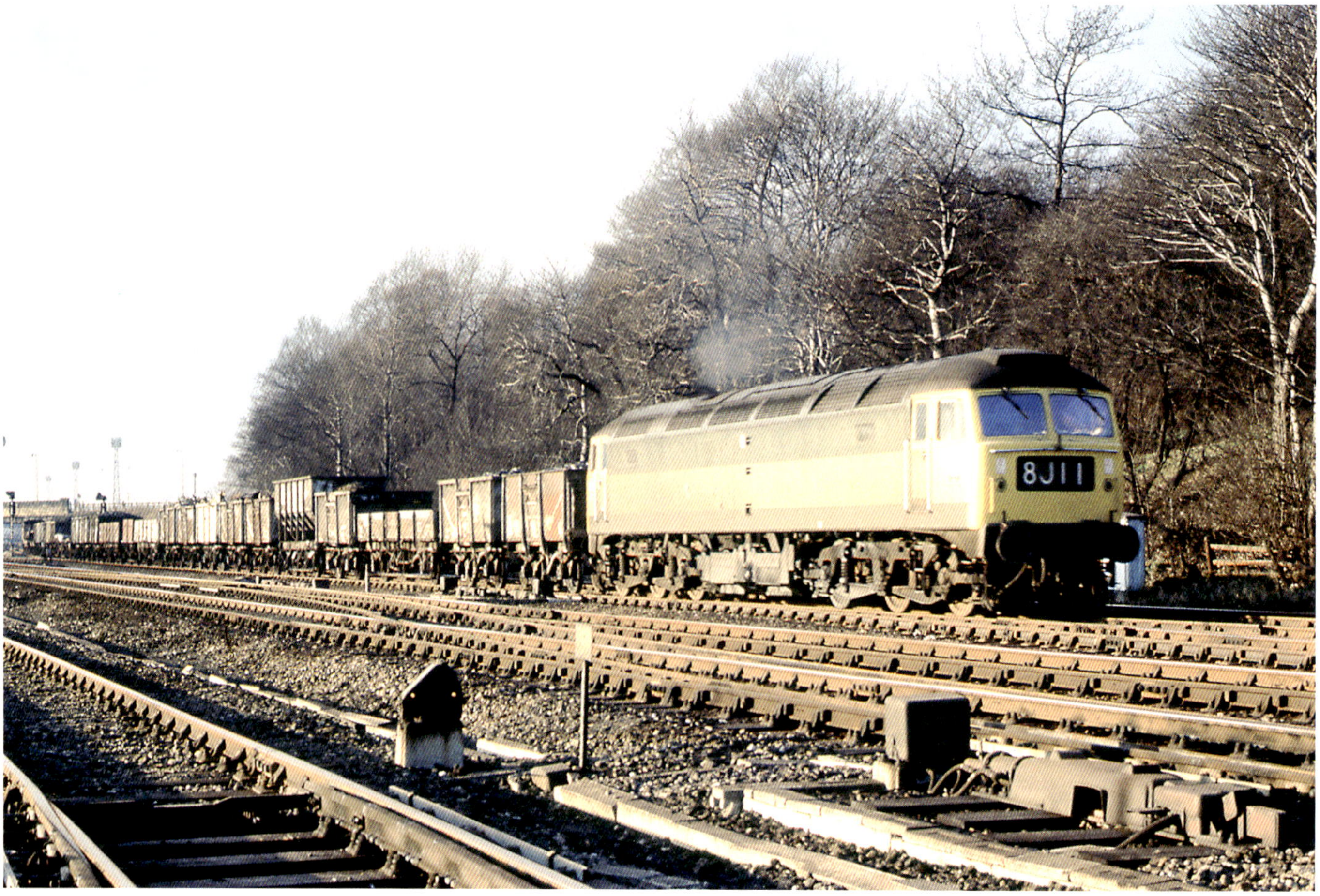

A fine mixture of wagons can be seen behind 1984 at Horbury in 1972 at a time before block workings became the norm. ***Roger Griffiths***

Doncaster built 56033 makes its way back onto the mainline from the loop at Hatfield and Stainforth in 1979 with yet another coal working. ***Arthur Wilson***

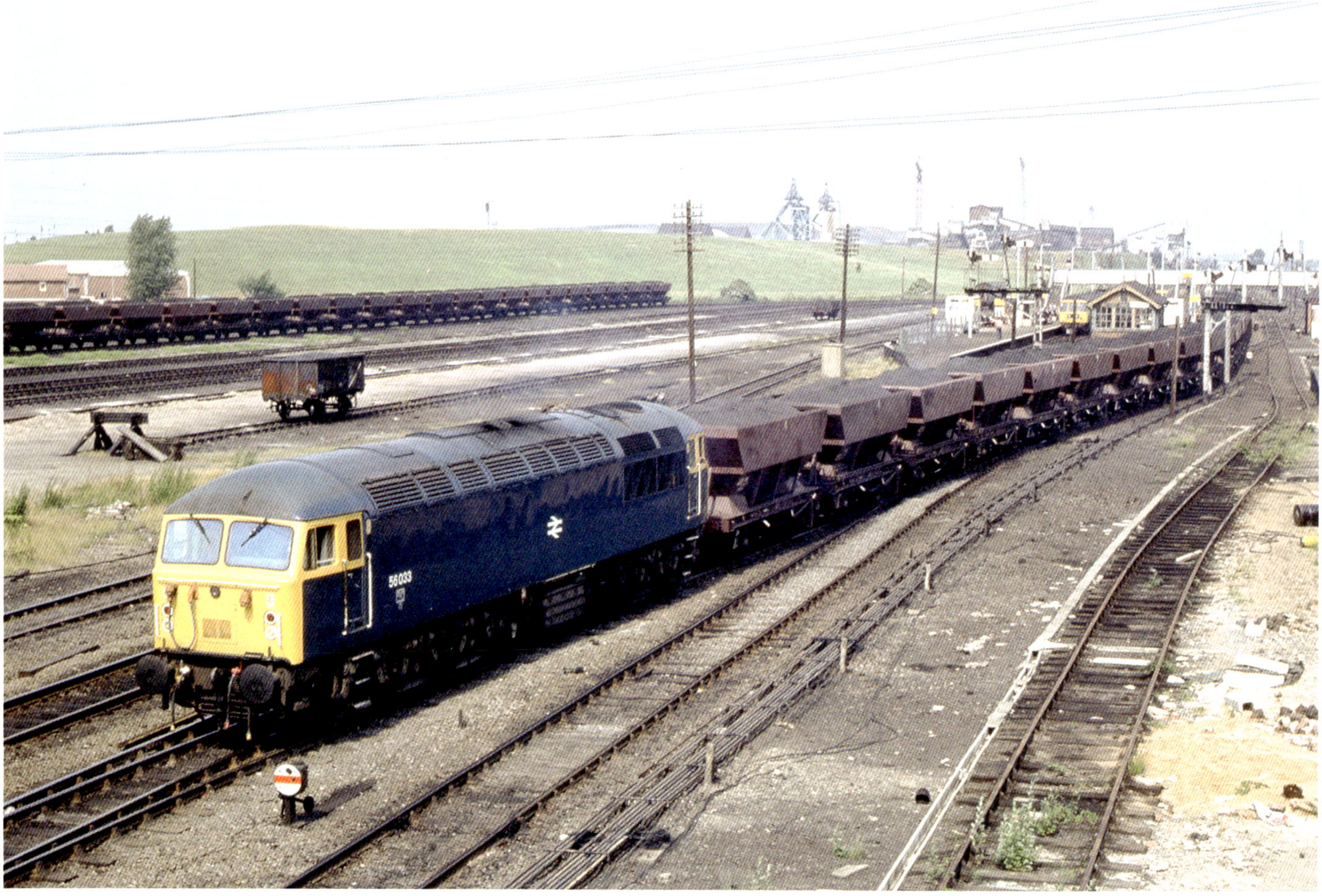

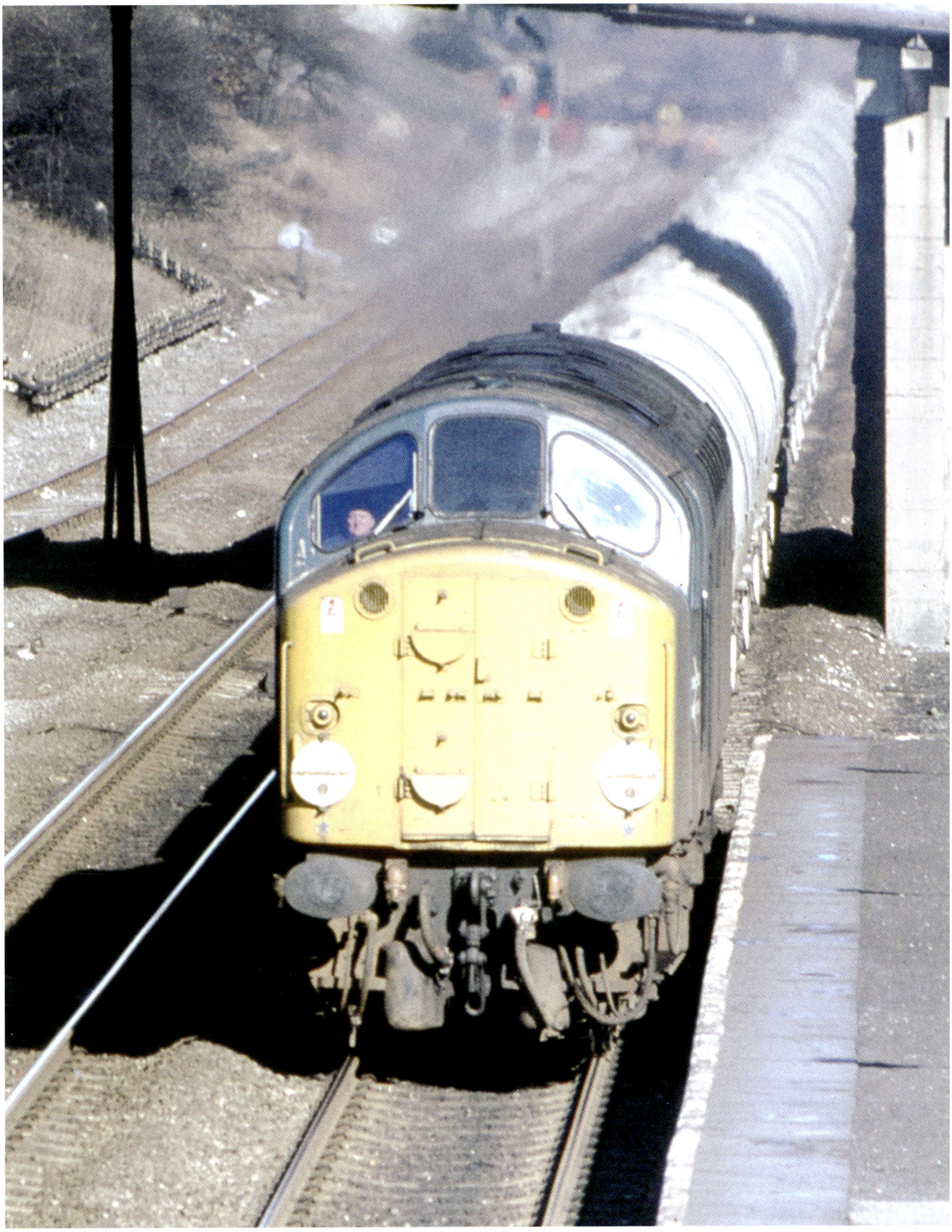

It is one of those block workings that has the driver of 40100 squinting in the low winter sunshine as his Class 40 storms past Brightside on 8 March 1978. The Hitchhiker's Guide to the Galaxy was first broadcast by BBC Radio 4 also on this day. ***Strathwood Library Collection***

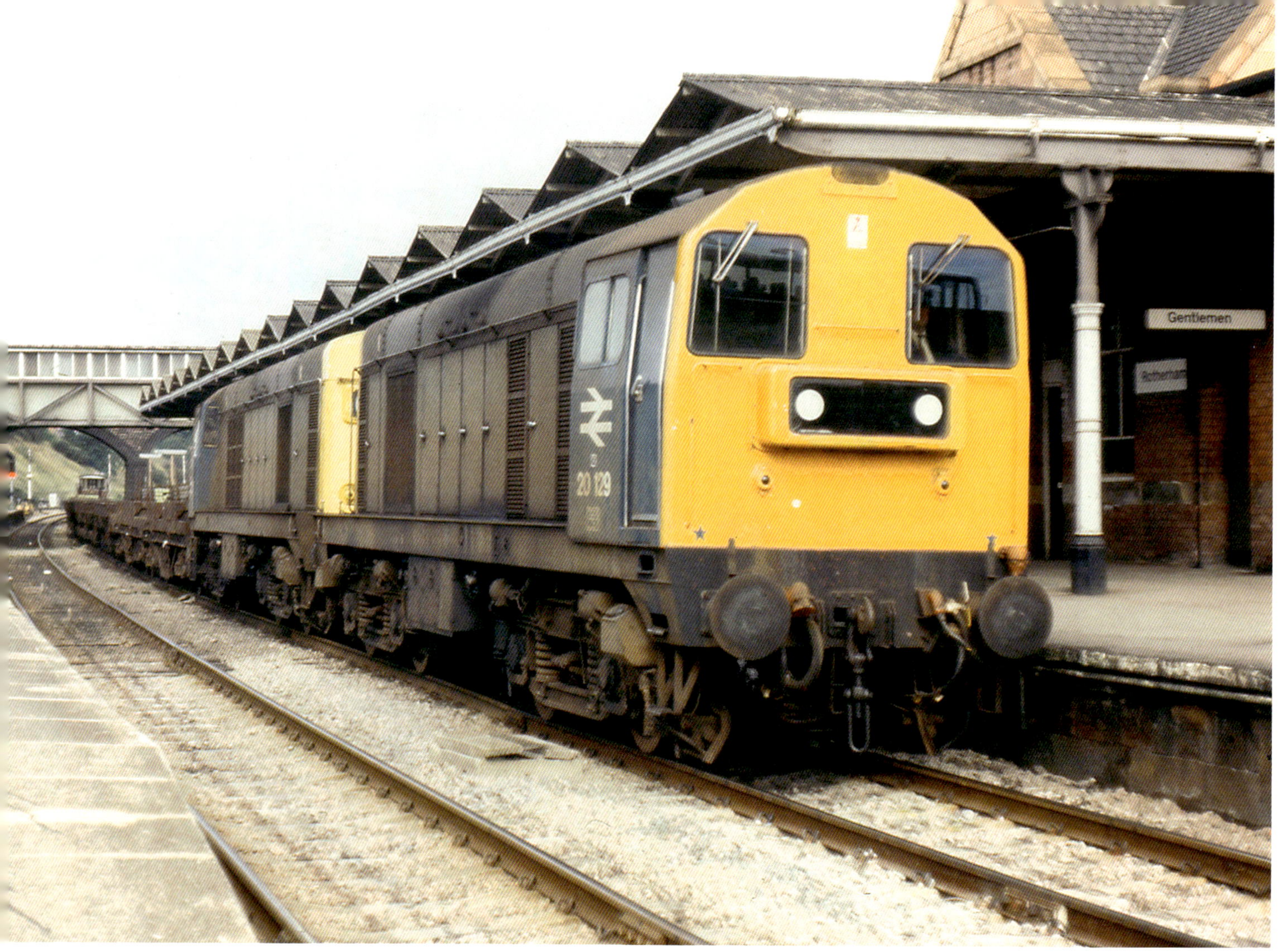

A rake of bogie bolster wagons is brought through freshly relaid track at Rotherham on 12 September 1978 behind a Tinsley based pairing of 20129 and 20209. ***Brian Daniels.***

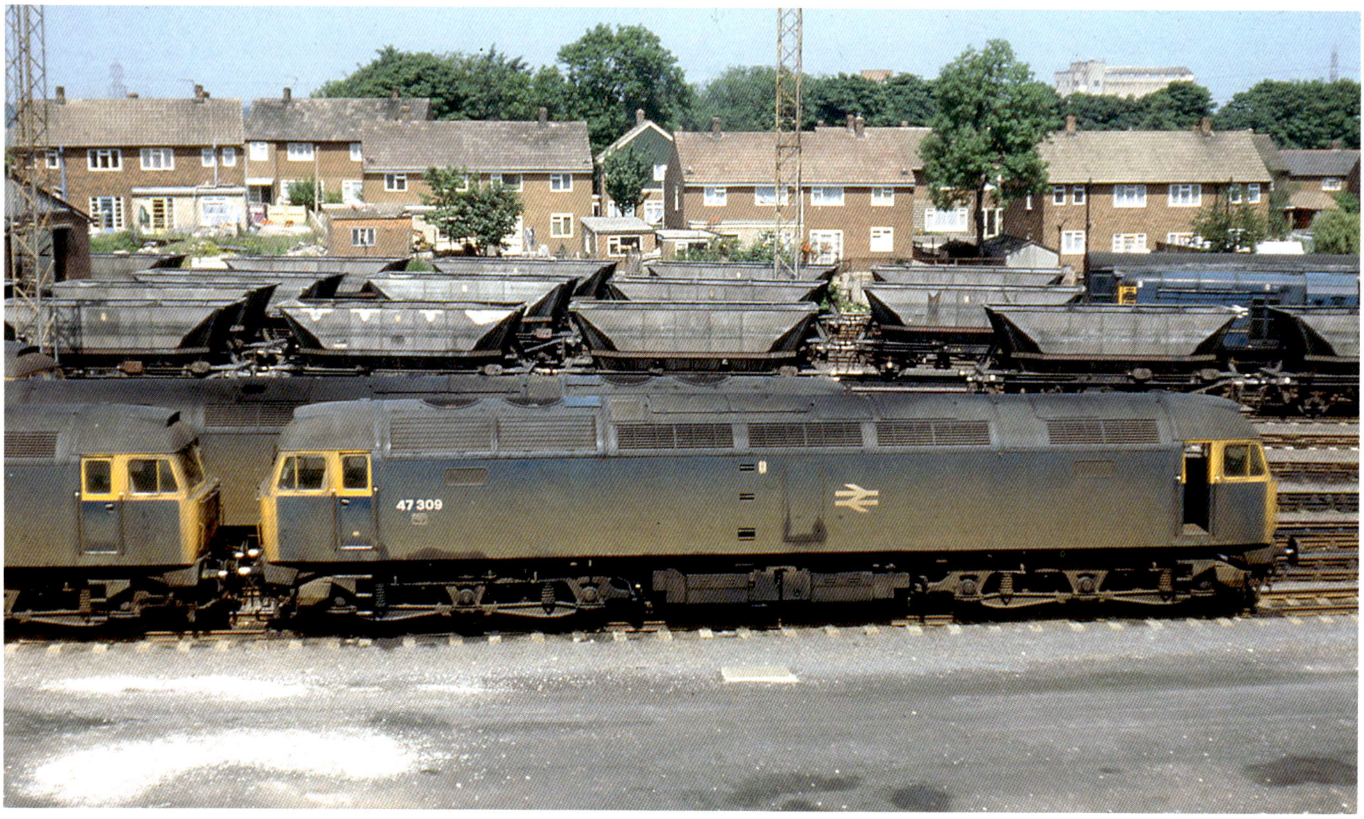

Knottingley depot opened on 1 July 1967 with an allocation of dedicated Class 47s for the heavy local coal traffic. On 18 June 1978 whilst many spotters were strolling around Doncaster Works for their Open Day others would drop in to record 47309 among those laid over for the weekend. ***Brian Daniels***

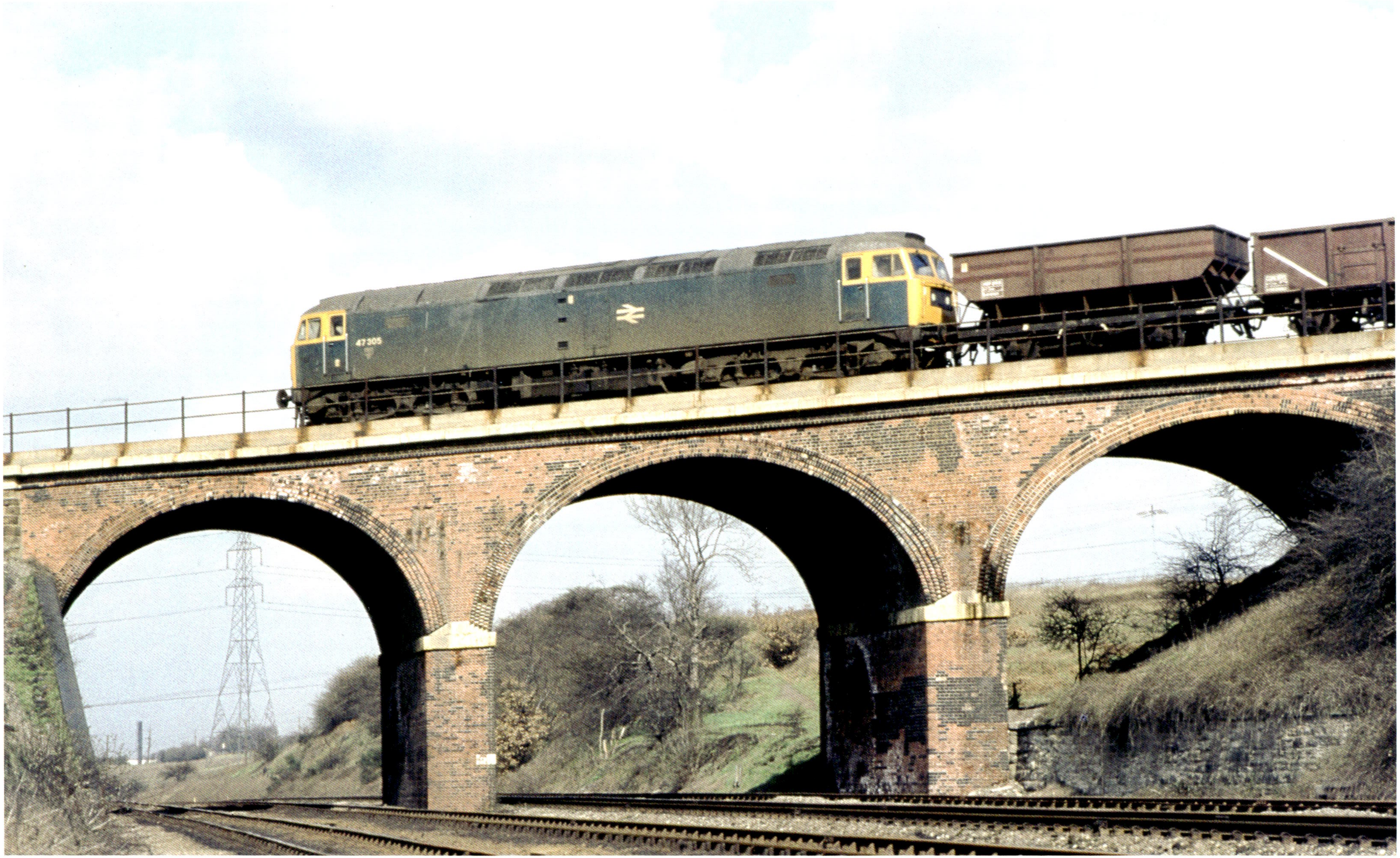

Based out of Tinsley when seen at Beighton on 29 March 1977 was 47305 with a rake of mixed coal empties. The Britsih entry for the Eurovision song contest that year was sung by Lynsey de Paul and Mike Moran and appropriately for later years perhaps was entitled Rock Bottom, ironically it came second! ***Jeffrey Lane***

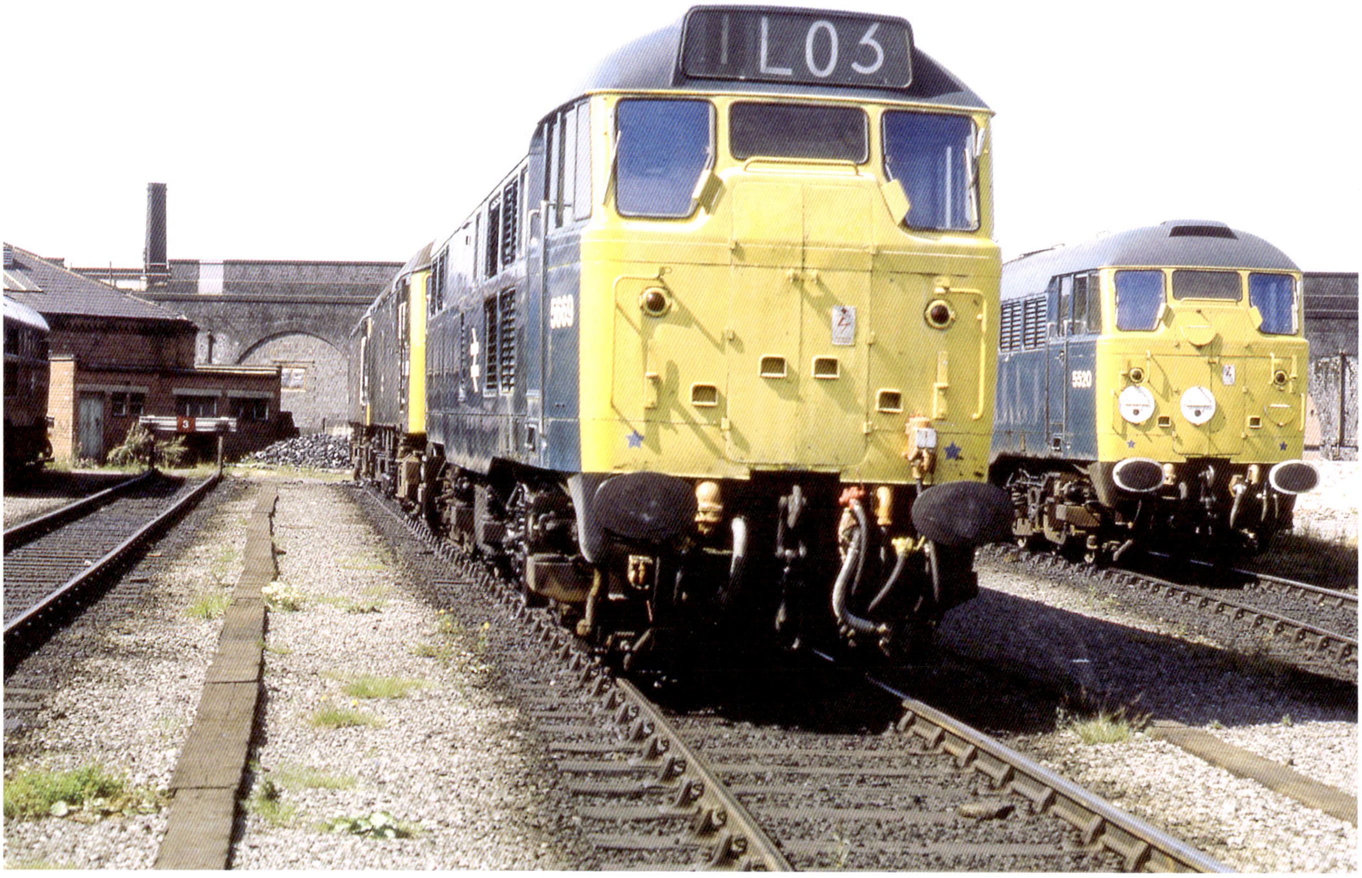

Leeds Holbeck enjoyed both freight and passenger rosters which brought workings for both Classes 25 and Class 31s when this view was exposed in January 1974. ***Ian King***

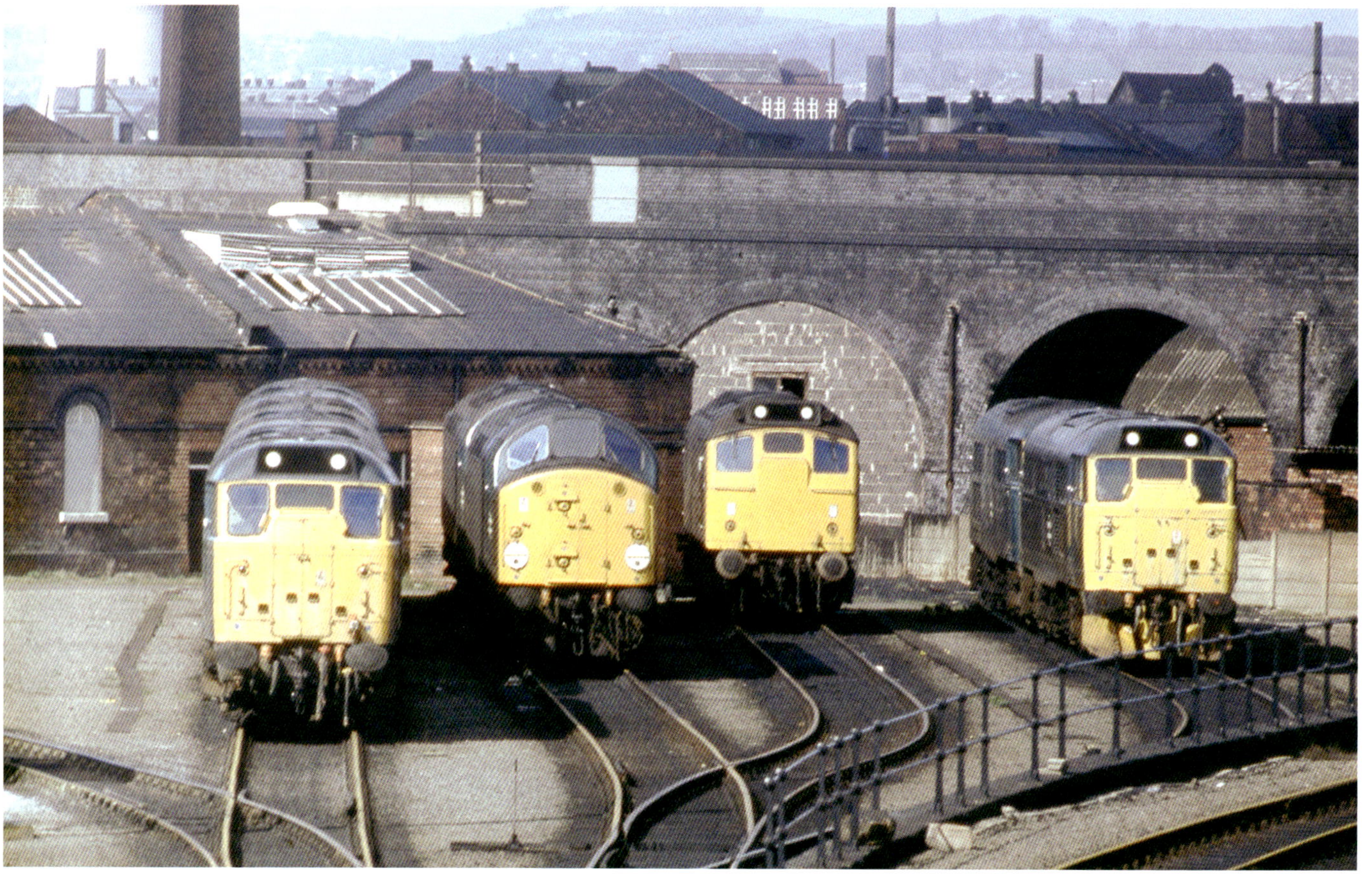

Another view taken here on 27 March 1978 throws up a couple of Class 40s as well the Type 2s this time for the notebooks of any spotters bunking the shed today. ***Strathwood Library Collection***

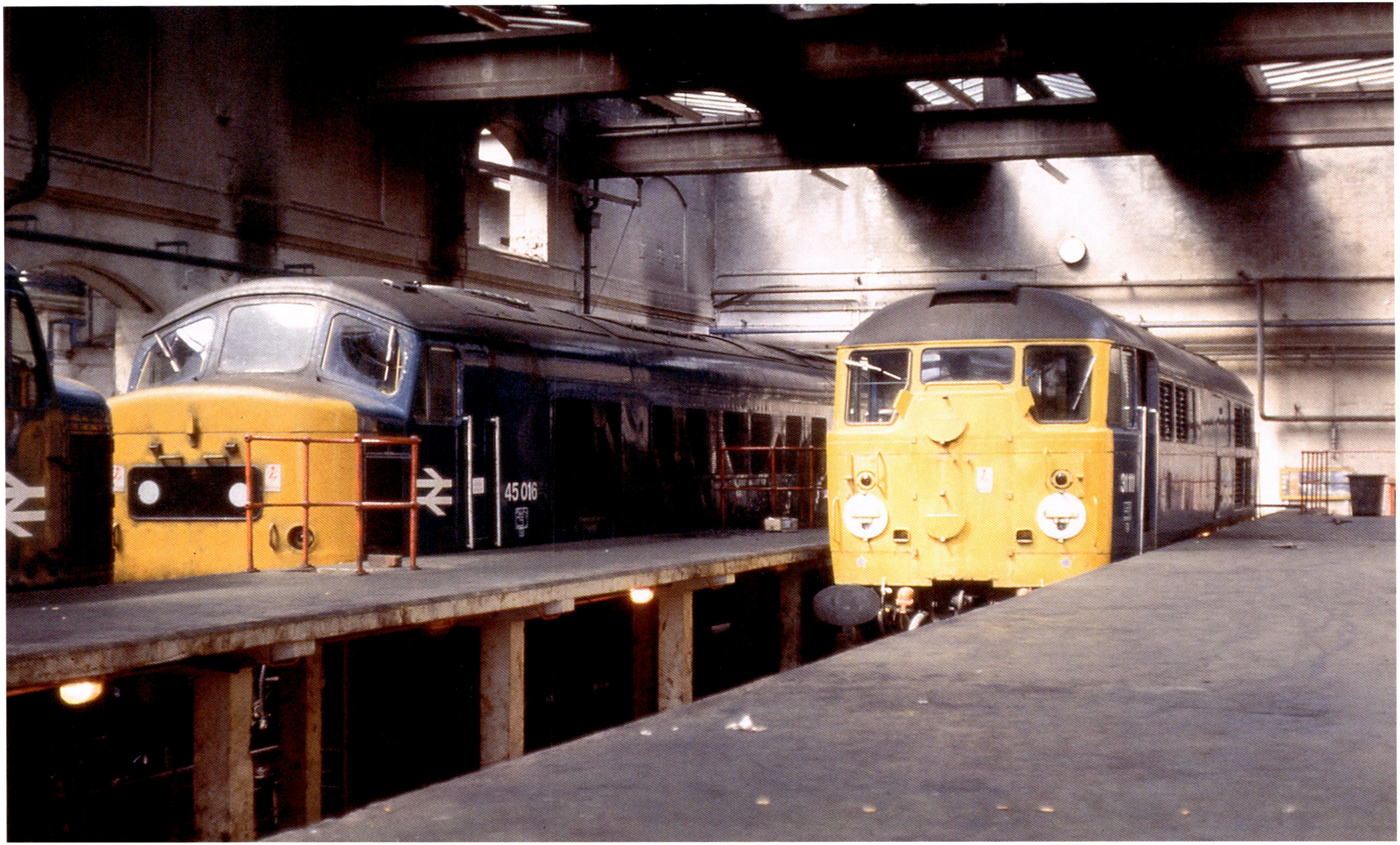

An interesting view taken inside the straight shed at Holbeck again over the weekend of the Doncaster Works Open Day yields 45016 alongside 31111 both locomotives recieveing some attention under cover. This shed had been the original machine shops here as in steam days locomotives had been stabled in the expansive roundhouse building with this conversion work taking place in the early sixties. ***Brian Daniels***

Passenger Turns

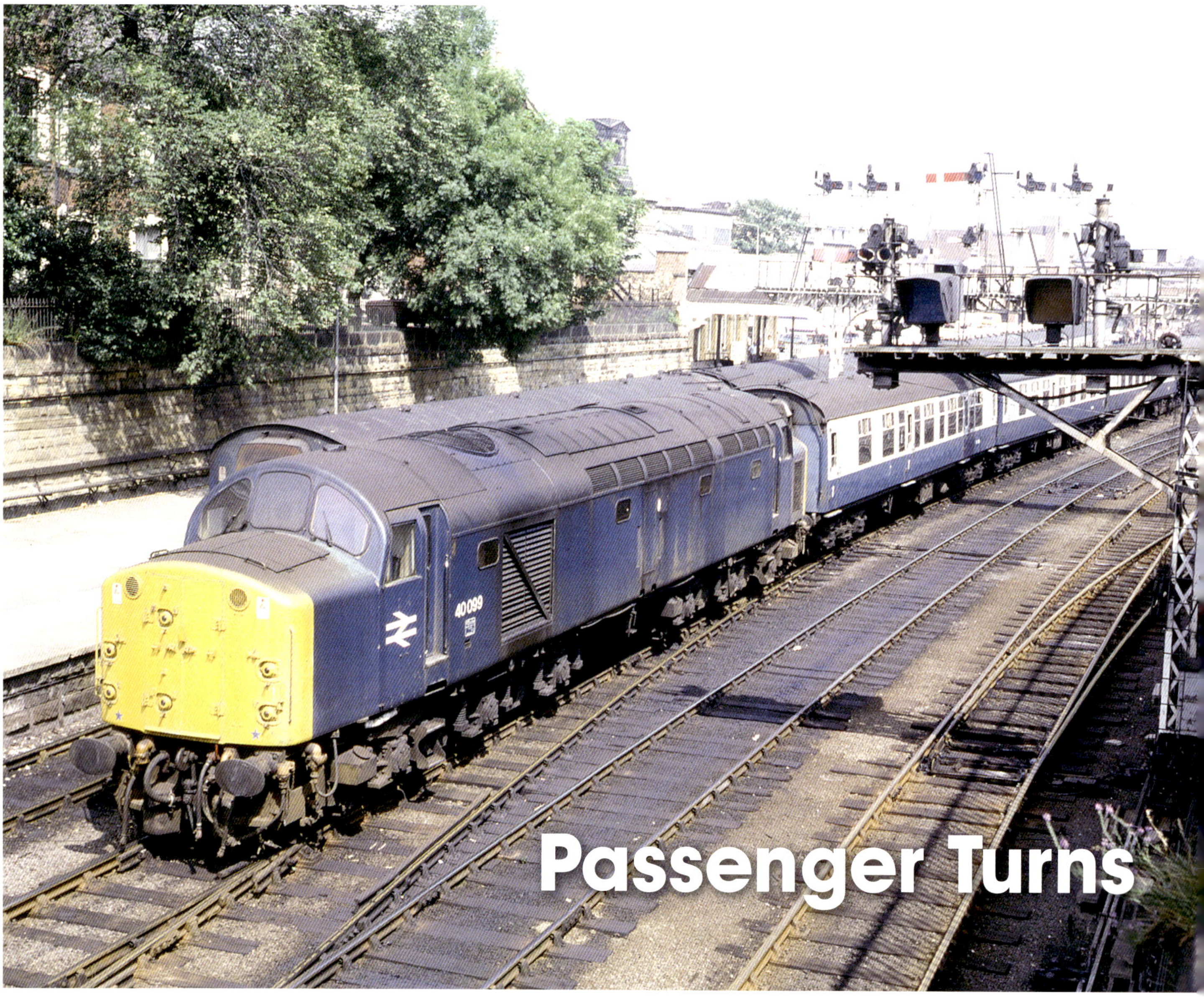

When seen having a day out by the seaside at Scarborough in 1979, 40099 was on the books of Longsight depot in Manchester for allocation of maintenance and duties. ***Strathwood Library Collection***

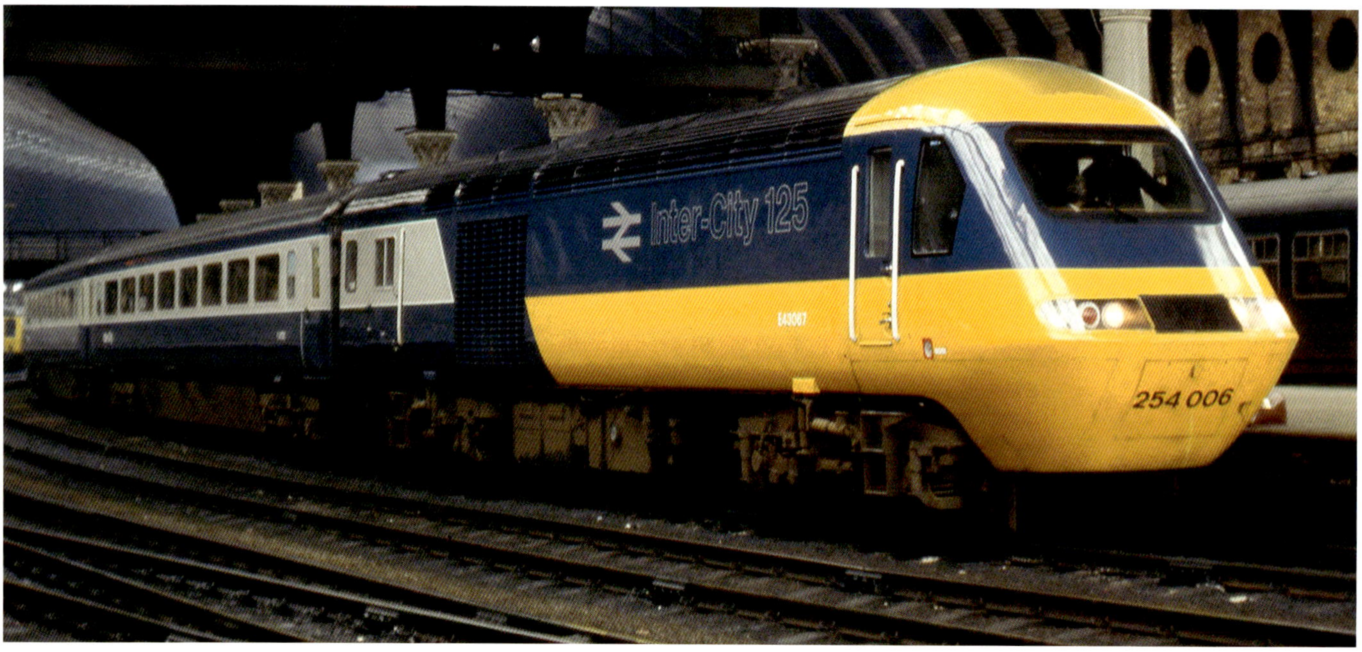

The new order at York on 3 May 1978 with E43067 leading an HST set northbound, Deltics best fear for the future from now on. ***Brian Daniels***

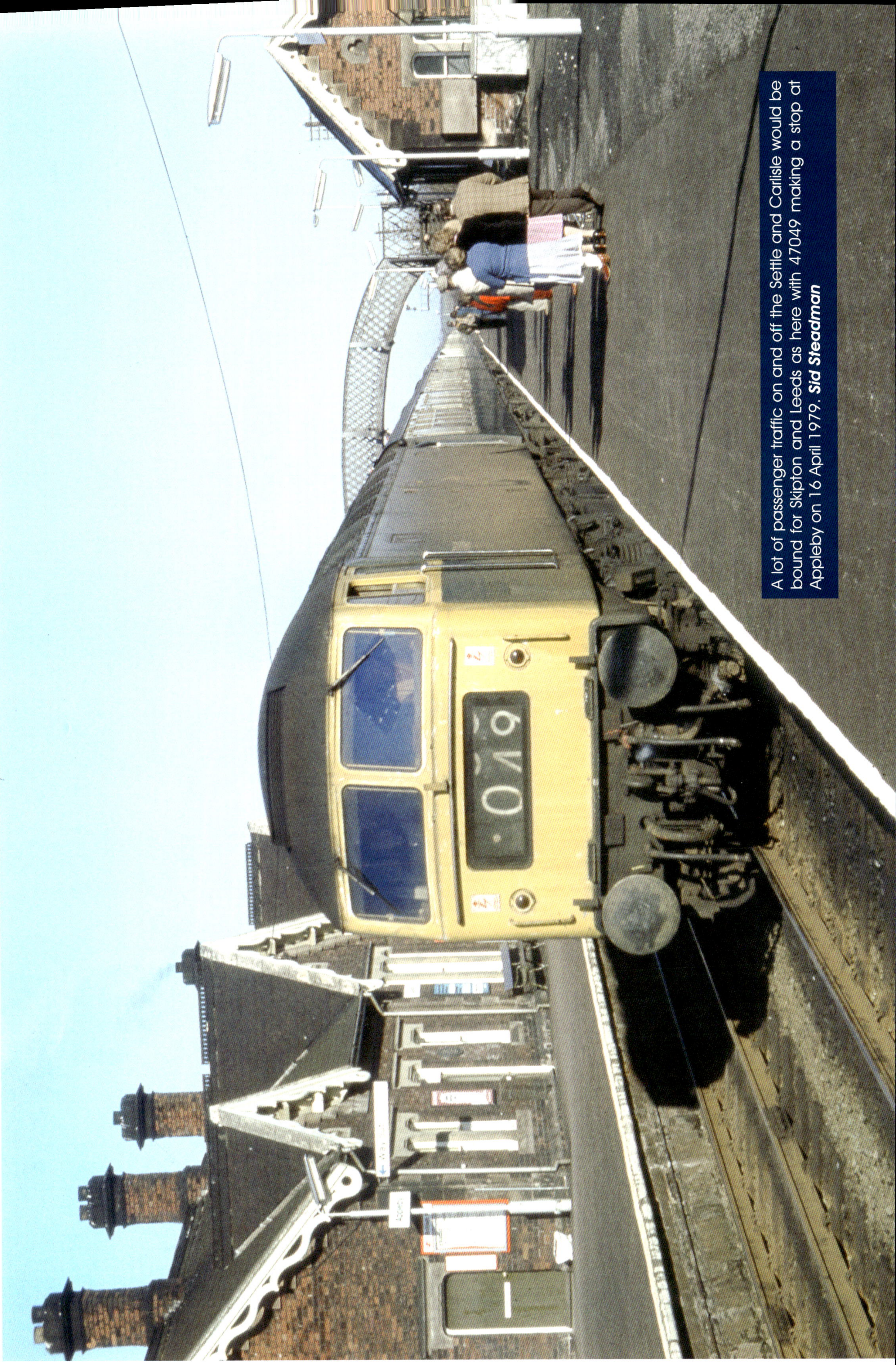

A lot of passenger traffic on and off the Settle and Carlisle would be bound for Skipton and Leeds as here with 47049 making a stop at Appleby on 16 April 1979. ***Sid Steadman***

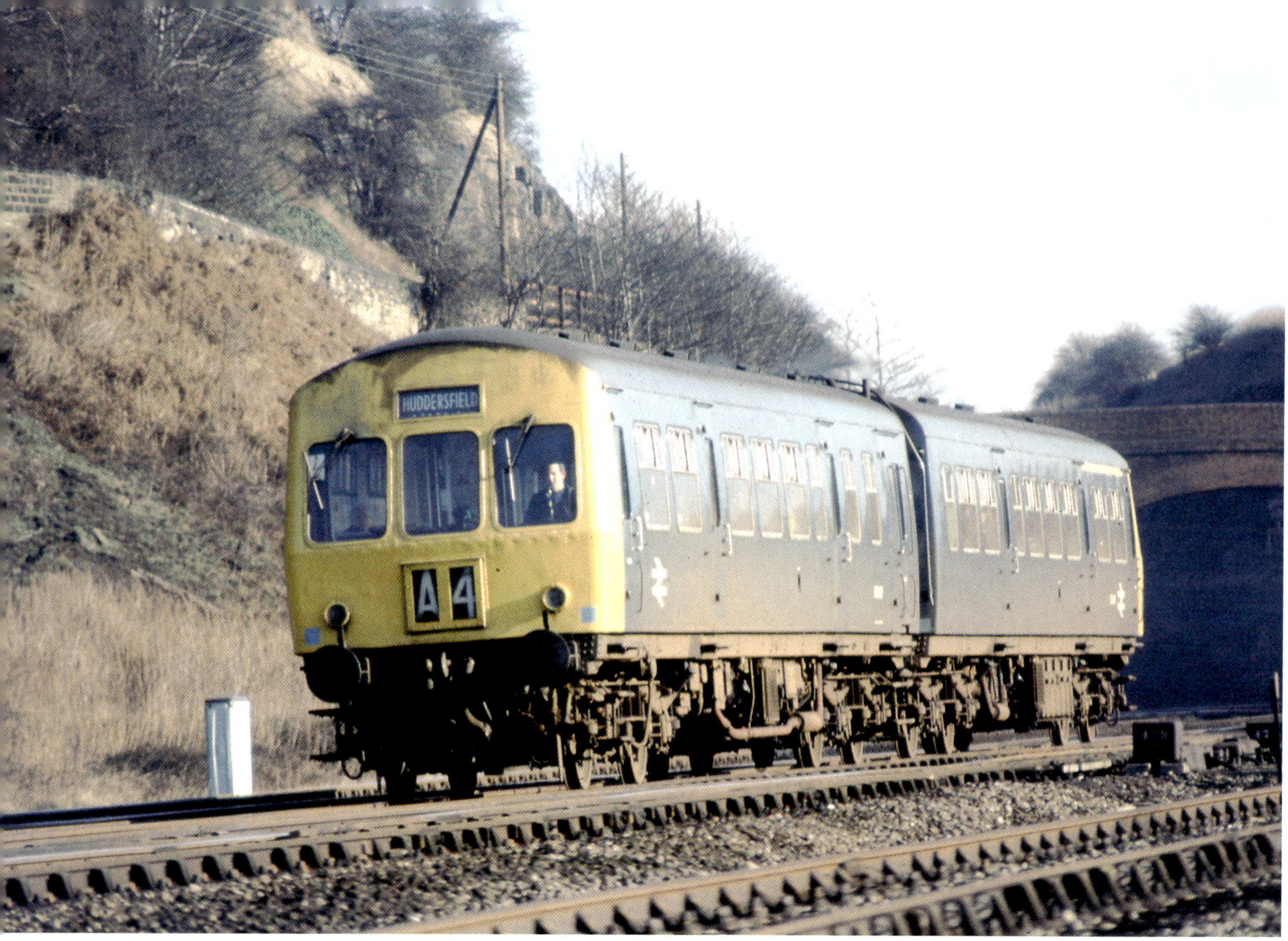

A two car Metropolitan Cammell DMU is more than suffcient to meet the needs of local traffic through Horbury cutting to and from Huddersfield during 1972. ***Roger Griffiths***

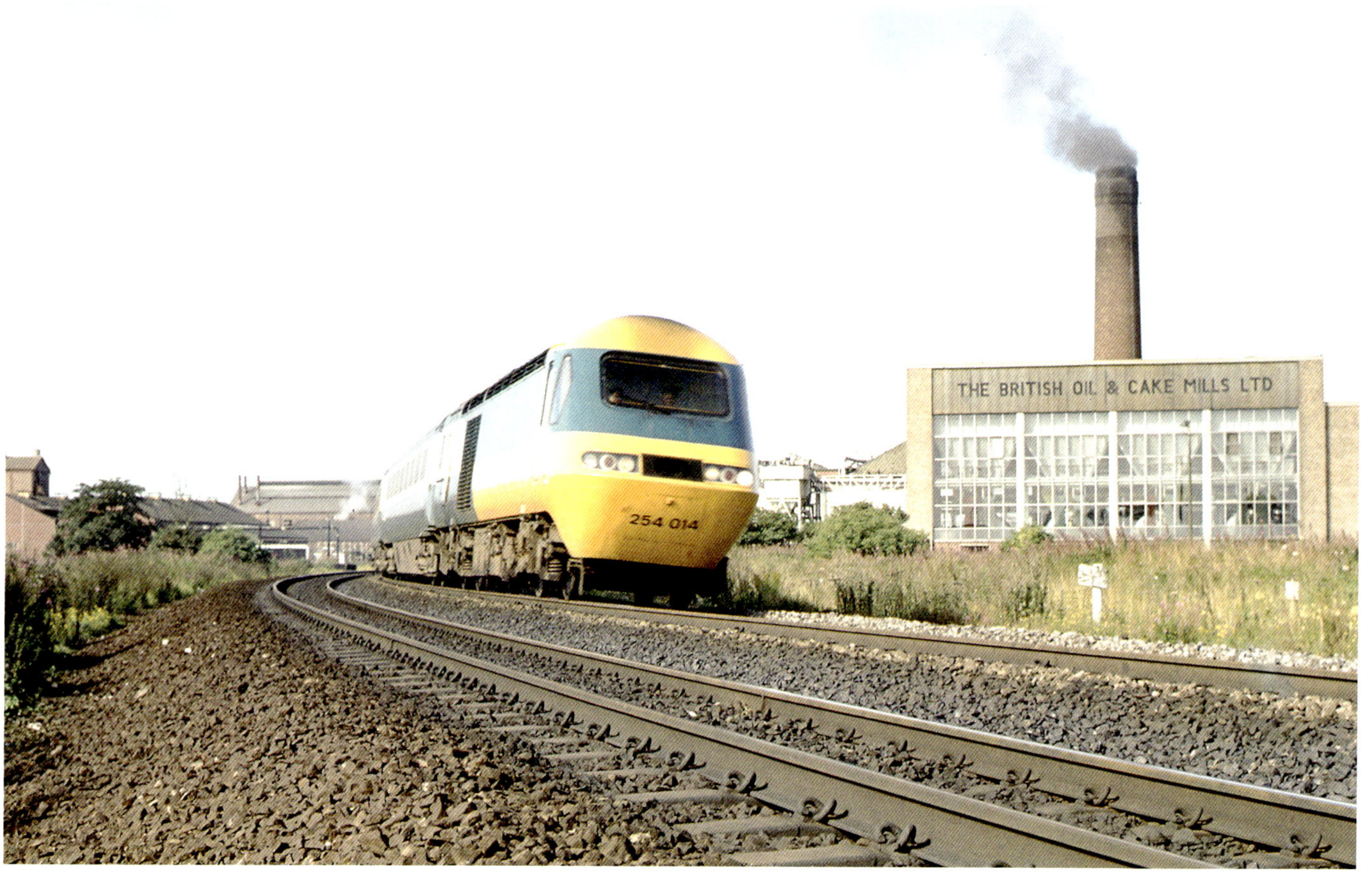

The animal feeds premises of British Oil & Cake Mills Ltd at Selby forms the backdrop to this HST working heading northwards on the East Coast Main Line on 2 September 1978. ***Nic Gledhill***

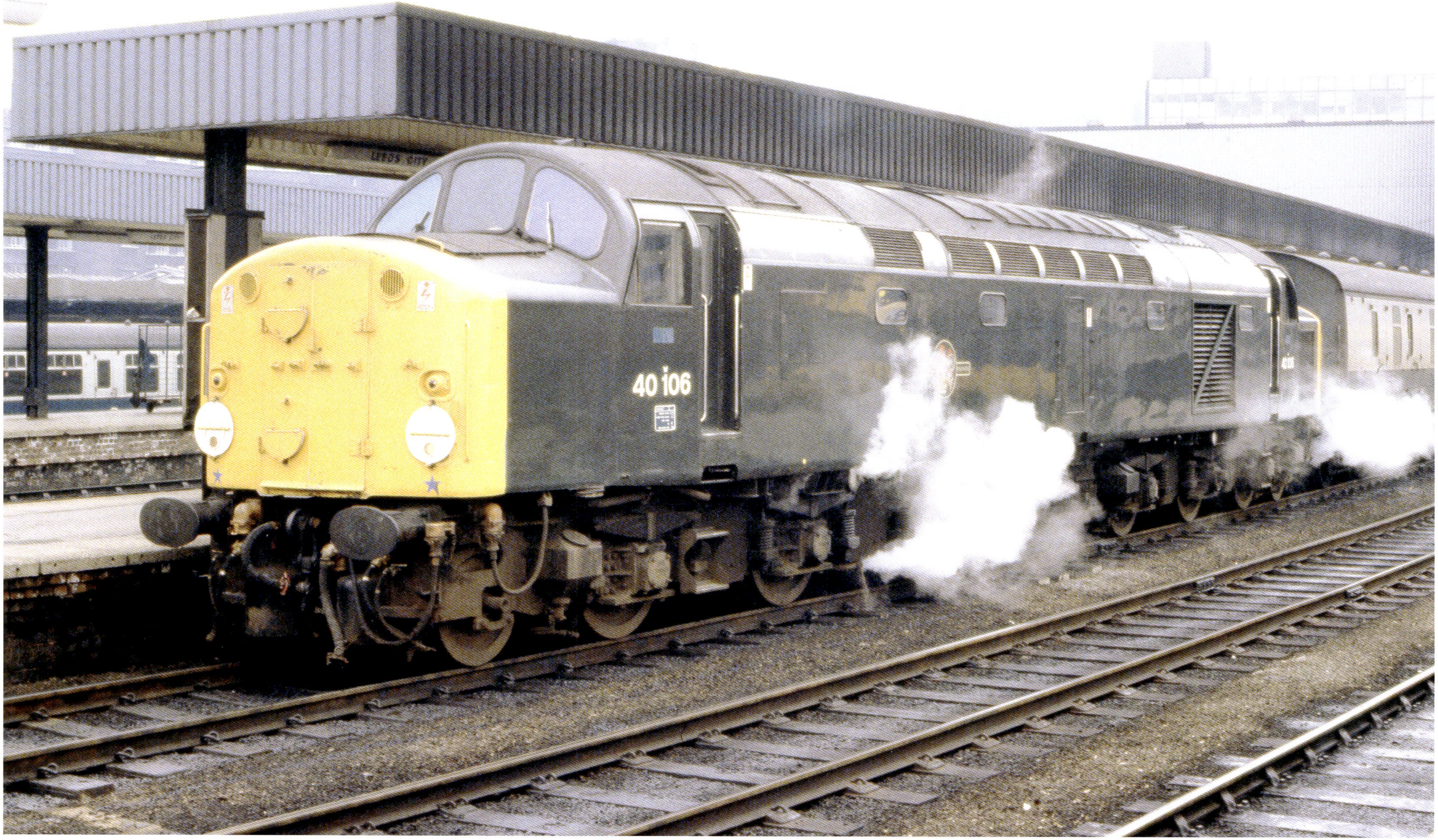

On 5 April 1979 the steam heating boiler is brewing nicely onboard 40106 keeping the passengers warm on its train at Leeds City for a working along the Settle & Carlisle. One of the most endearing sitcoms from the era was the Yorkshire based Open All Hours which first aired in 1976 and ran until 1985. It featured Arkwright as a tight-fisted shop owner in Doncaster, who would stop at nothing to keep his profits high and his overheads low, even if it meant harassing his nephew Granville. Arkwright's only weakness is his love - Nurse Gladys Emanuel, the much loved series featured Ronnie Barker and David Jason. ***Stuart Broughton***

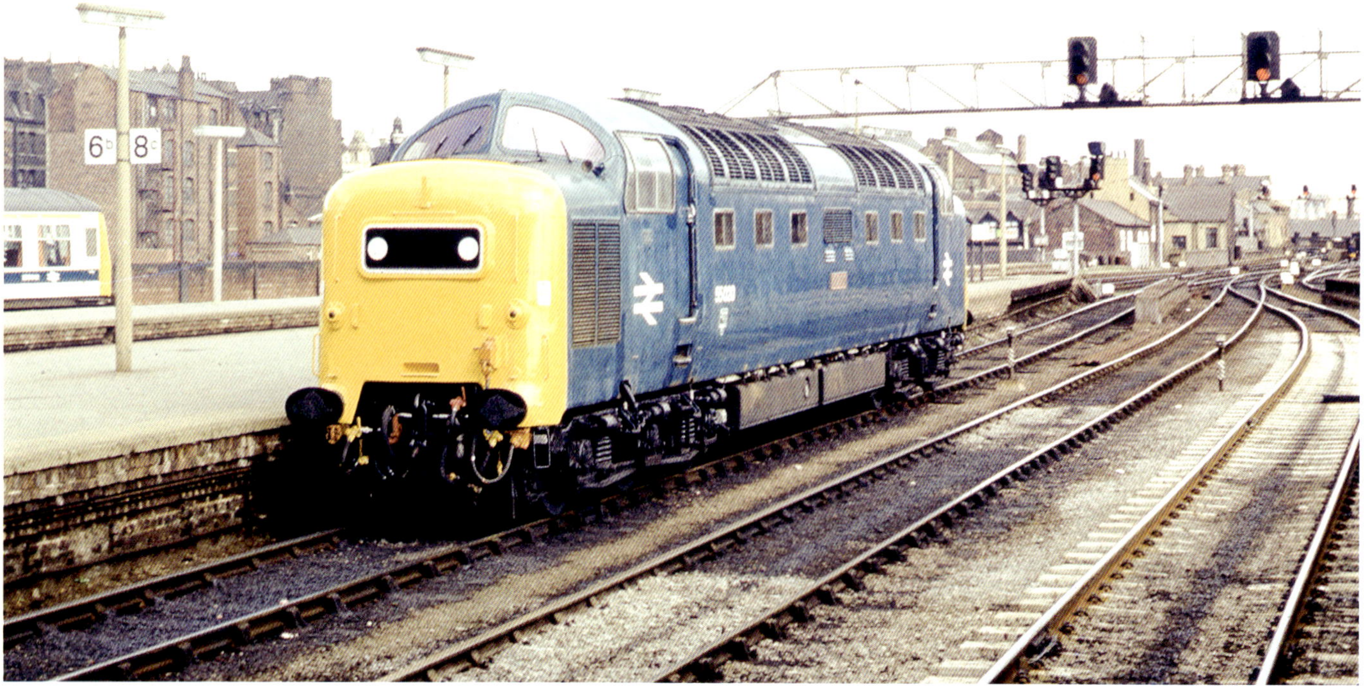

We catch sight once again of that ealry Deltic casualty 55020 Nimbus this time at Leeds City having come off an arrival on 12 September 1977. Another Yorkshire based sitcom started its incredible thirty seven year run in 1973 based around the small town of Holmfirth as the home of Last of the Summer Wine. ***Nev Sloper***

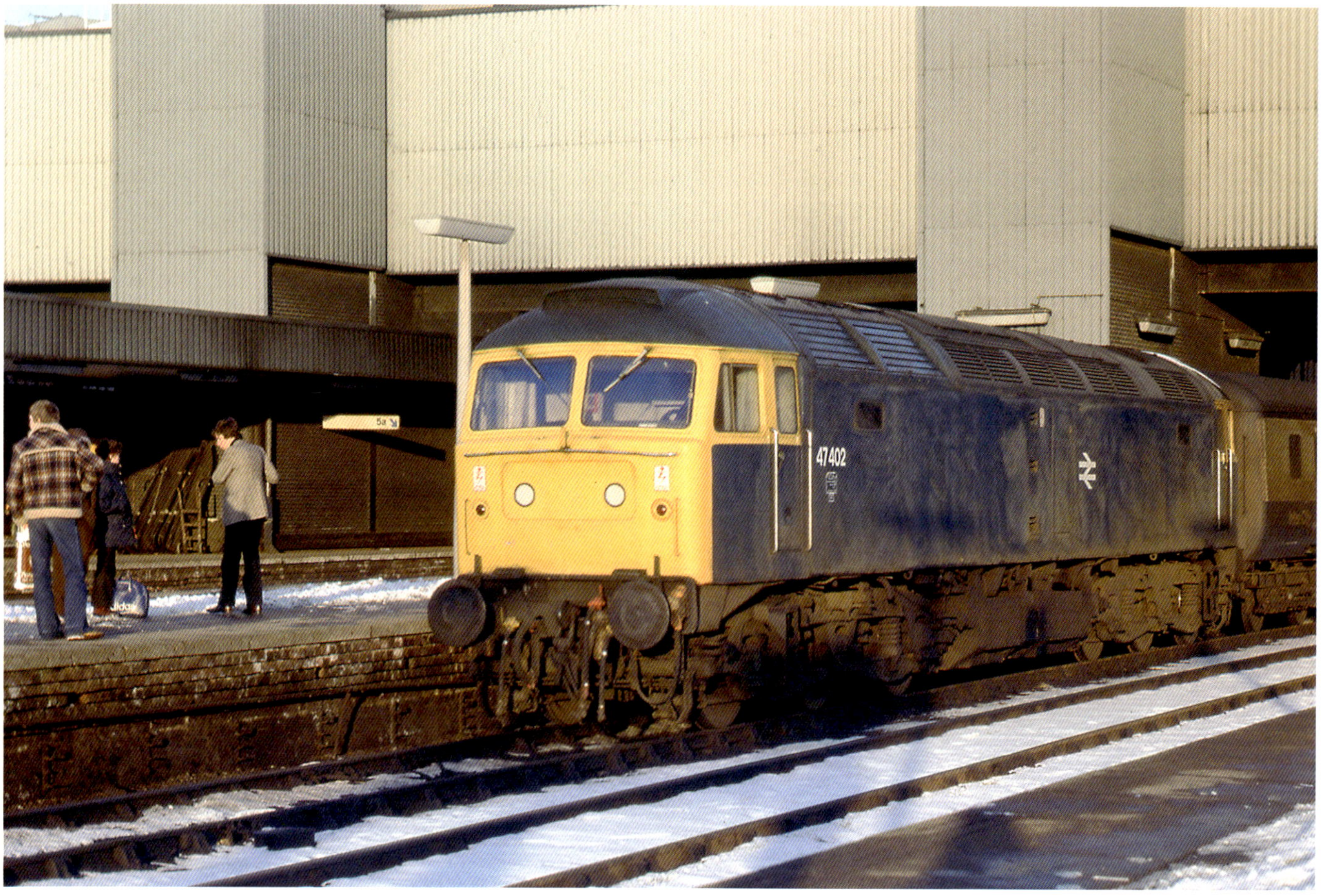

It will be electric train heating employed today to keep the passengers warm on their journey behind 47402 through the sow in March 1979 from Leeds. This locomtive was the second of its class to enter service as D1501 in November 1962 first allocated to Finsbury Park, by the close of the seventies it would be based at Gateshead who would name it after the depot on 25 November 1981. ***Roger Bradley***

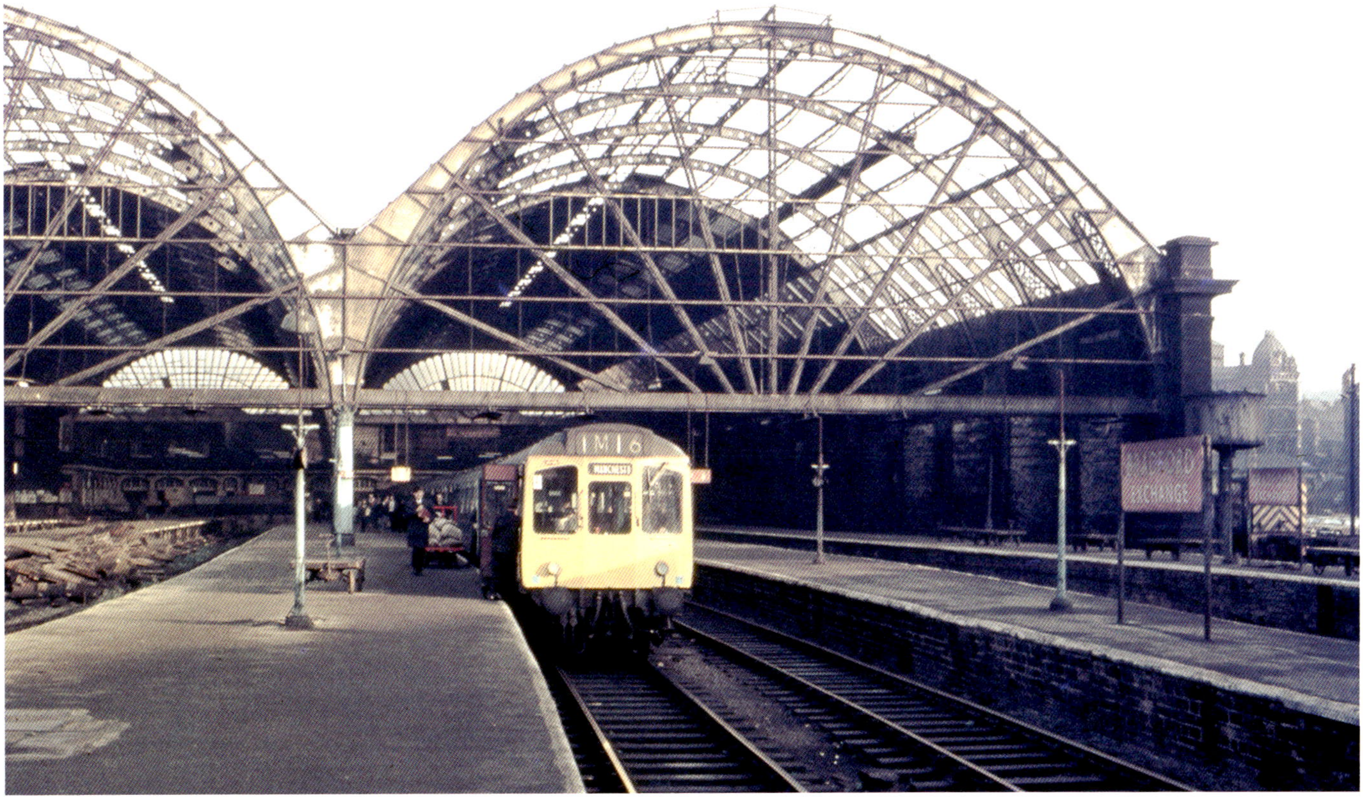

The old Bradford Exchange station was being progressivly abandoned when visited on 25 October 1972, although the eagle-eyed will spot a Class 03 pilot still attracting some useful employmment stabled in the background. ***Late Derek Whitnell/Strathwood Library Collection***

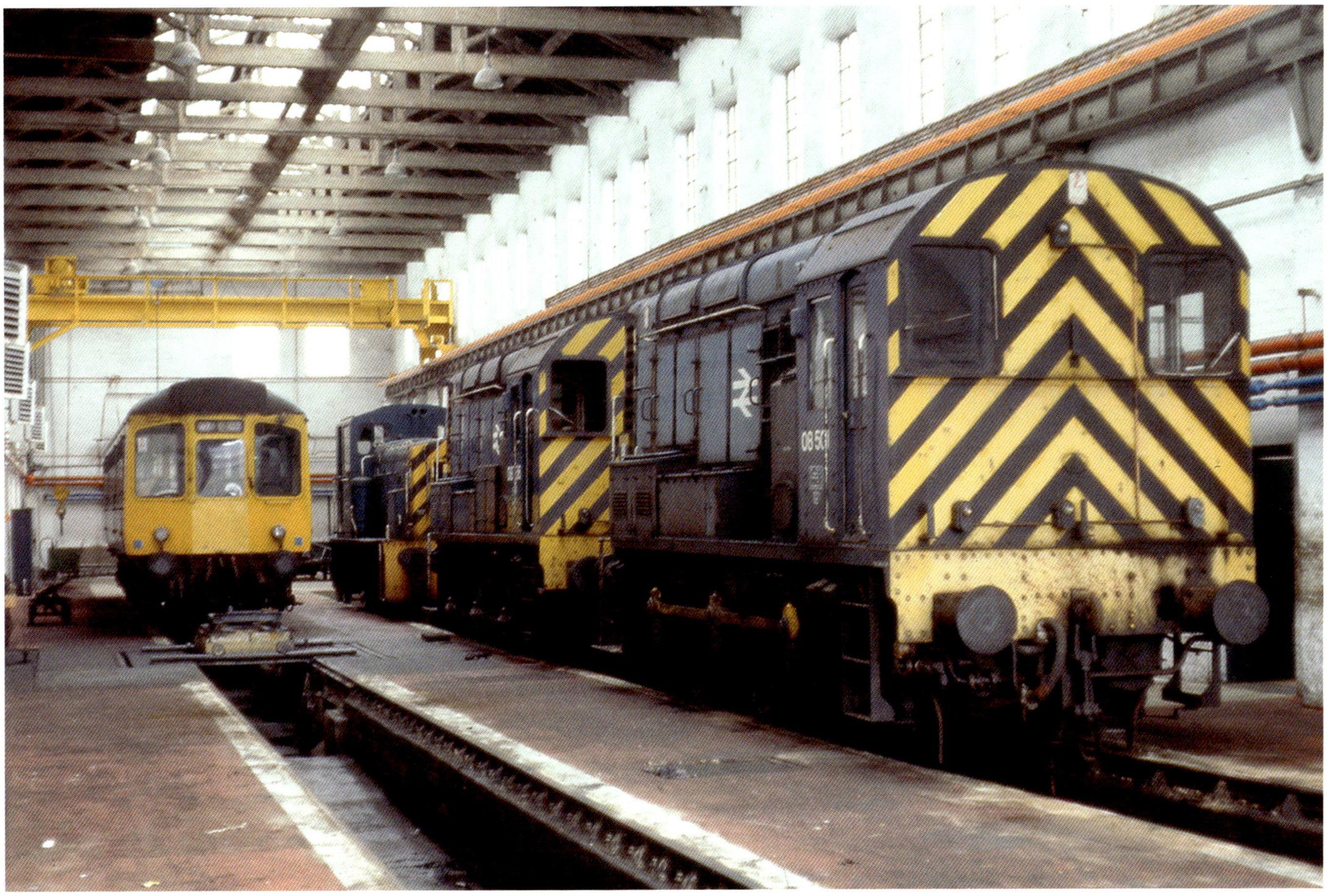

Bradford's Hammerton Street depot looked after a wide selection of DMUs with a Birmingham Railway Carriage & Wagon Co. set in the company of 08501, 08776 and 03371 on 22 April 1979. ***Brian Daniels***

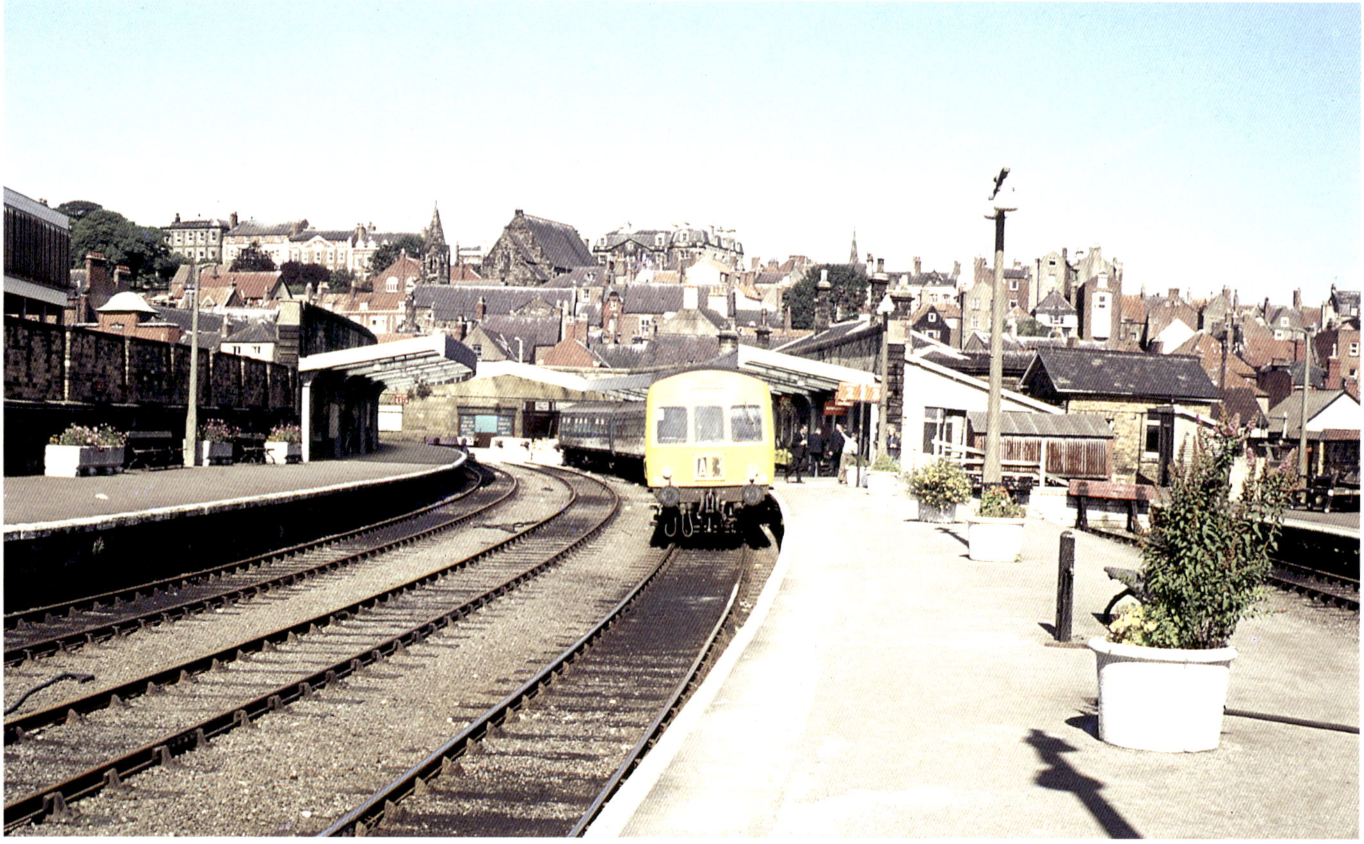

It is another product from Metropolitan Cammell that awaits departure away from the coast at Whitby Town on 3 September 1975. The fishing port here emerged during the Middle Ages and developed important herring and whaling fleets, and was where Captain Cook learned seamanship. Tourism started in Whitby in Georgian times and developed with the coming of the railway in 1839 and remains a popular destination for a day out to this day. ***Late Derek Whitnell/Strathwood Library Collection***

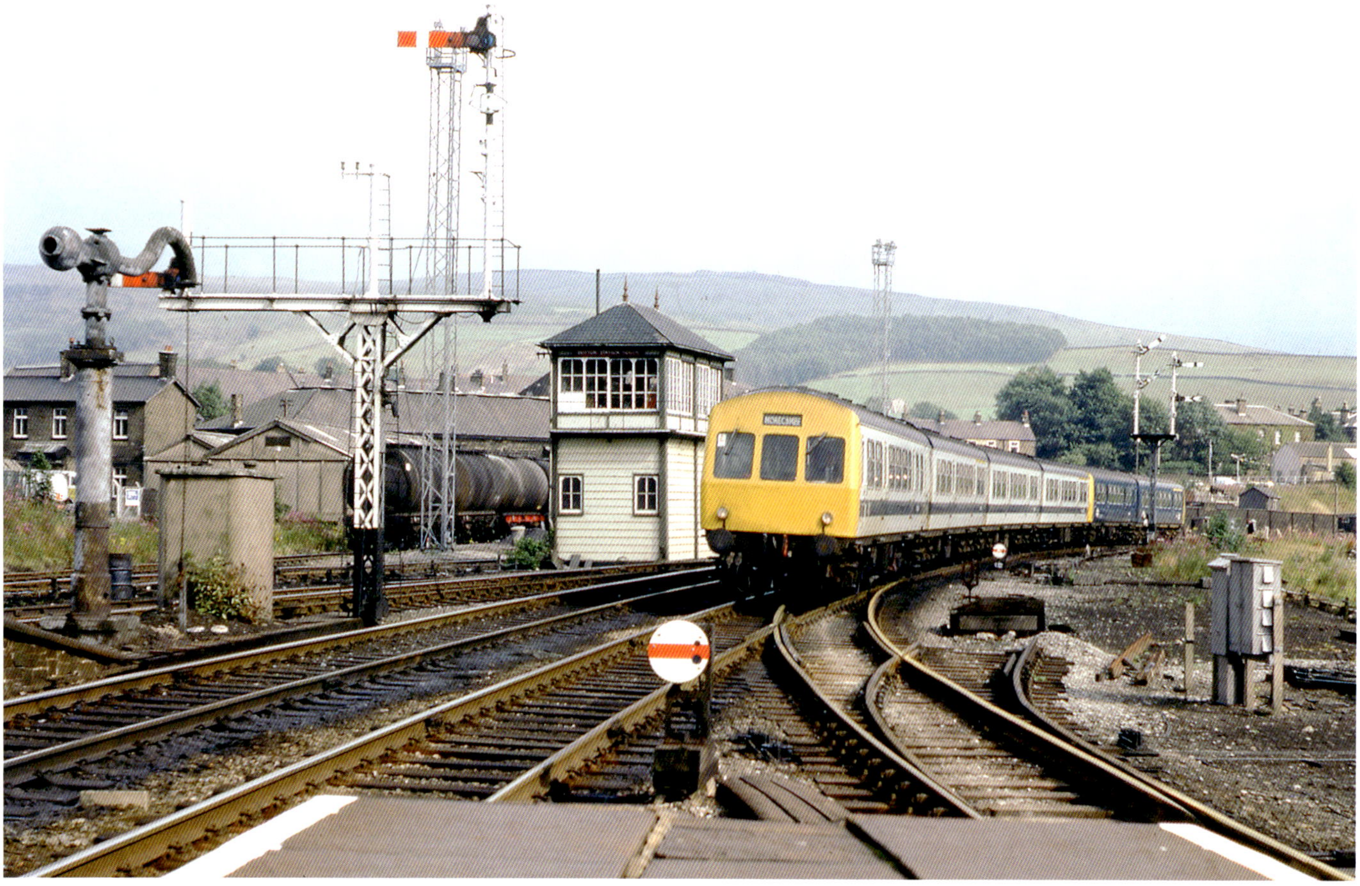

The refurbishment programme to get a longer life out of the ageing DMU fleet was started in the mid seventies with many units being turned out in an almost white livery with a blue stripe, hardly practical to maintain a clean appearance, although the leading coaches of this arrival at Skipton on 19 August 1977 from Leeds look smart enough. ***Strathwood Library Collection***

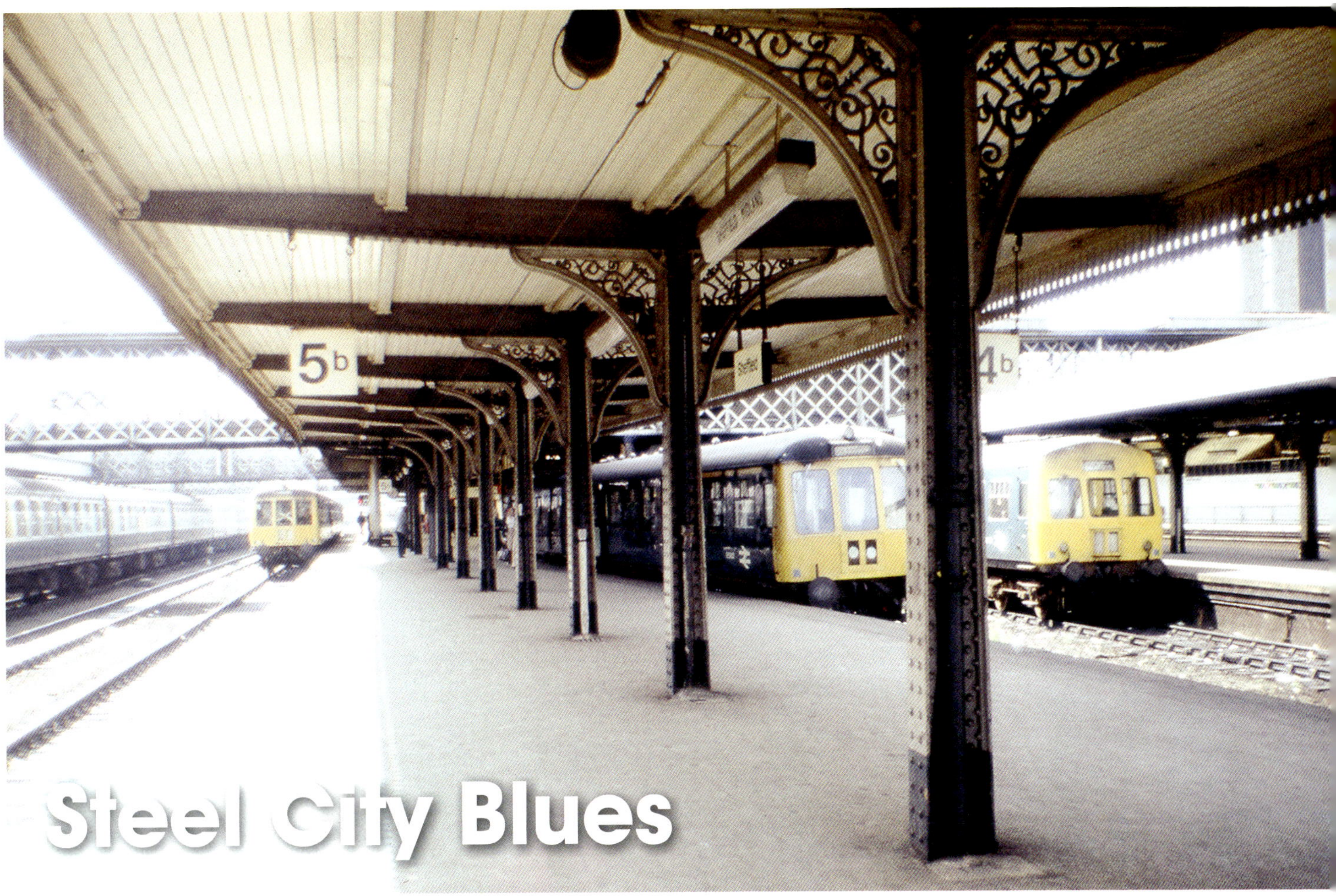

Steel City Blues

A selection of DMU types from Derby Works and Metropolitan Cammell's Birmingham factory greet our arrival at Sheffield Midland, but no locally built Cravens units to be seen on 30 July 1977. ***Phil Bidwell***

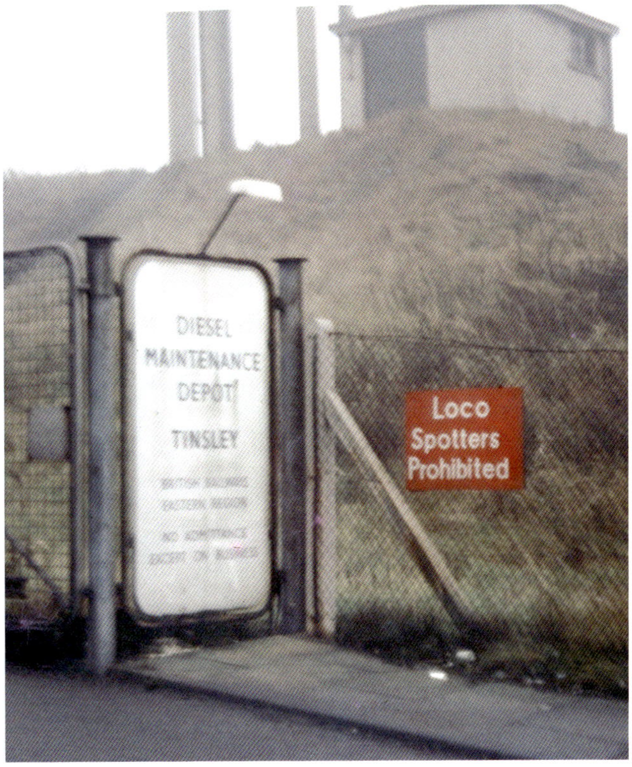

Many of us would have visited Tinsley over the years with mixed results if you did not have a permit unless you were not put off by the signs to greet visitors from afar. Local lads would know the ropes on how, when and whether to bunk the depot. This was the scene in 1975, the new diesel depot opened as 41A on 26 April 1964 to be coded as TI from 6 May 1973 when the TOPS codes went live. facility. In 1998 the shed closed and by June 2006 the site had been completely cleared for new development and all that remained was the abutments of the rail overbridge once used for access. ***Phil Bidwell***

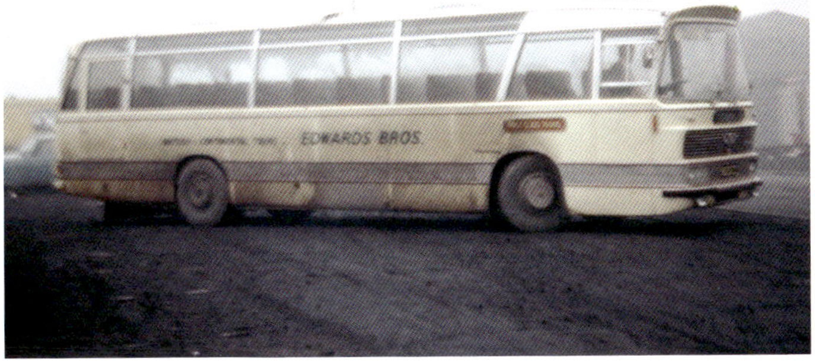

The warmth of the society hired coach would be welcome after a walk around the shed yards on a freezing winter's day and the chance to see what you had copped before the next location. ***Phil Bidwell***

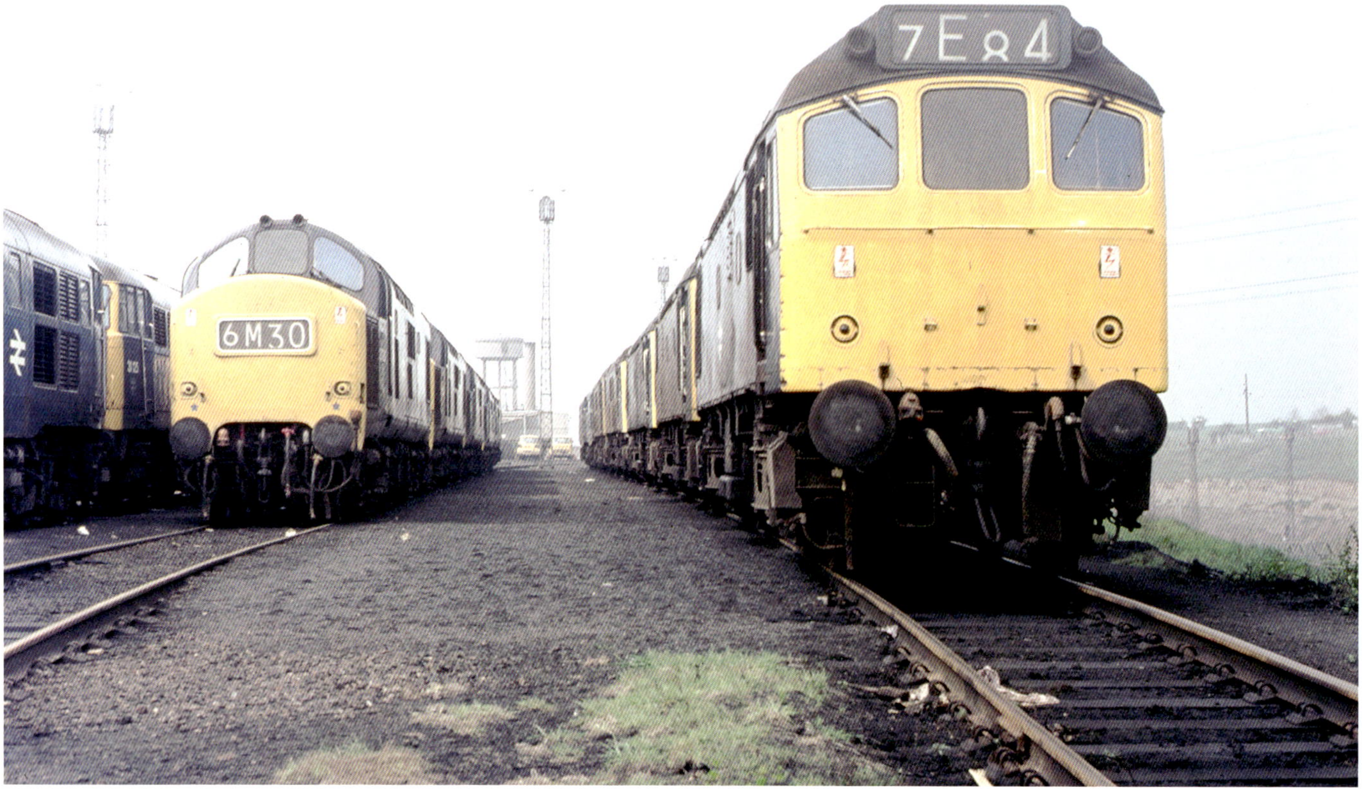

Visits to depots such as Tinsley that supplied mainly freight turns on sundays would always result in long lines of locomotives awaiting the start of the next working week, such as here on 26 April 1975. If you arrived home in time that evening you could have settled down to watch That's Life hosted by Esther Rantzen along with Cyril Fletcher who would recite some of his 'Odd Odes'. He proved such a success with the audience that he became a fixture of the show for eight years. ***Phil Bidwell***

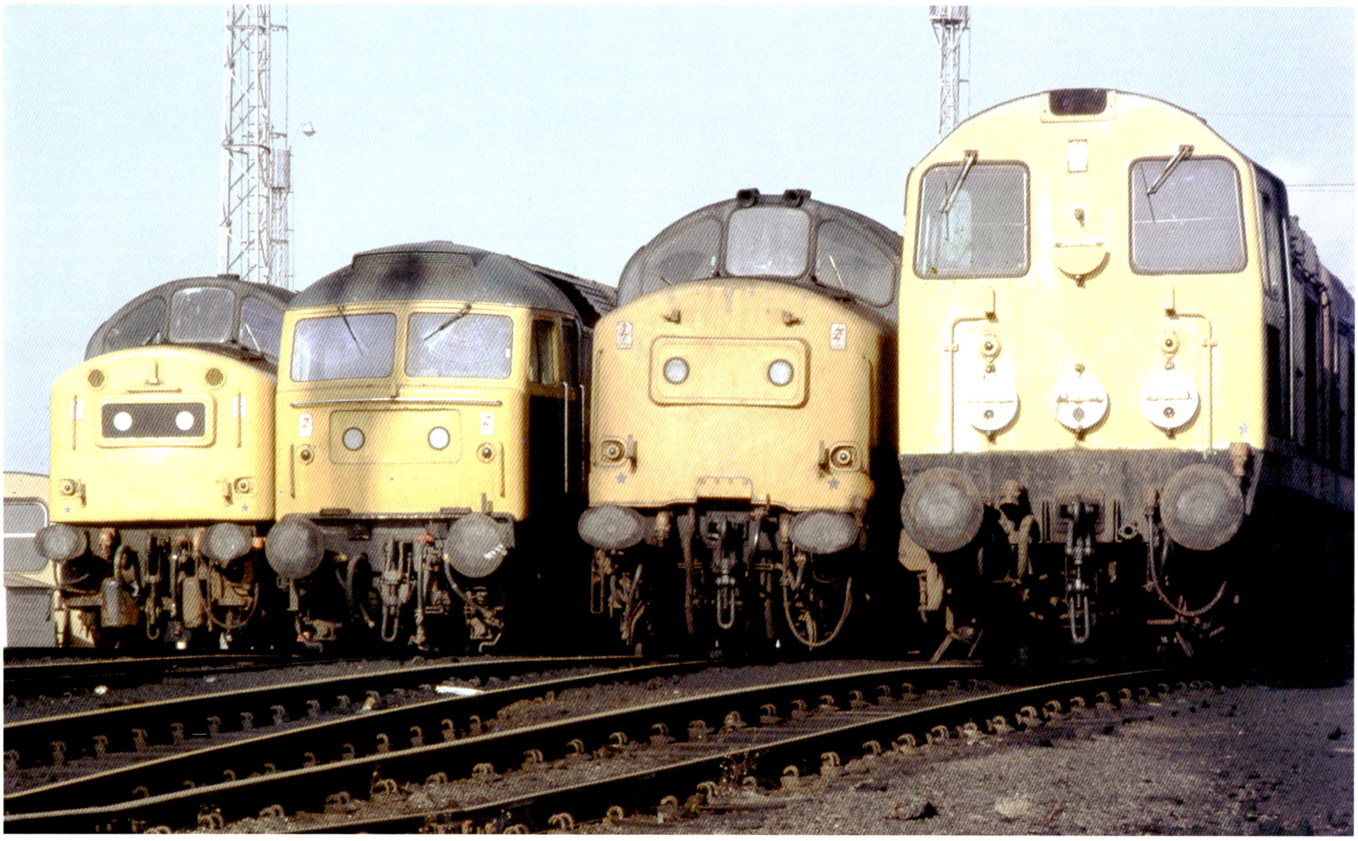

Tinsley enjoyed a large allocation of locomotive types and would also host visitors such as Wigan Springs Branch alocated 40180 alongside 47029, 37122 and 20071. This view dates from the last winter of the seventies. ***Bruce Smetham***

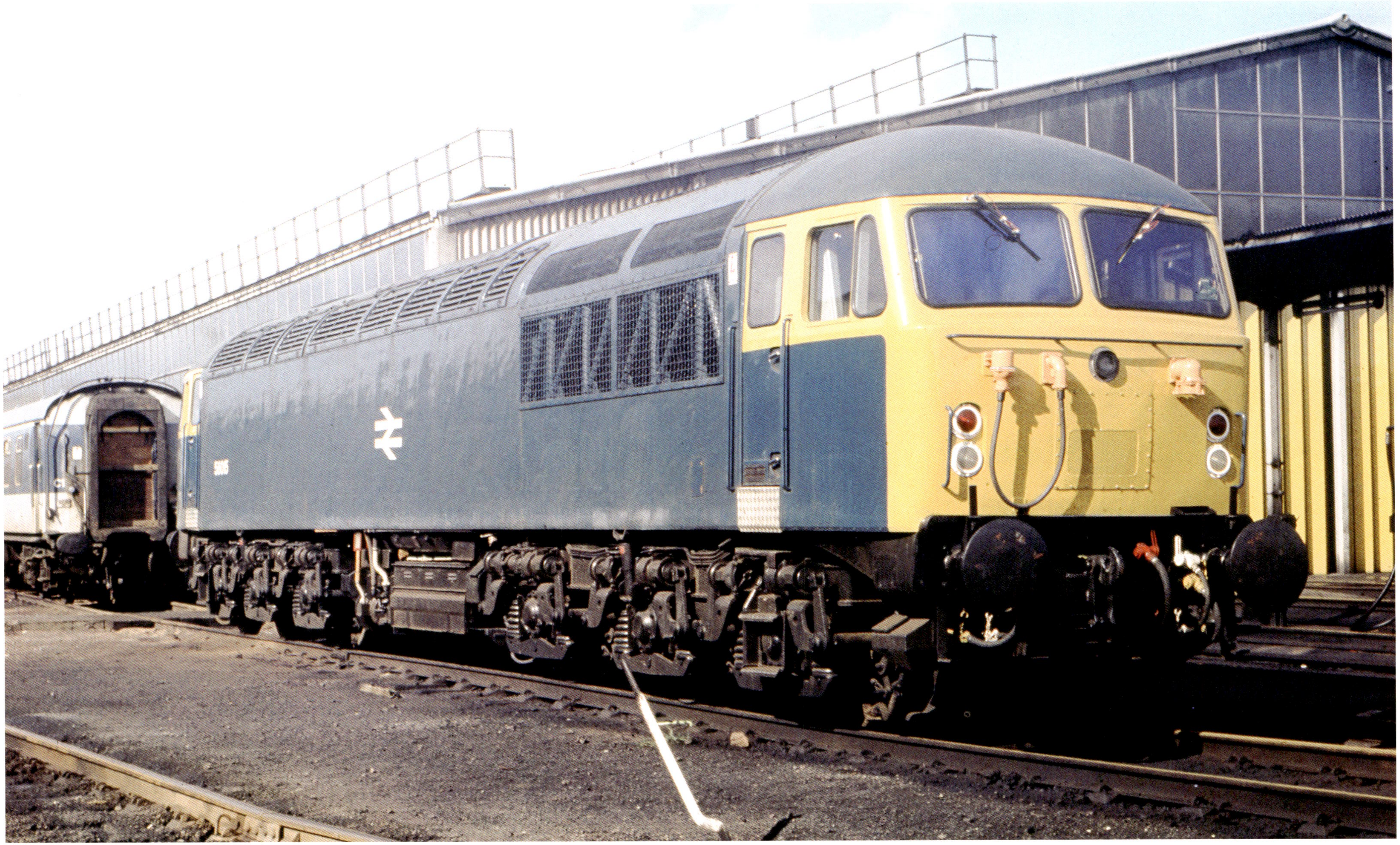

When the first of the Romanian built Class 56s arrived in the country it was via Harwich with 56015 being sent onwards to Tinsley usually via Stratford's Works in early January 1977. Once at Tinsley many of the new locomotives were sent to Barrow Hill and stored in the roundhouse there where modifications were carried out. By 16 March, 56015 has returned to Tinsley to take up service on the 21st, note the ECML Pullman coach behind the locomotive. ***John Arthur Bennett/Strathwood Library Collection***

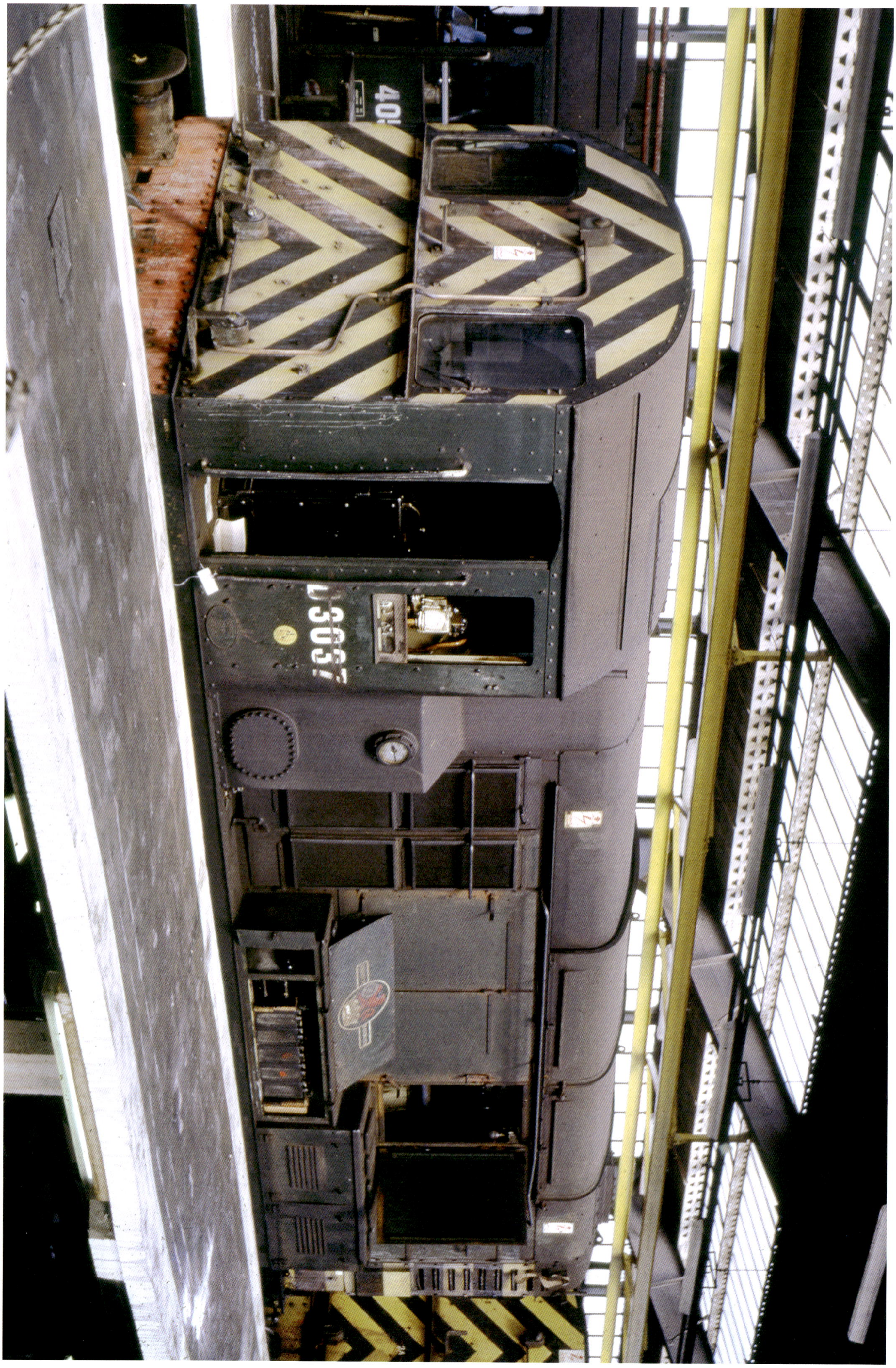

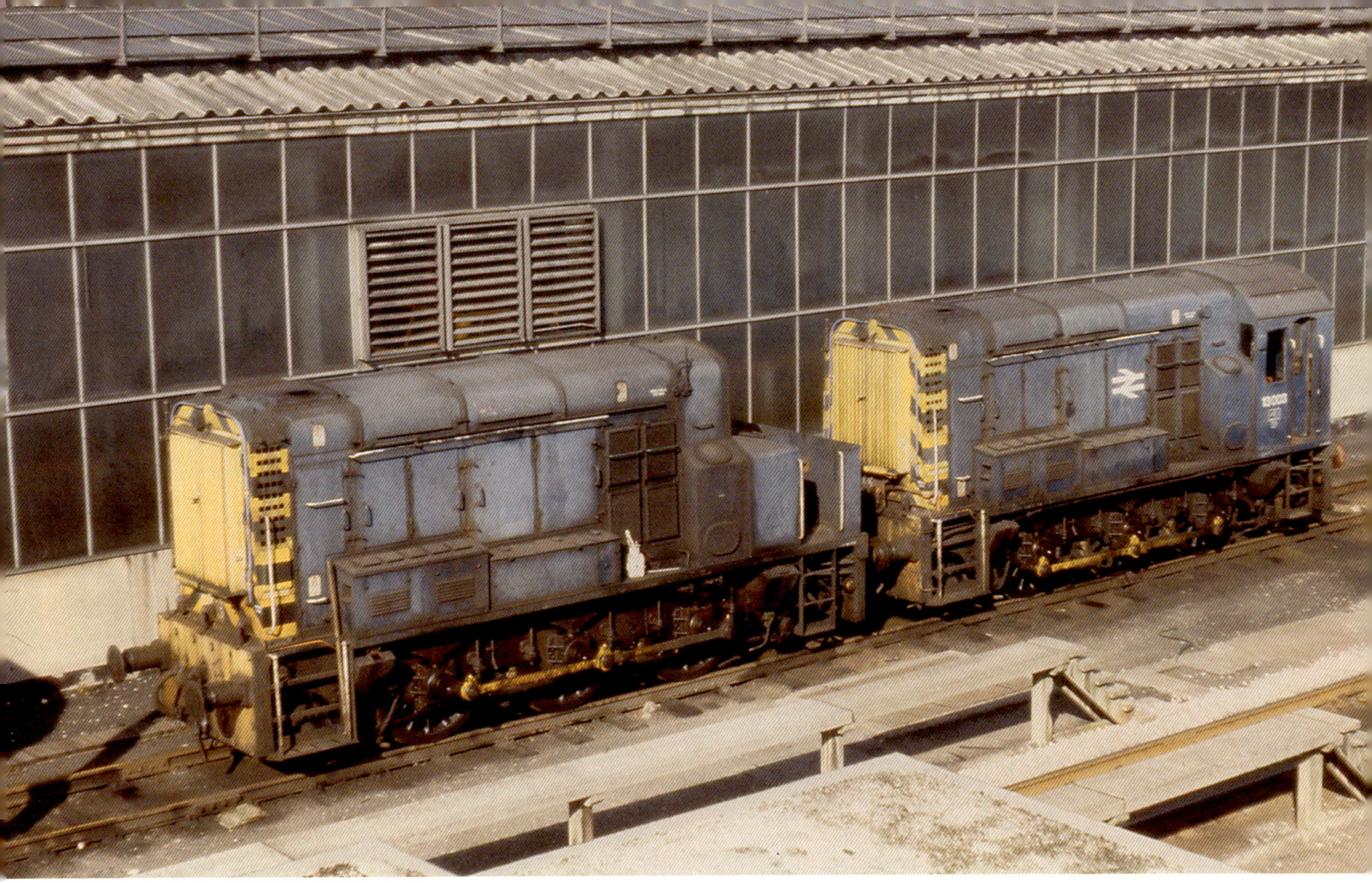

Spotters just had to go to Tinsley if they wanted to get the three Class 13 Hump Shunters, unless they caught them on their rare works visits. Looking down from the embankment alongside the depot on 18 June 1978 we find 13003 which was formed from D4188 and D3698 in May 1965. ***Brian Daniels.***

In 1973, 6833 moved from Stratford to join the fleet at Tinsley where we see it having arrived with a household domestic coal working down in the once busy marshalling yard, not so many homes around Yorkshire enjoyed gas central heating back then. ***Phil Bidwell***

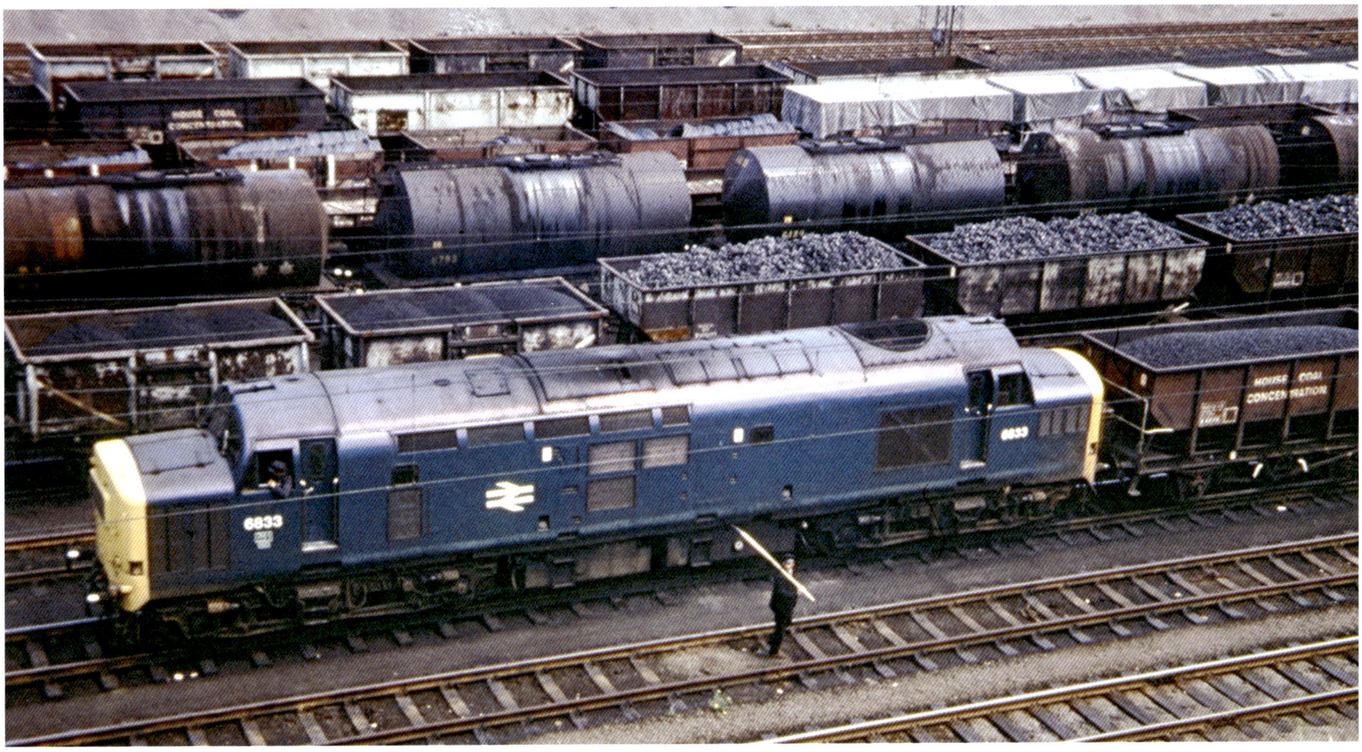

Page left: Built in 1953, D3037 had only just been transferred to Tinsley from Derby when recorded inside the shed on 8 July 1972. Things did not go well as the shunter was declared withdrawn as it was rundown and surplus just before that Christmas. However someone must have thought a shunter was for life as it lingered around Tinsley before being converted to a snowplough at Doncaster Works and numbered as ADB966510 which it survived as until recalled to The Plant and cut up in March 1979. ***Strathwood Library Collection***

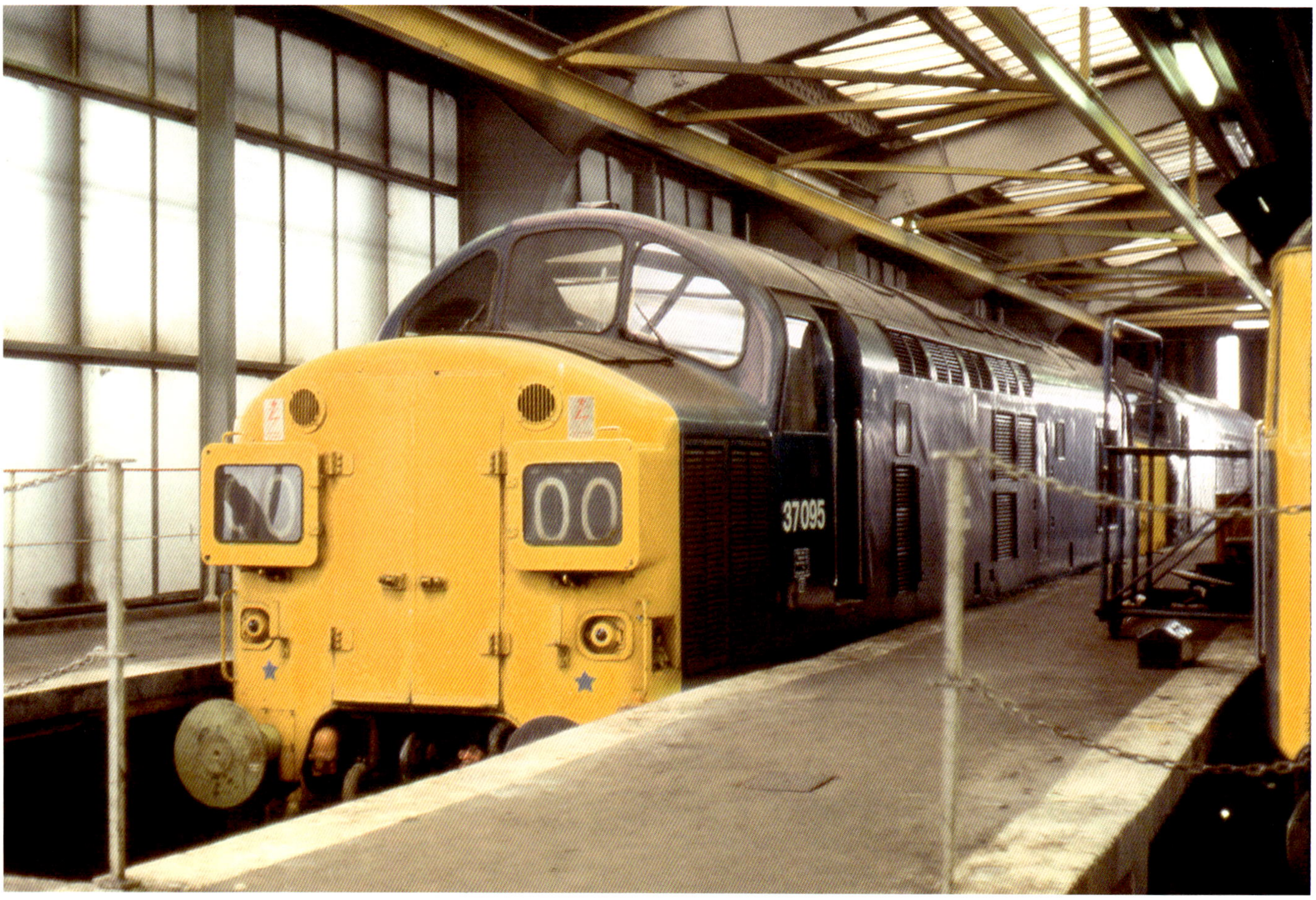

Recieving some maintenance inside it's home shed on 14 May 1978 was 37095, this Class 37 would be allocated variously to Gateshead, Thornaby, Immingham and Healey Mills as well during the decade. ***Brian Daniels***

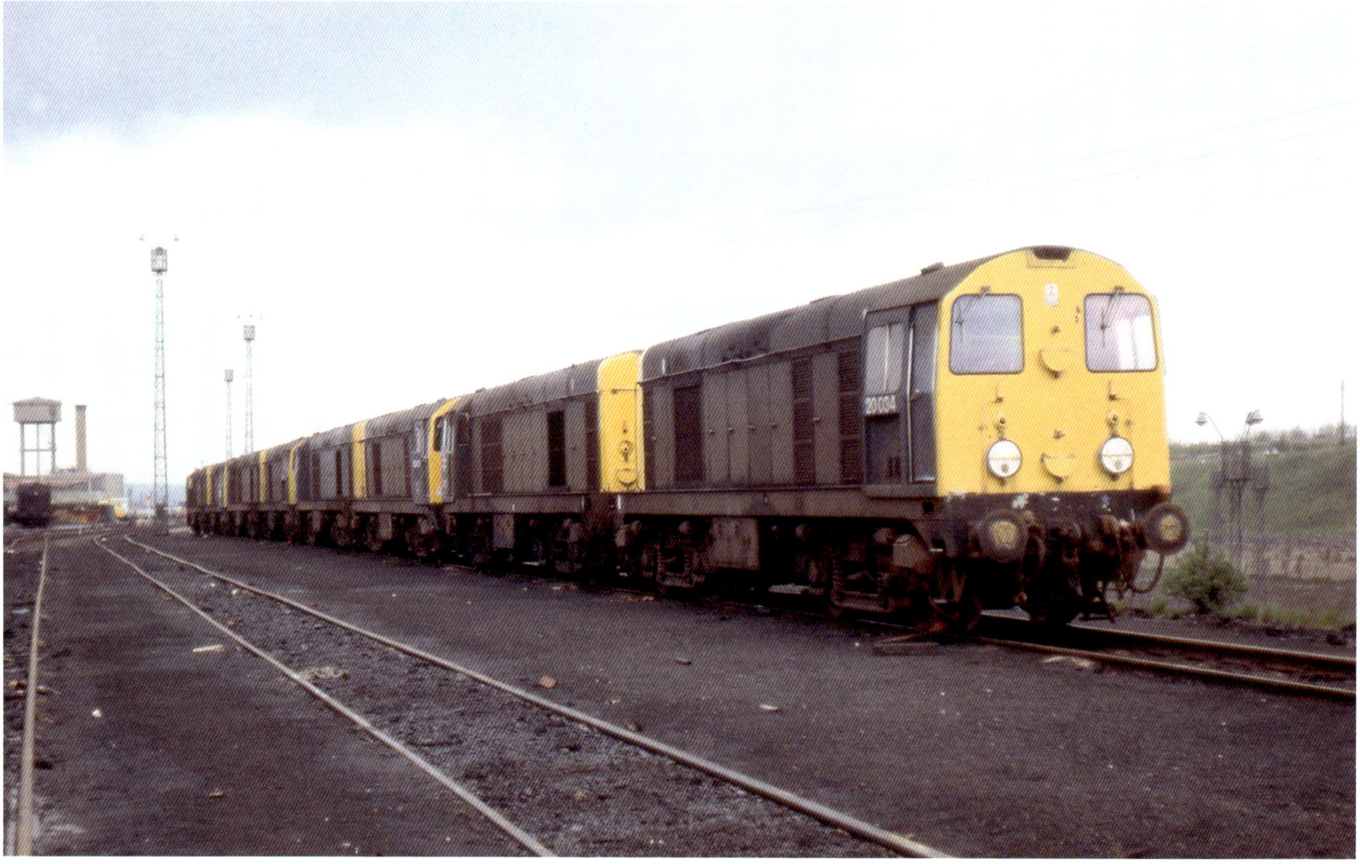

For 20034 at the head of the lines of Class 20s the same day at Tinsley it was a different story. Starting the seventies based at Toton as part of the D16 Nottingham Division it was then transferred to 41A Tinsley before a move back to Scotland taking in Eastfield, Haymarket and back to Eastfield, before a return to Tinsley for Christmas 1976 before moving onwards once agin in October 1982 to find work at Immingham. ***Brian Daniels***

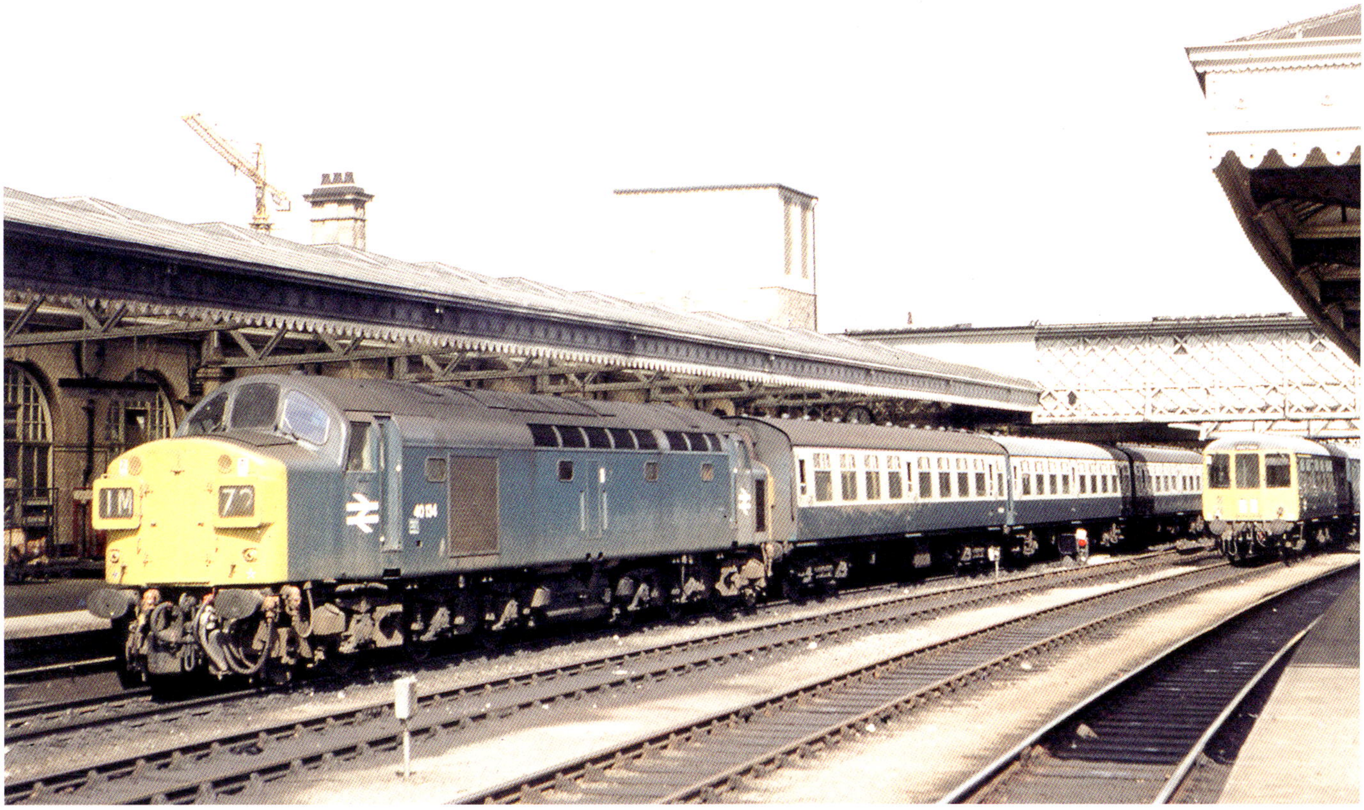

A trans-Pennine passenger working has brought Wigan Springs Branch allocated 40134 to Sheffield Midland on 16 August 1974. In the charts George McCrae was just about to drop off from three weeks at Number 1 with Rock Your Baby, to make room for the Three degrees with When Will I See You Again. ***Strathwood Library Collection***

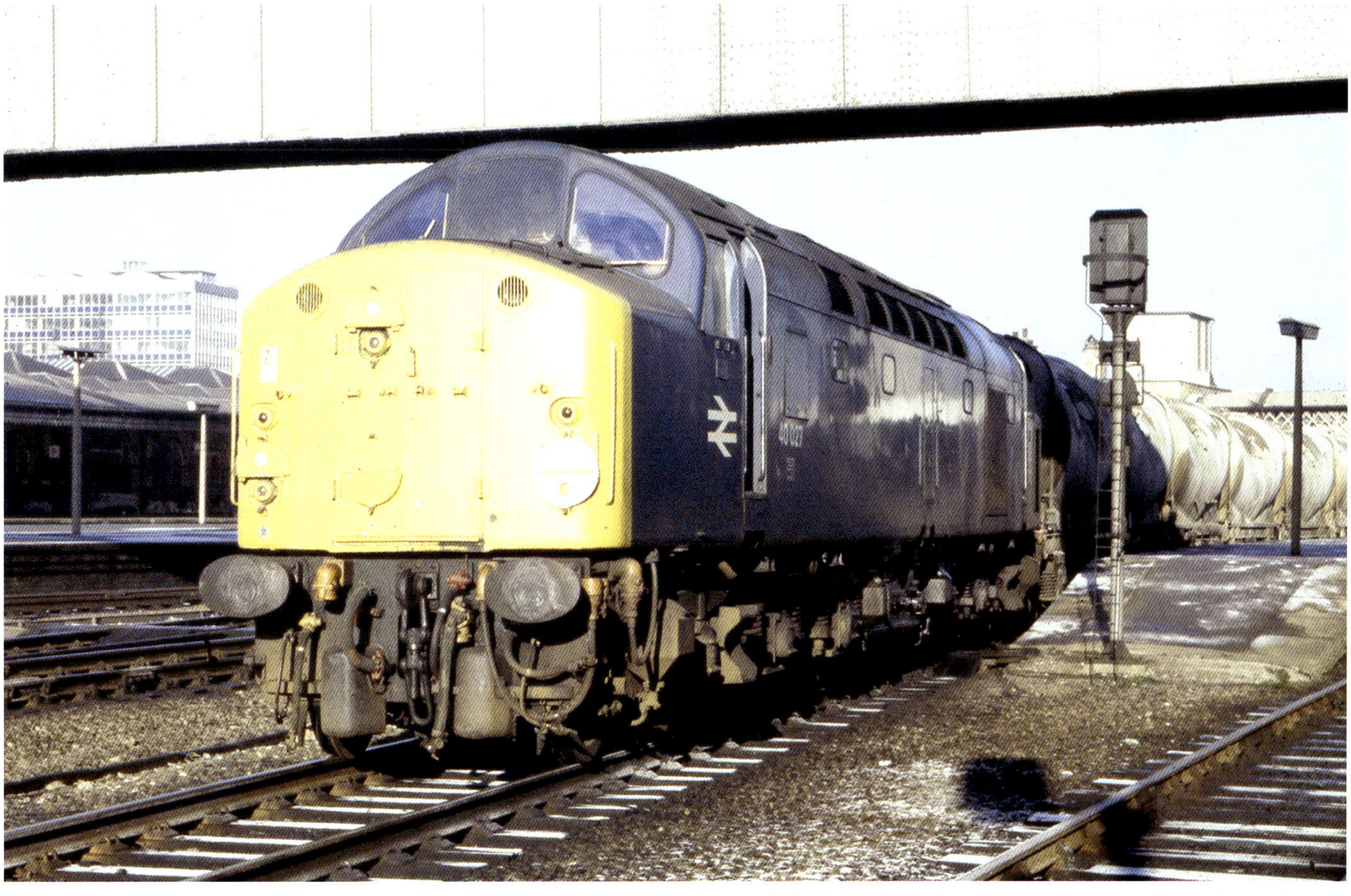

More whistling across the Steel City on 18 January as 40027 now devoid of it's Parthia nameplates draws through Sheffield Midland, once again the other side of the Pennines from it's base at Longsight. ***Nev Sloper***

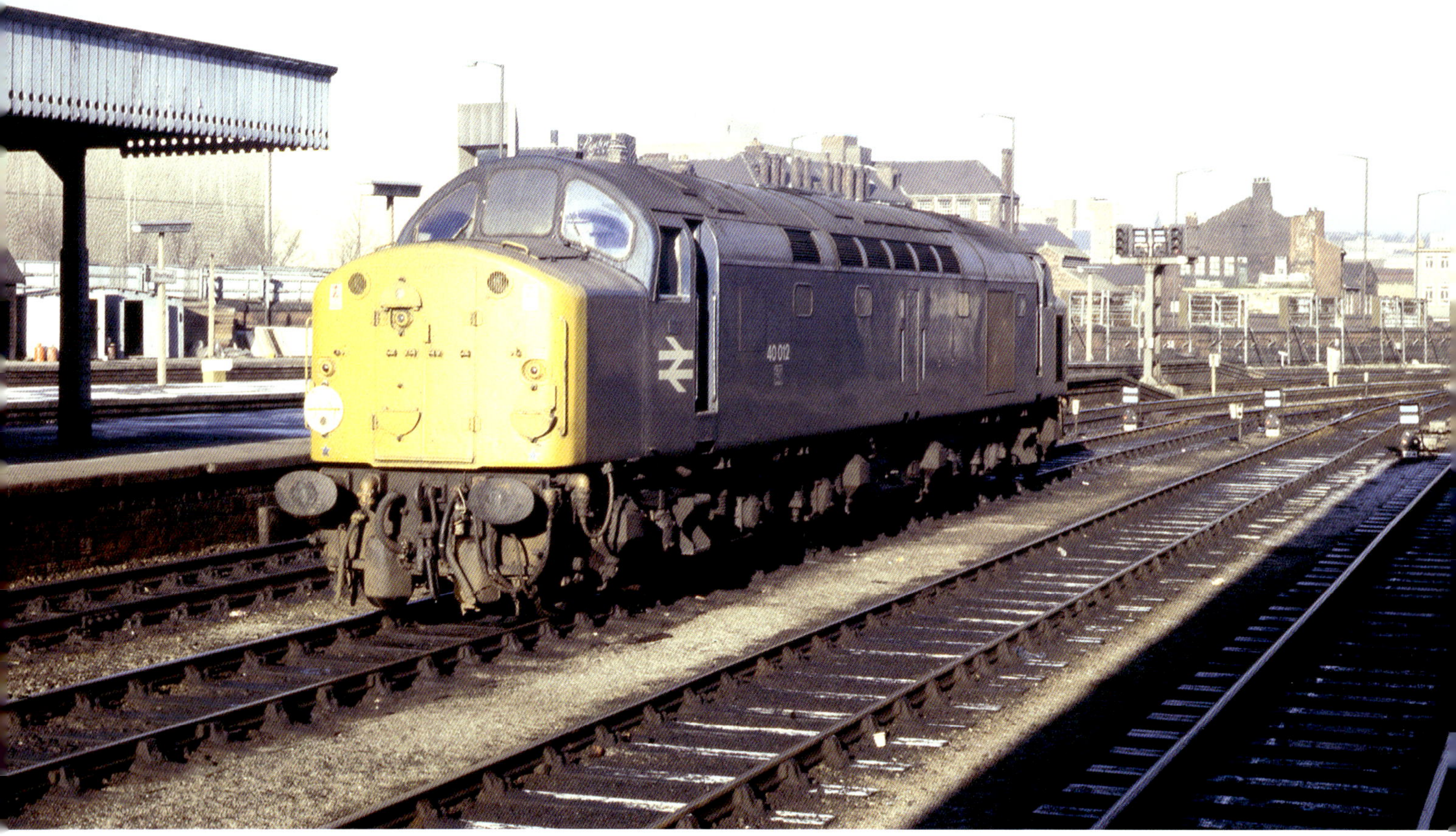

It would seem that Class 40s such as 40069 were more commonplace than regulars in the shape of 45134 on 18 January 1978. But it seems that as Peaks were so frequent here that many cameramen often ignored them much of the time. ***Both: Nev sloper***

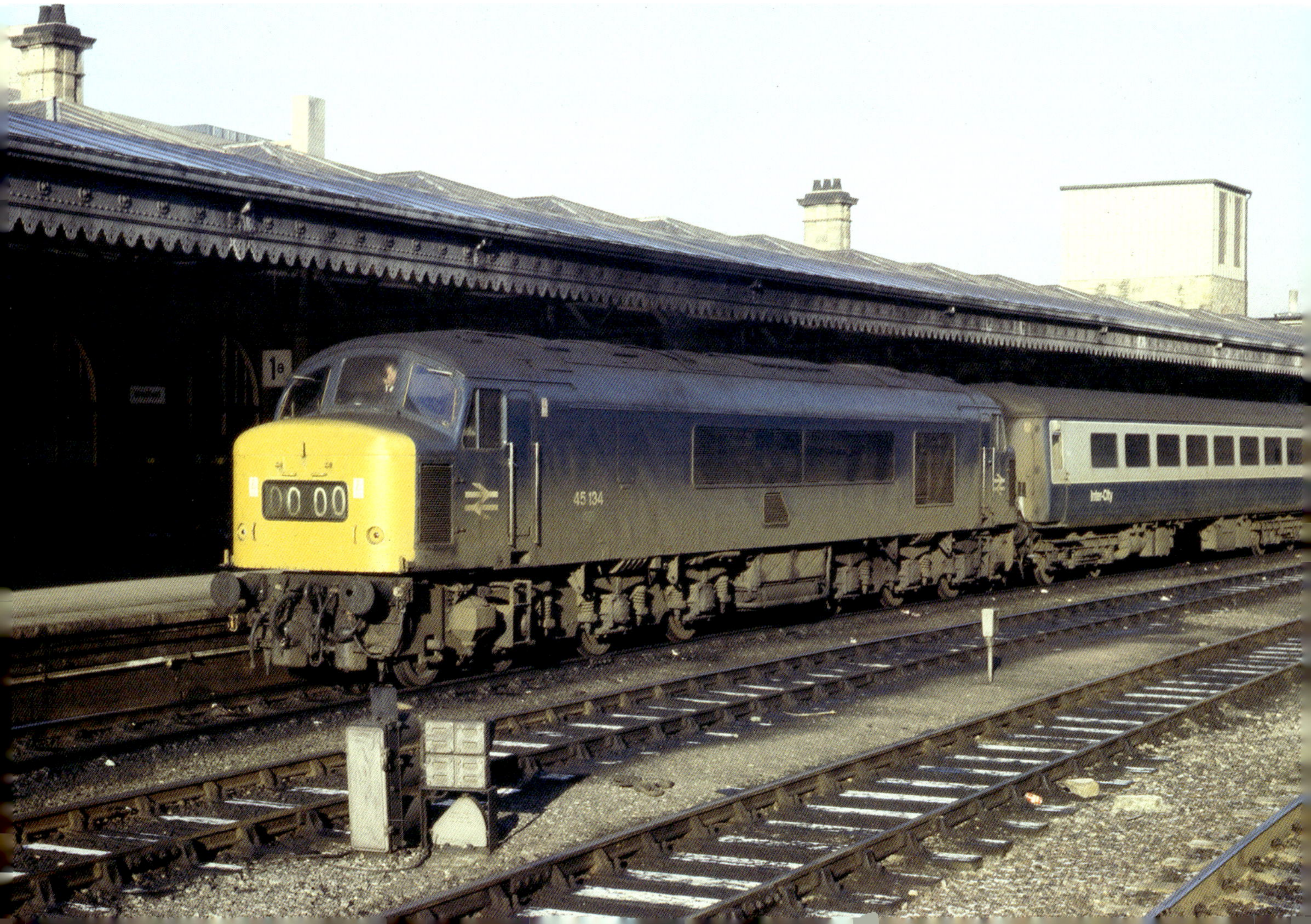

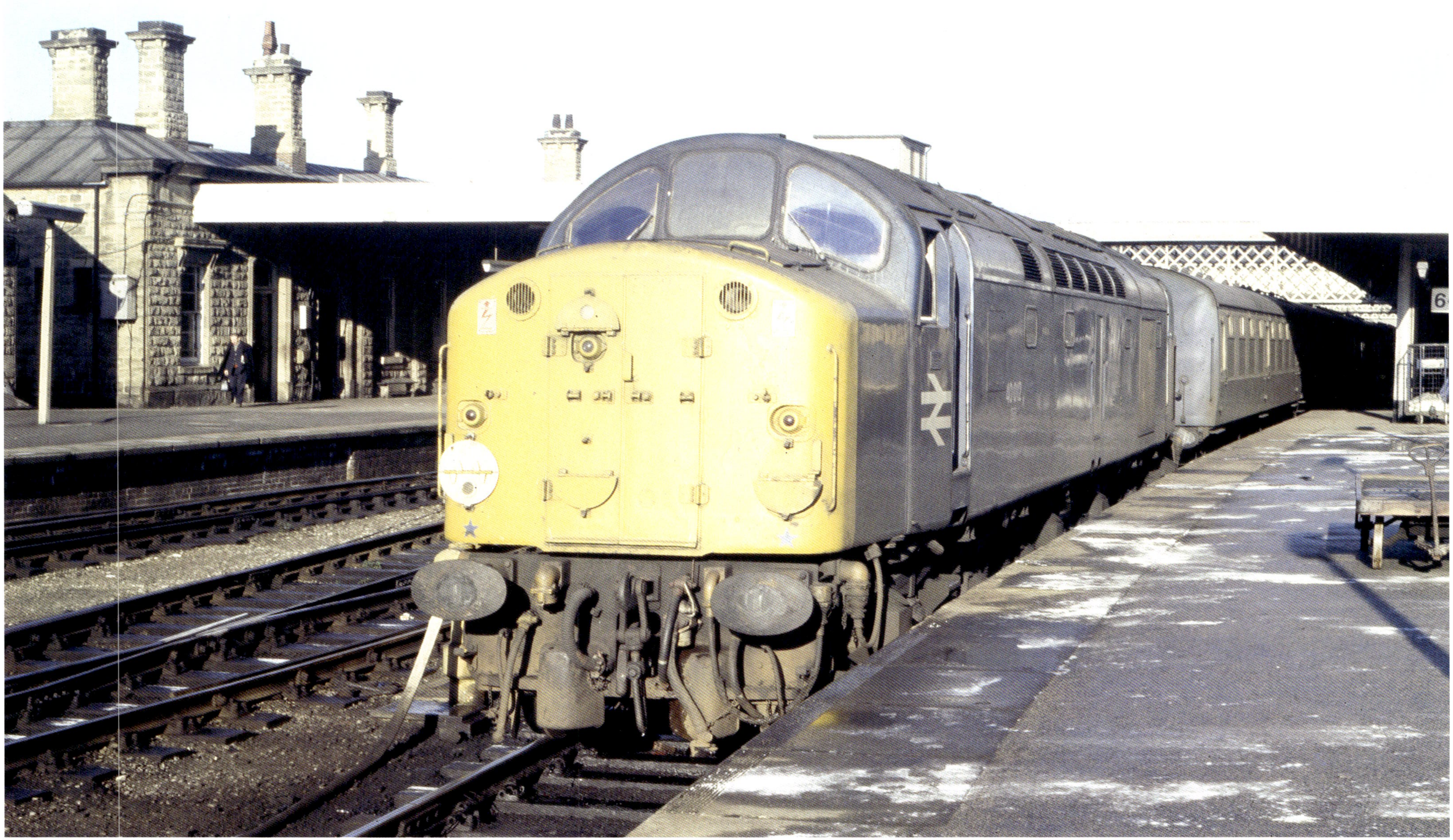

Here we go again on 18 January 1978 as this time we find 40012 the erstwhile Aureol on passenger work again at Sheffield Midland. Across the Irish Sea the troubles were raging away with outrages also on the mainland as well. Meanwhile across the English Channel, The European Court of Human Rights found the British government guilty of mistreating prisoners in Northern Ireland, but not guilty of torture on this day. A few days beforehand across the Atlantic this time the punk rock band The Sex Pistols had broke up amidst their US tour, anarchy in the UK indeed! ***Nev Sloper***

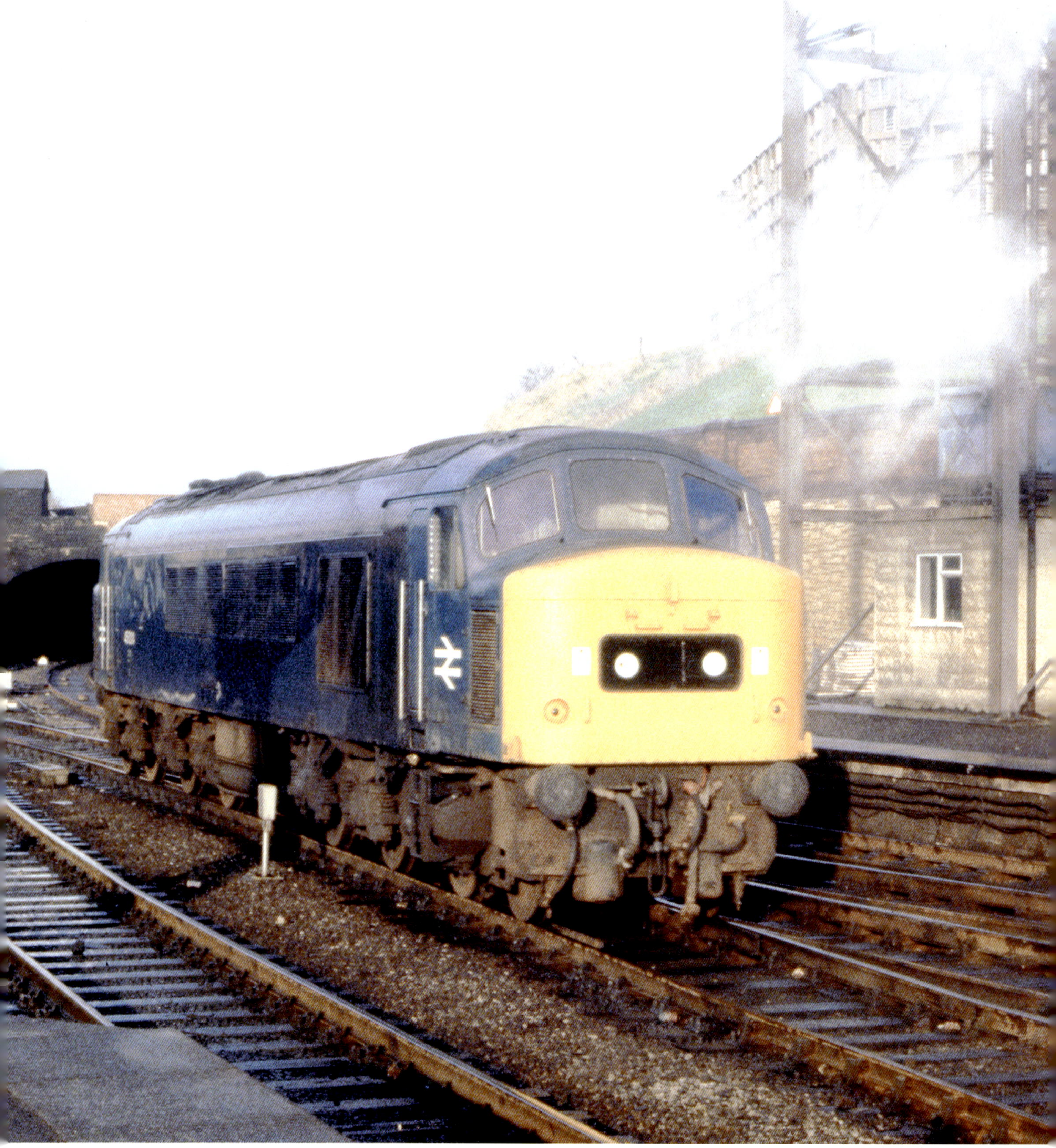

A return to the then traditional locomotive power at Sheffield Midland before the influx of HSTs in the guise of Tinsley's 45024 on 10 November 1979. Incredibly on this same day in Canada, the evacuation of a quarter of a million residents of the city of Mississauga, Ontario took place, in the aftermath of the derailment of a freight train carrying hazardous materials. It was, at that time, the largest peacetime evacuation ever conducted in North America. It took place with little panic or injury, no deaths, and no apparent resistance to evacuation advice. Not surprisingly, then, the success of the Mississauga evacuation has attracted the interest, and raised the hopes, of emergency planners, governments, and industry officials across the globe. It was of course another Peak numbered 46009 that would be destroyed on 23 July 1984 in the nuclear flask stunt at the Old Dalby testrack. ***Nev Sloper***

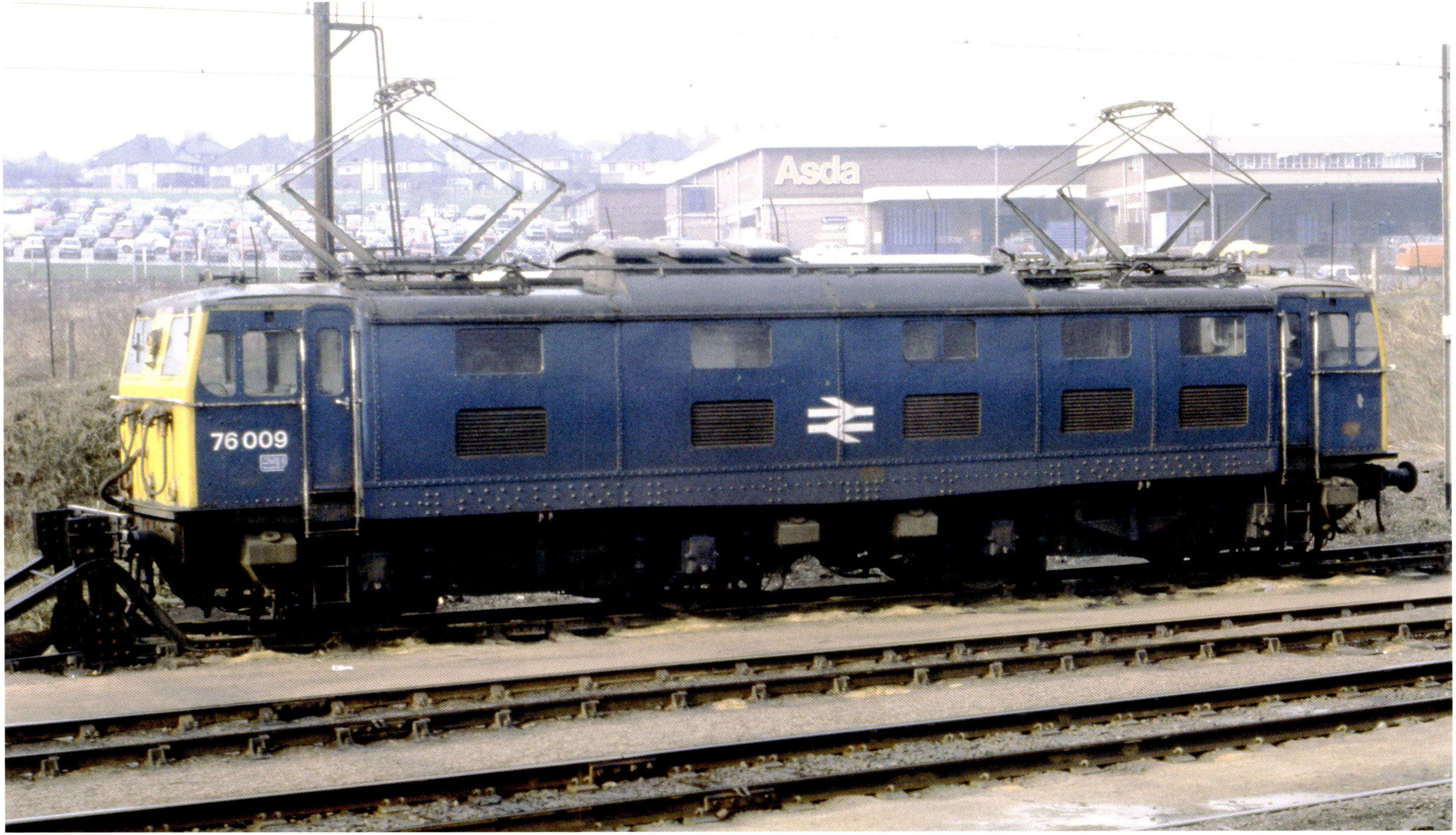

Staying in 1979 we find 76009 stabled close to the city centre in Sheffield on the once electrified lines awaiting something to do on 7 April. In the background can be seen the then distribution depot of ASDA which was still very much a part of Yorkshire life then. Asda Stores Limited was founded as Associated Dairies & Farm Stores Limited in 1949 in Leeds. The adoption of the Asda name occurred in 1965 with the merger of the Asquith chain of three supermarkets and Associated Dairies; Asda is an abbreviation of Asquith and Dairies, often capitalised. From 1990 until the close of the 1992 season the company also sponsored Sheffield Wednesday F.C. continueing their association with the city. ***Stuart Broughton***

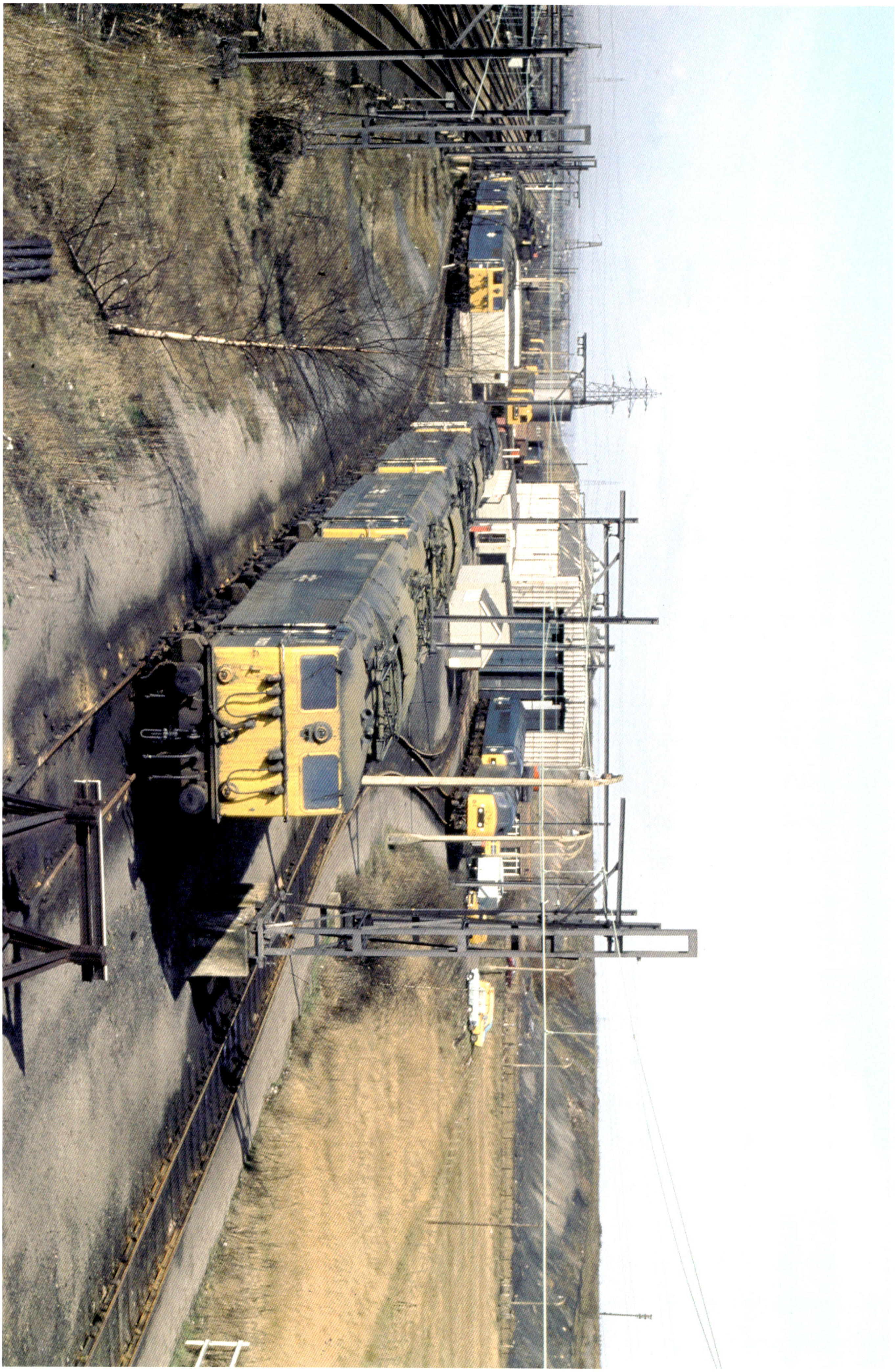

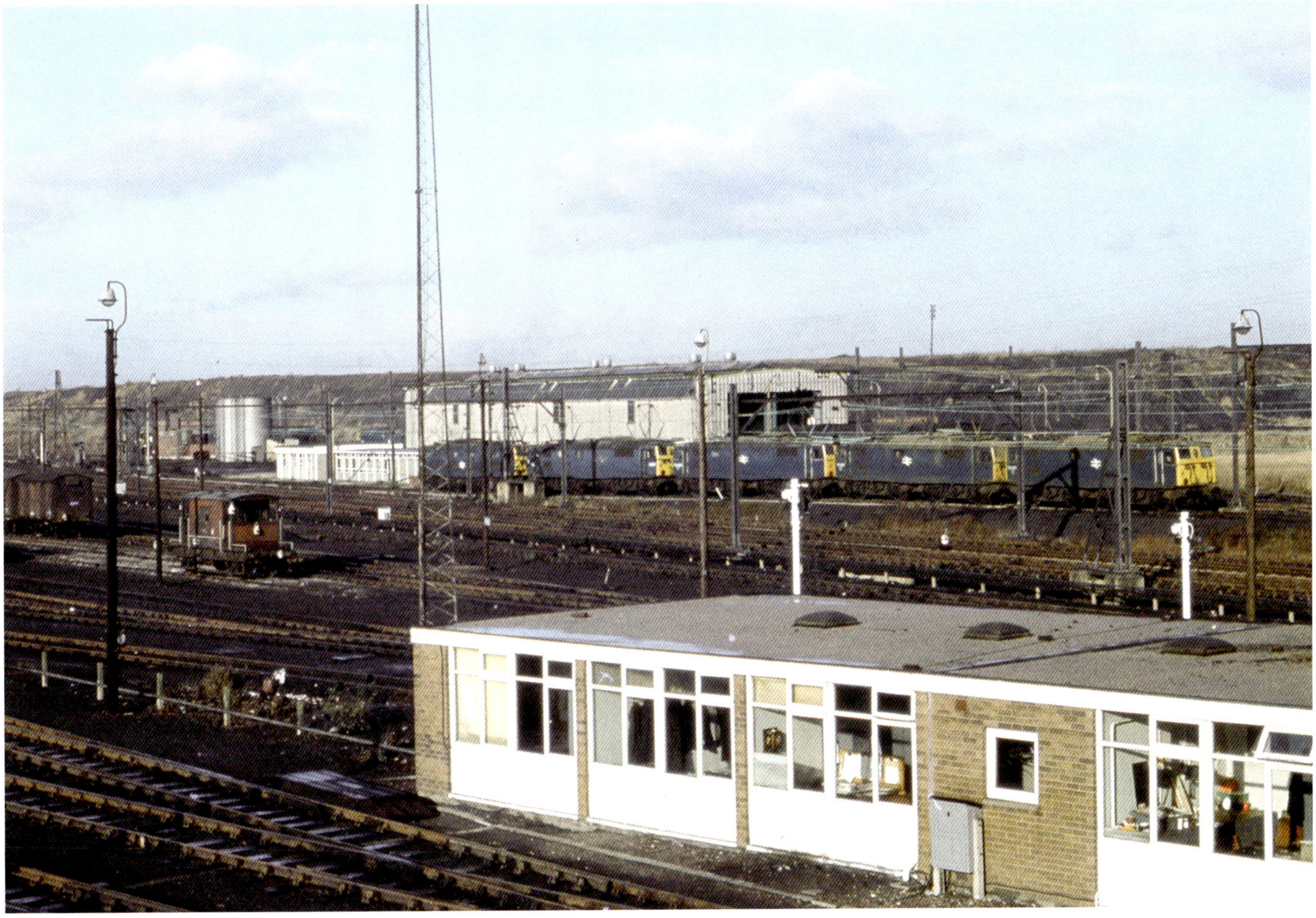

Maintenance for the fleet of Class 76s on the Yorkshire side of the Pennines was carried at Wath who also looked after the diesels working through the once busy marshalling yards here. This was the scene on 25 November 1978. ***This page and opposite: Arthur Wilson***

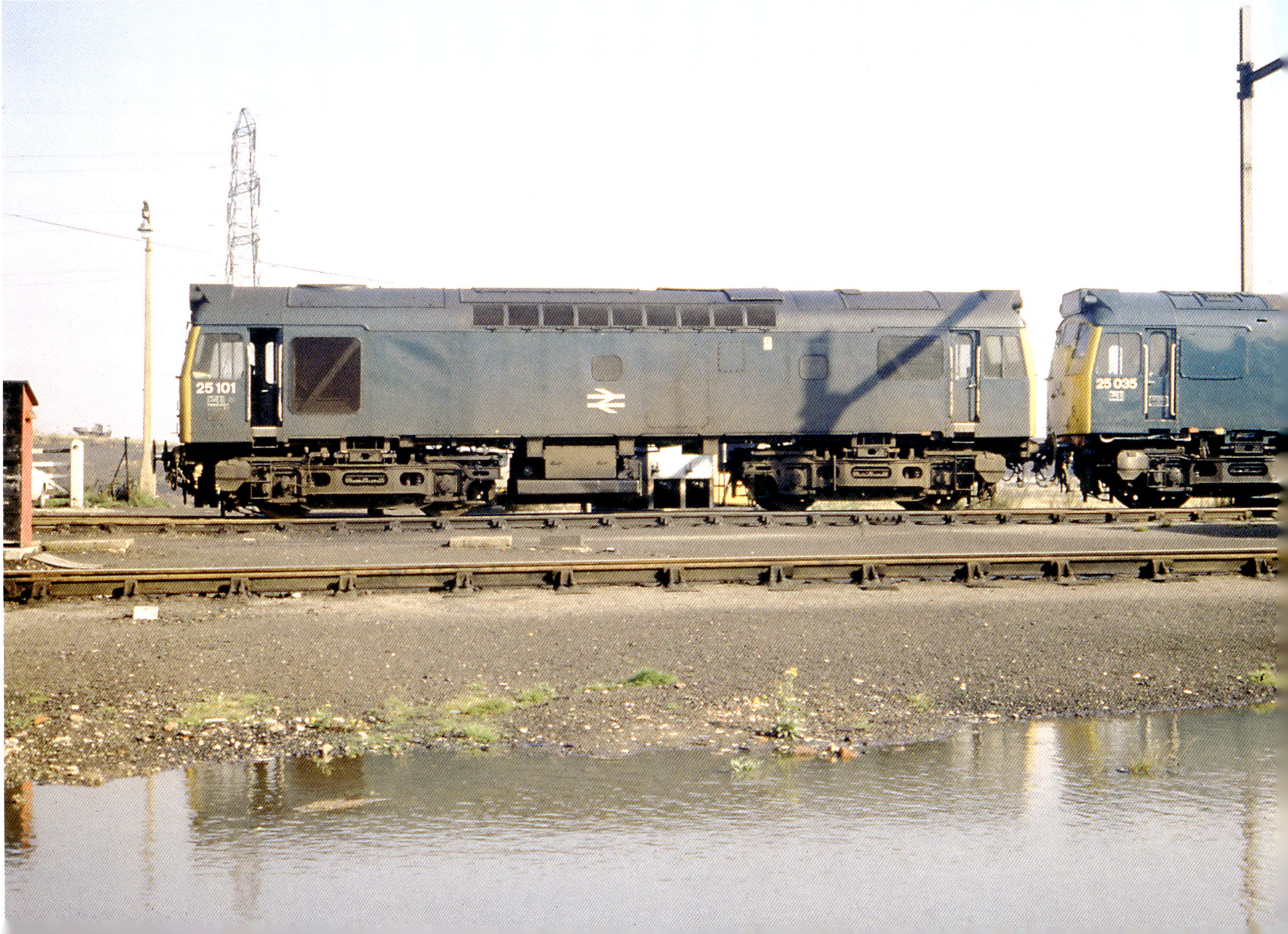

One of Tinsley's Class 25s, 25101 reflects on its next duties with a classmate at the back of the depot at Wath on 28 September 1974. ***Frank Hornby***

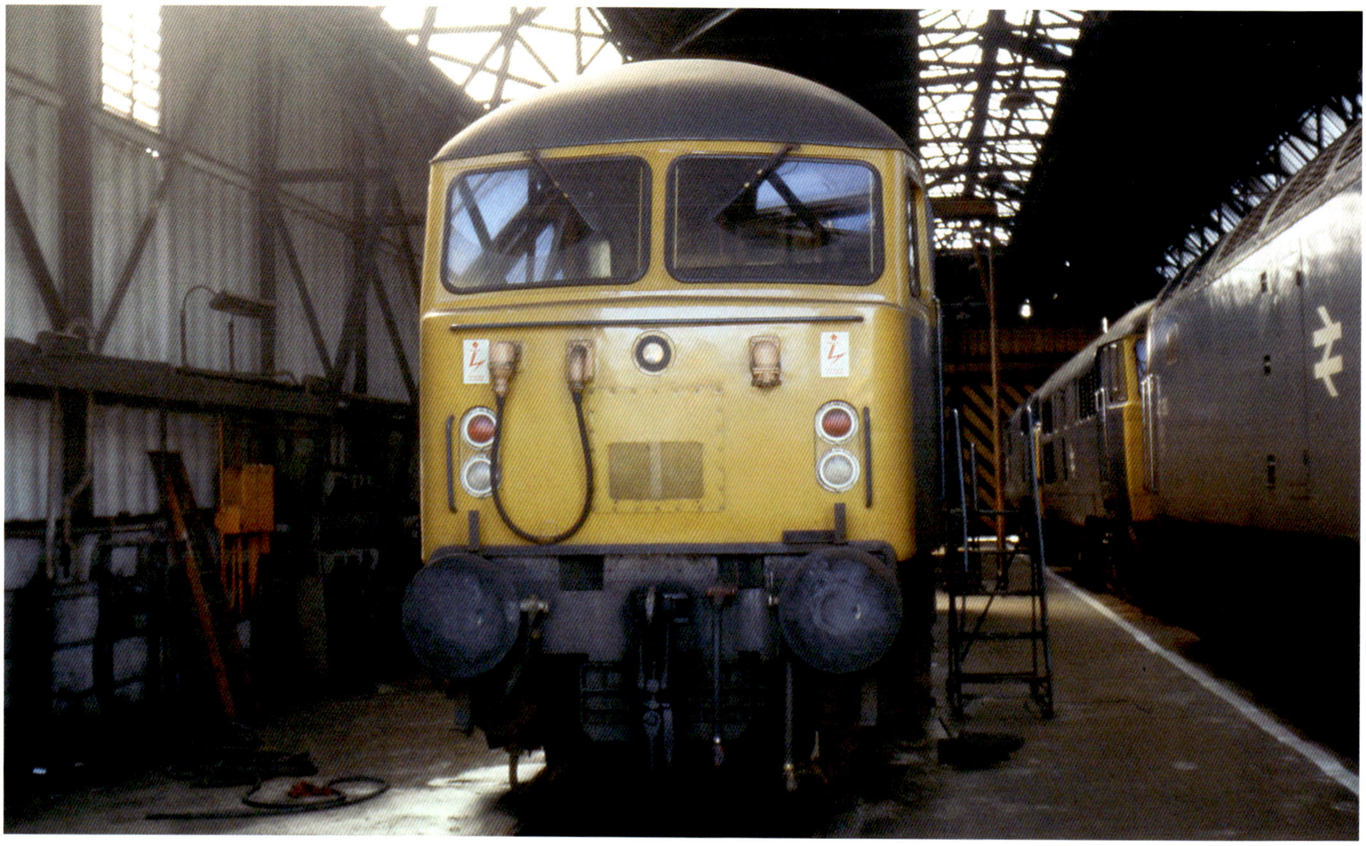

Venturing inside the gloom of the shed at Wath on 18 June 1978 we find a mix of motive power alongside 56011 awaiting the attention of fitters. This shed was built in the 1950s when the route was electrified. then in 1963 as a result of the replacement of steam with diesel locomotives on the non-electrified lines in the area Mexborough shed closed and a small diesel depot was built on the site of the old turntable in the centre of Wath yard, although diesel locomotives were also stabled at the electric locomotive shed. ***Brian Daniels***

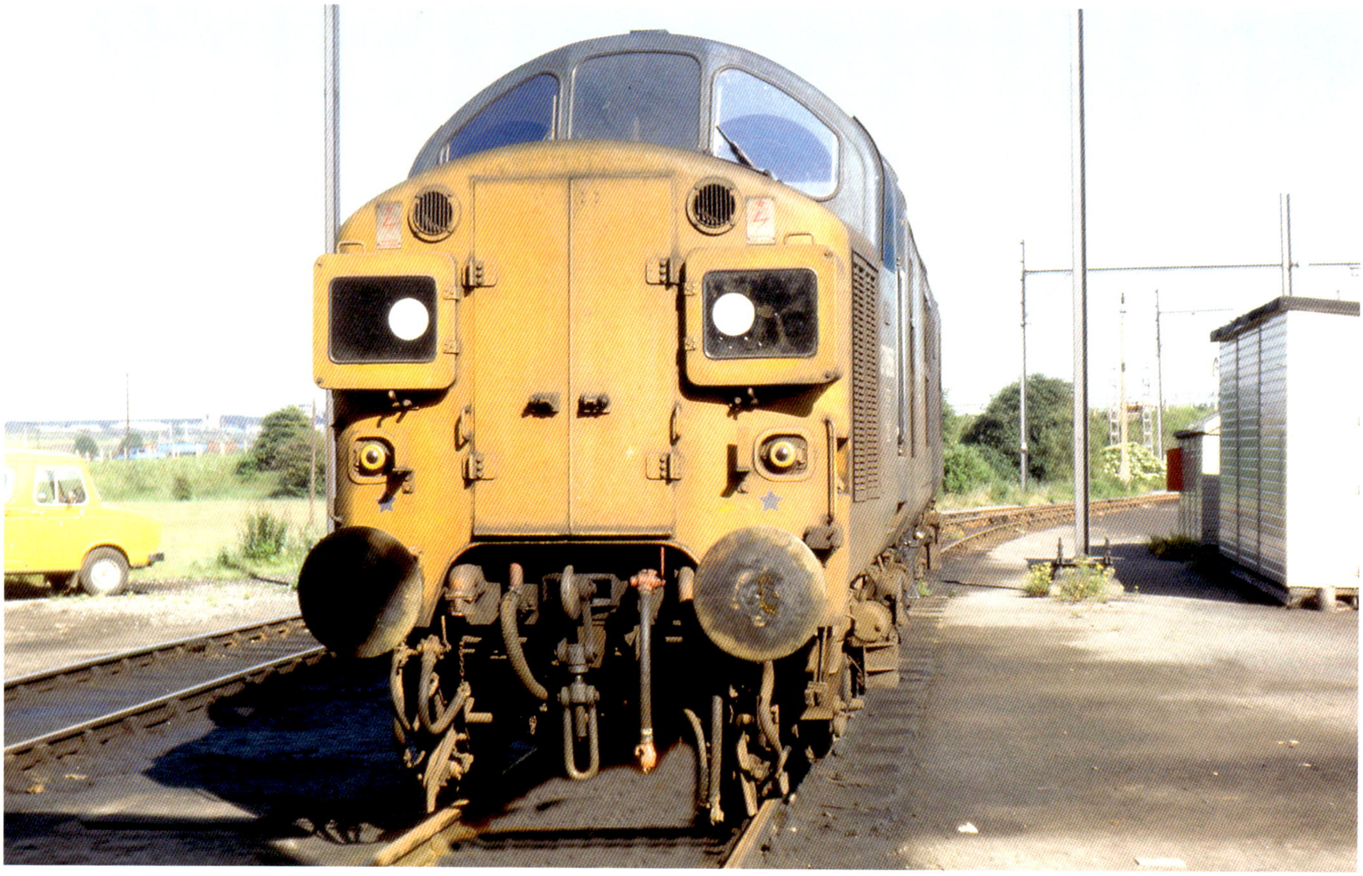

Back outside the same day we have another Tinsley locomotive outstabled with 37056 enjoying the sunshine. This shed closed in 1983, after then a shunter was provided as a trip from Tinsley until closure. After closure of the depot and yard in 1988, the locomotive shed was for a few years the home of a toxic waste processing company, which resulted in a local protest movement being formed., today there is very little to show of the railway's presence at this point. ***Brian Daniels***

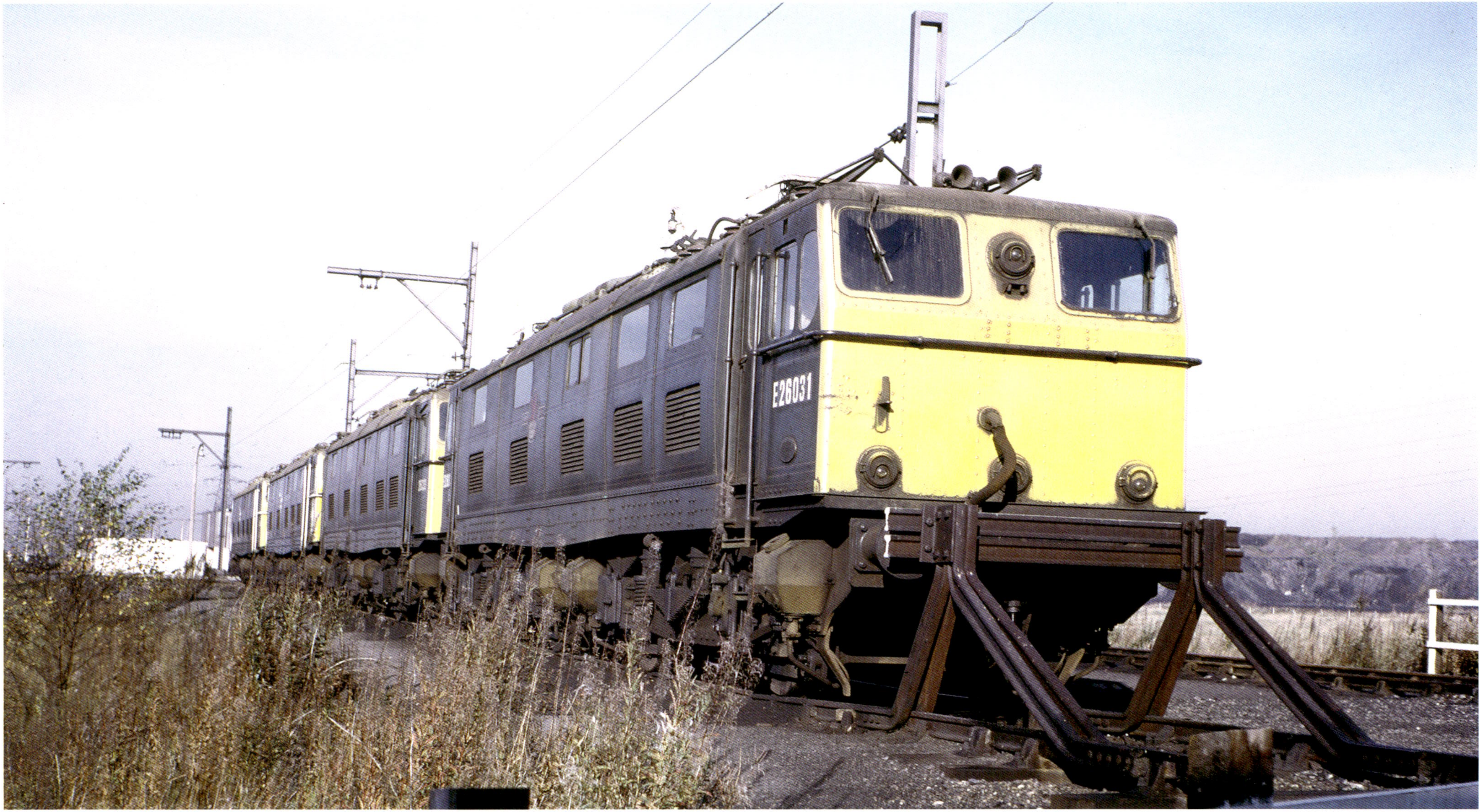

At the start of the seventies the area was rich with coal mines and the nearby Manvers Main Coking Plant which employed a fleet of ex-British Railways shunters. Greeting the visitor on 23 October 1971 was E26031 at the head of the once familiar snake of Class 76s always stabled here. With a total length of over 1¼ miles, between Wath Central railway station and Elsecar Junction, and with over 36 miles of track this was a busy location. Eastbound traffic was received in eight reception sidings feeding thirty one departure sidings and controlled by "B" Box, whilst for westbound traffic there was a fan of nine reception sidings, again feeding thirty one departure sidings and controlled by "A" Box. The western entry and exit to the yard was under the control of Elsecar Junction signal box whilst the eastern end was controlled by Moor Road signal box, with additional control from the Wath Central signal box, which controlled the main lines through the yard and was situated by the station. The yard once handled as many as 5,000 wagons per day. ***Strathwood Library Collection***

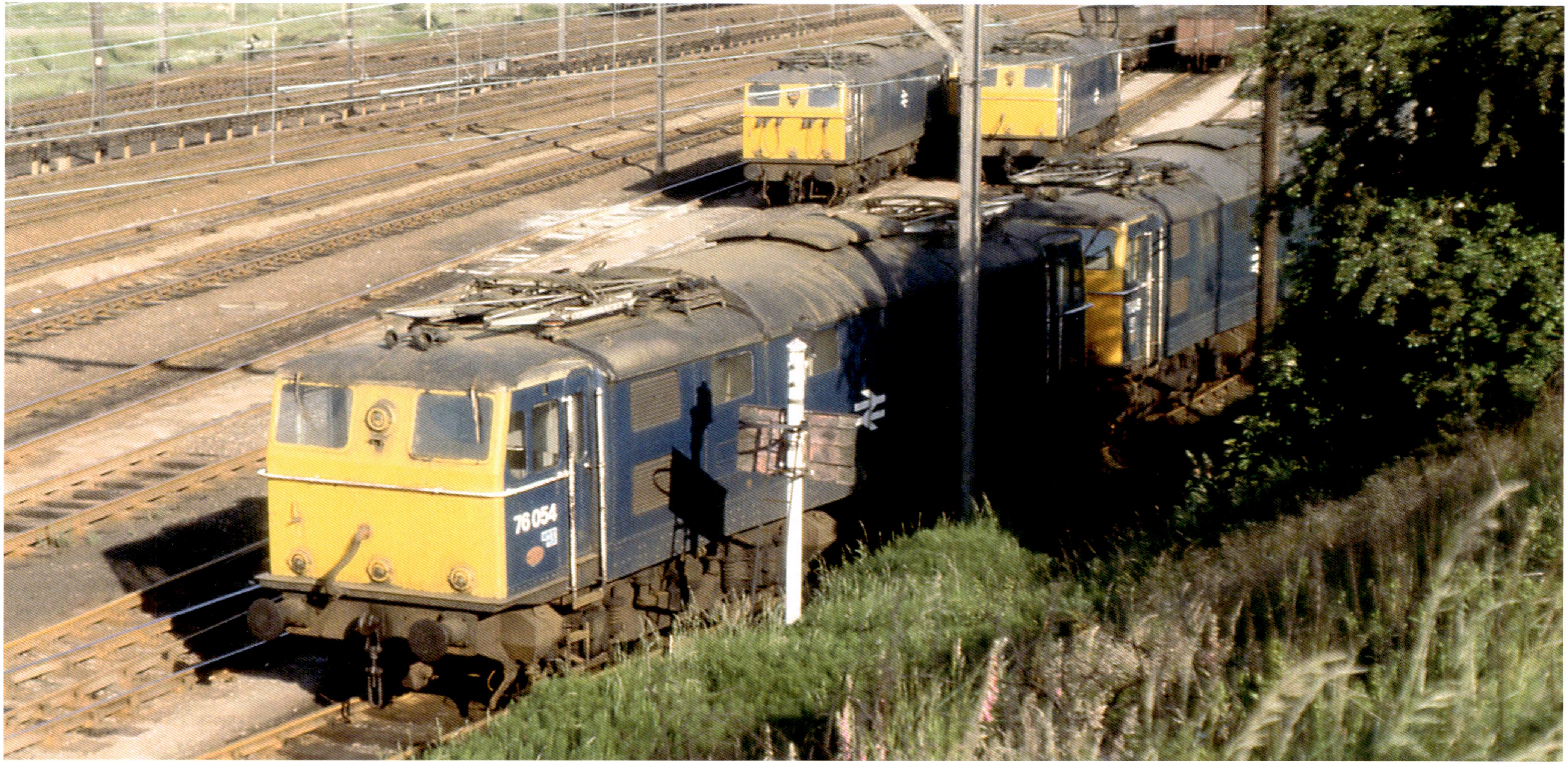

Spotters of the day could find a further selection of Class 76s stabled over the weekend at Rotherwood Yard as here on 18 June 1978 with 76054 which was once named Pluto after the ancient Greek name for the ruler of the underworld, nothing to do with the mafia and definately not the Walt Disney dog either! These exchange exchange sidings were set at the eastern extremity of the Manchester-Sheffield-Wath electrified lines between Orgreave Lane and Retford Road, on the south eastern boundary of the City of Sheffield in the Parish of Orgreave, within Rotherham. The Battle of Orgreave is the name given to a confrontation between police and picketing miners at the British Steel coking plant in Orgreave. Where during the miners' strike the National Union of Mineworkers organised a mass picket of Orgreave for 18 June 1984, with the intention of blockading the plant, and ideally forcing its temporary closure. Aware of the plans by means of MI5 infiltration, the police organised counter-measures. Between 5,000 and 6,000 pickets assembled here from across the UK. The police deployed between 4,000 and 8,000 officers, and were deployed from 10 counties. Of these, a small number had been trained in new riot tactics following the Toxteth and Brixton riots, while most had little or no experience in dealing with such events. There were between 40 and 50 mounted police and 58 police dogs. There were no women officers and only a handful of female picketers. Unlike most of the strikes of the time, where picketers were kept well away from their intended positions, the strikers were escorted to a field to the north of the Orgreave plant. The field was flanked by police on all sides except the south, where the Sheffield to Worksop railway line runs. ***Brian Daniels***

Days at Doncaster

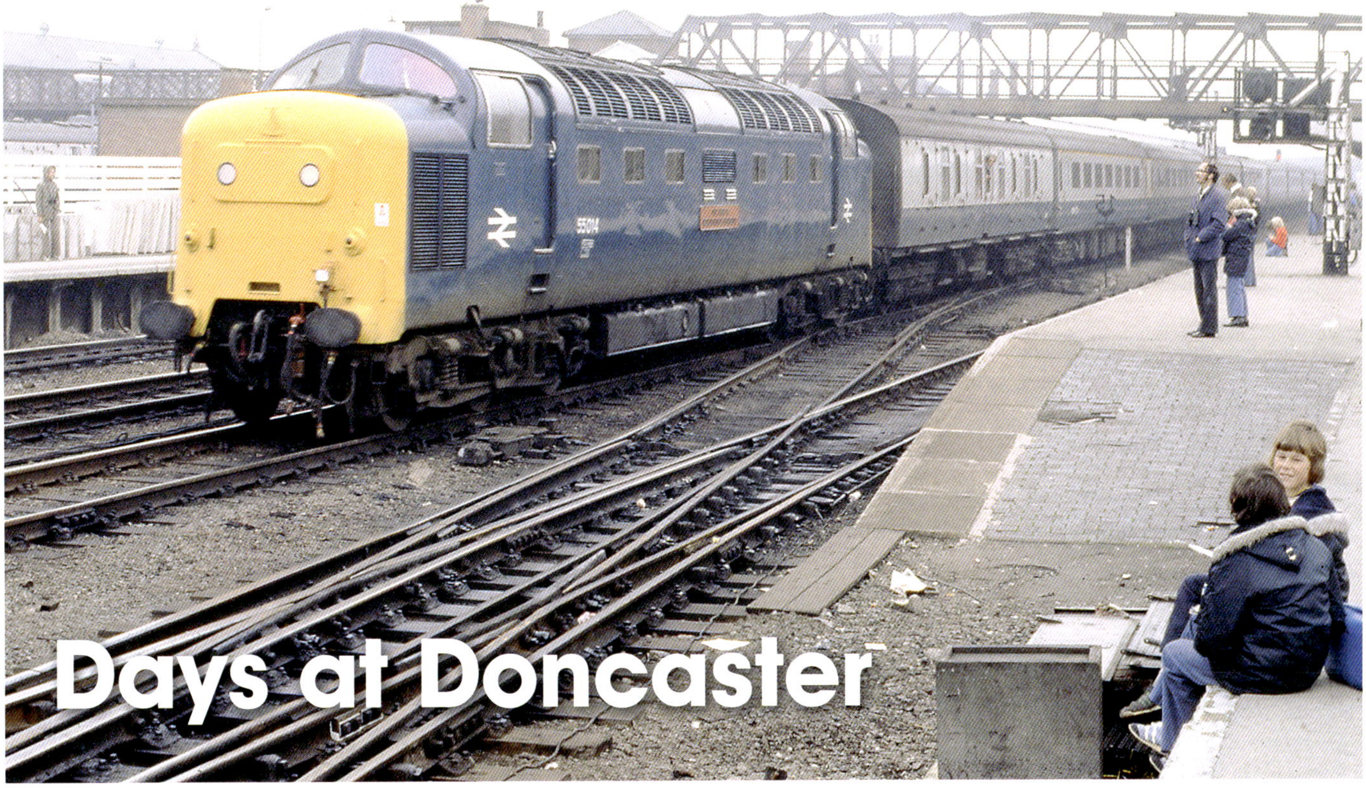

At least two of these spotters seem to be of the opinion "oh its only a Deltic" so they must be locals who have seen 55014 The Duke of Wellington's Regiment so many times it is no longer worth watching, as the Type 5 roars by with the 09.00 Edinburgh to Kings Cross on 14 October 1978. ***Len Ball***

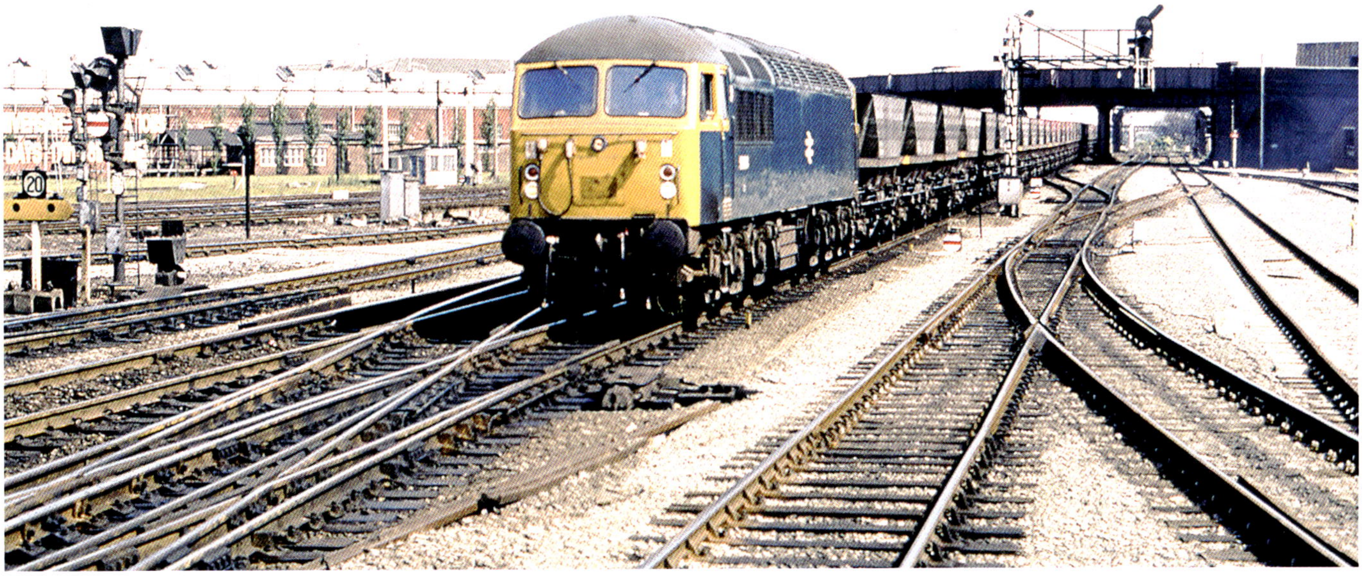

Old King Coal was well represented by traffic in the seventies across Yorkshire as 56024 brings a rake of merry-go-round empties into Doncaster on 20 June 1978, the Class 56 had been put to work on this type of workings on 23 August the previous year. ***Phil Bidwell***

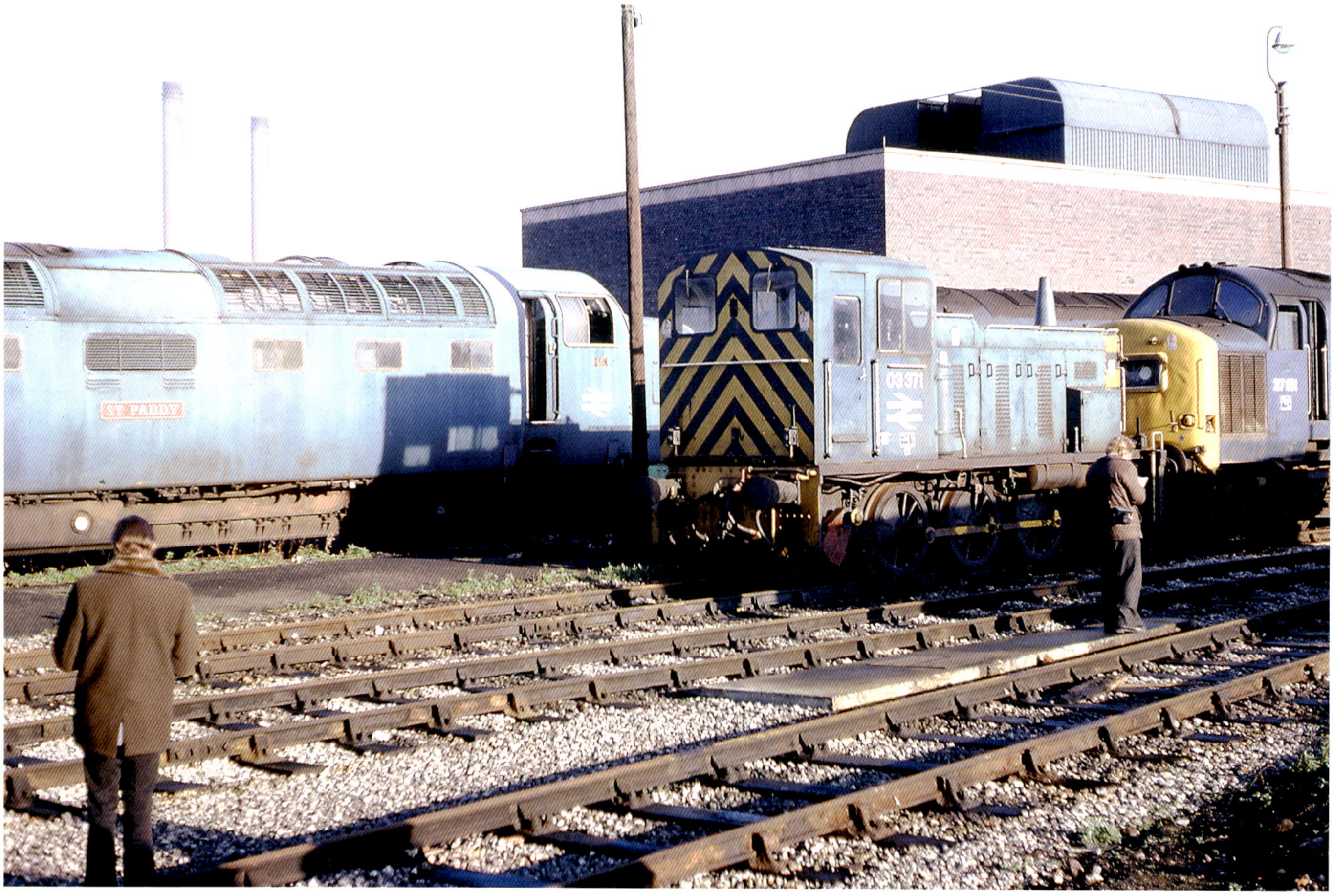

Society visits to Doncaster Works were quite relaxed really at the time with the guides allowing spotters to wander in fairly casual way around the yard to take notes of 03371 alongside the shabby hulk of 55001 St. Paddy in December 1979. This Deltic was posted as withdrawn on 18 December from Eastern Region Operating Stock and officially as of 5 January 1980. Within just a few weeks this racehorse was put to the torch with very little to identify it by late February. ***Strathwood Library Collection***

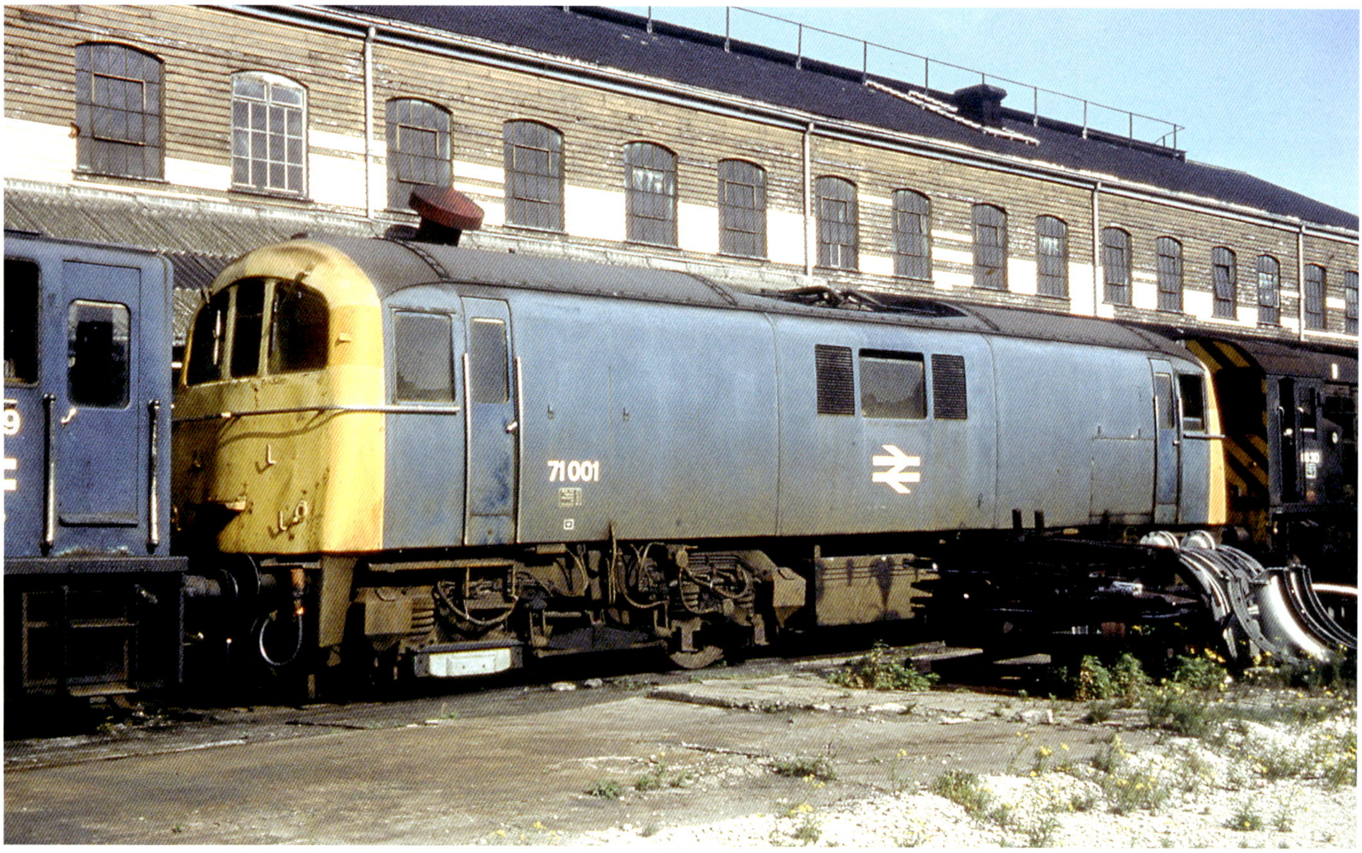

Another locomotive to spend some time in storage during the seventies was 71001 which was laid up at Ashford in Kent from October 1976 until June 1978. It was withdrawn officially in November 1977, however the authorities decided it was worthy of preservation and when seen on 24 September 1978 it was awaiting restoration outside the works where it had been built twenty years beforehand. ***Strathwood Library Collection***

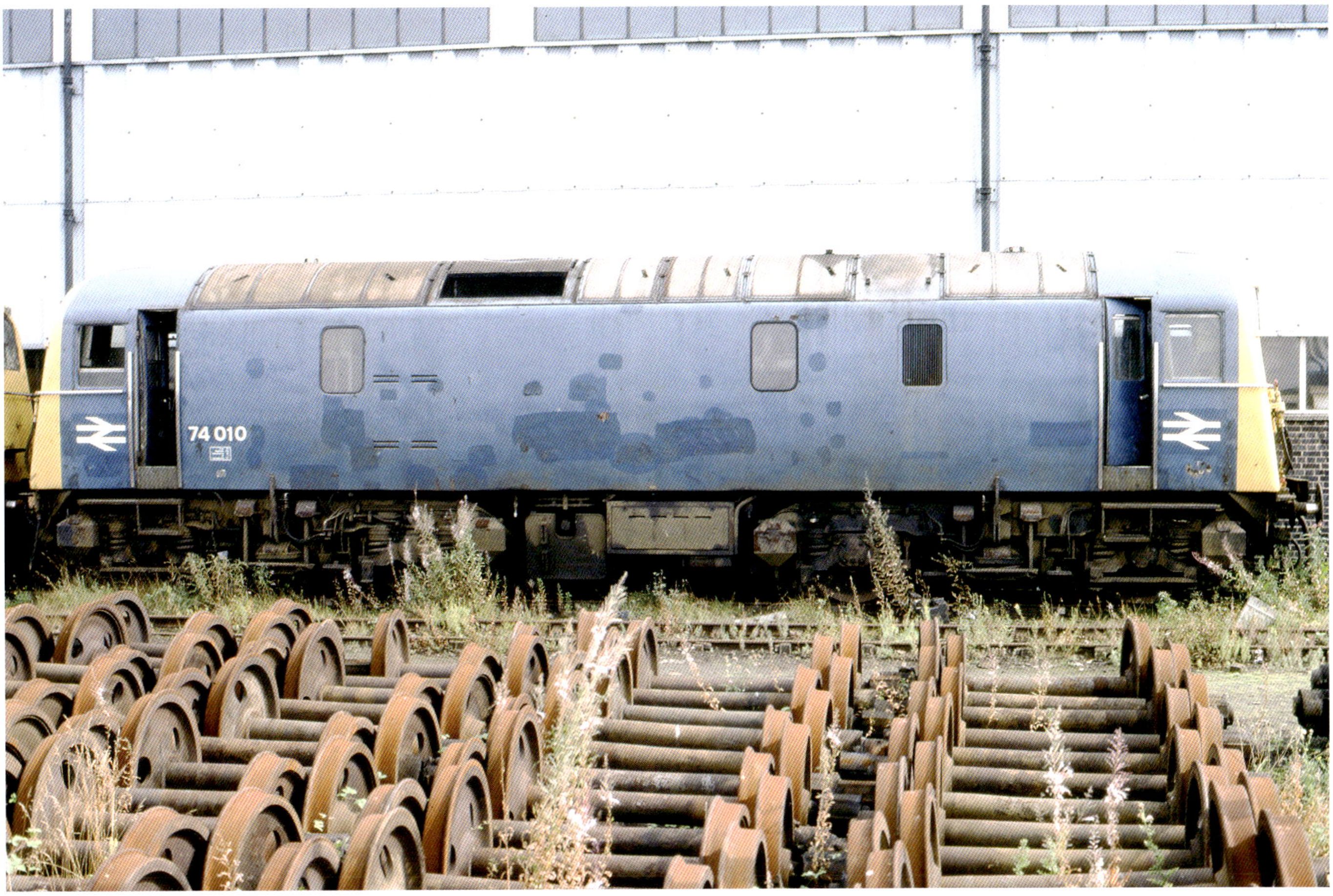

Less fortunate was 74010 which on 19 August 1979 was awaiting its turn in front of the cutters which would come during October a few weeks later. ***Strathwood Library Collection***

More raw material for the cutters was brought down this time from Scotland in the shape of 24095 which was swiftly dealt with during June 1976. ***Late John Ferneyhaugh/ Strathwood Library Collection***

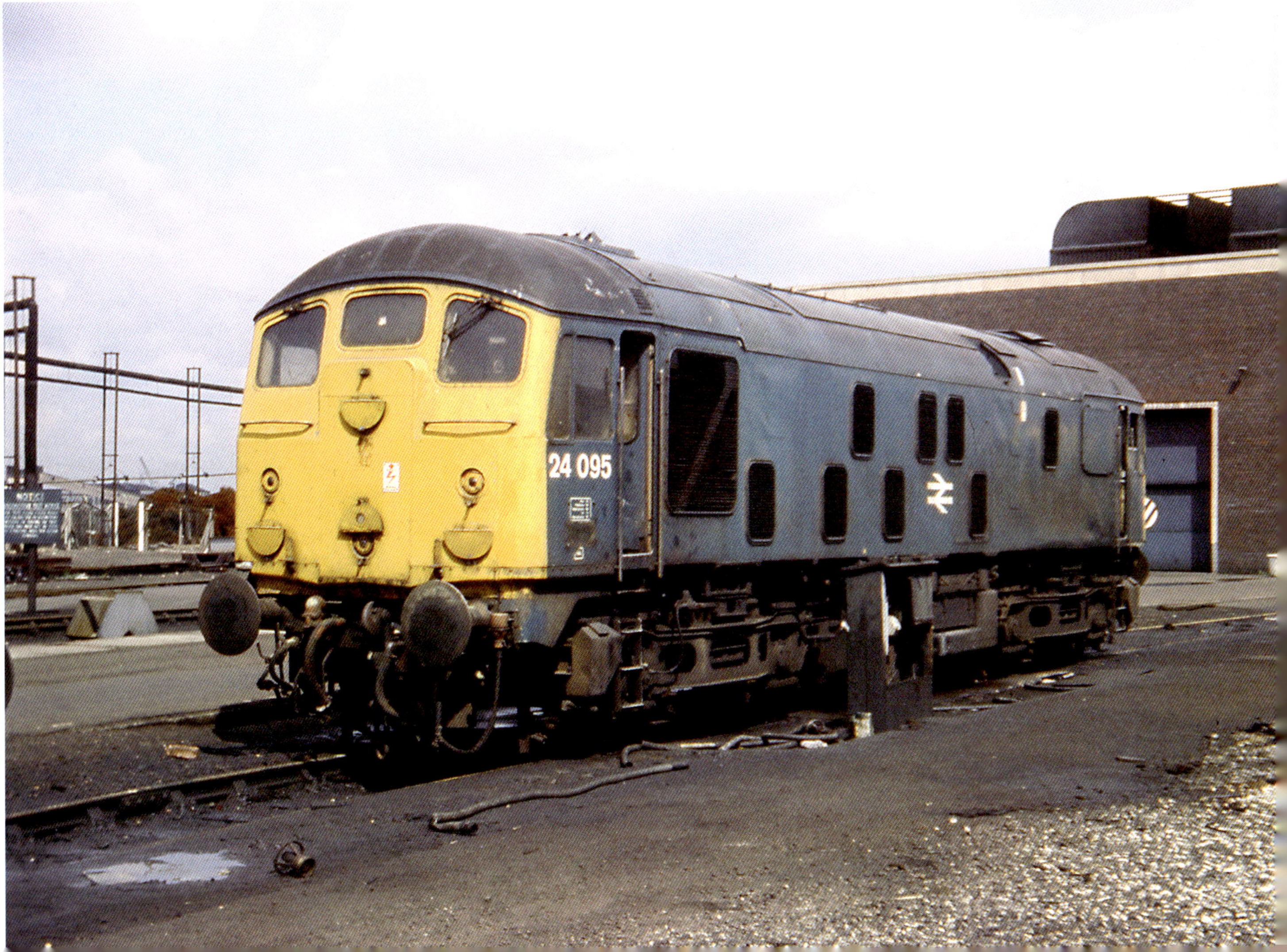

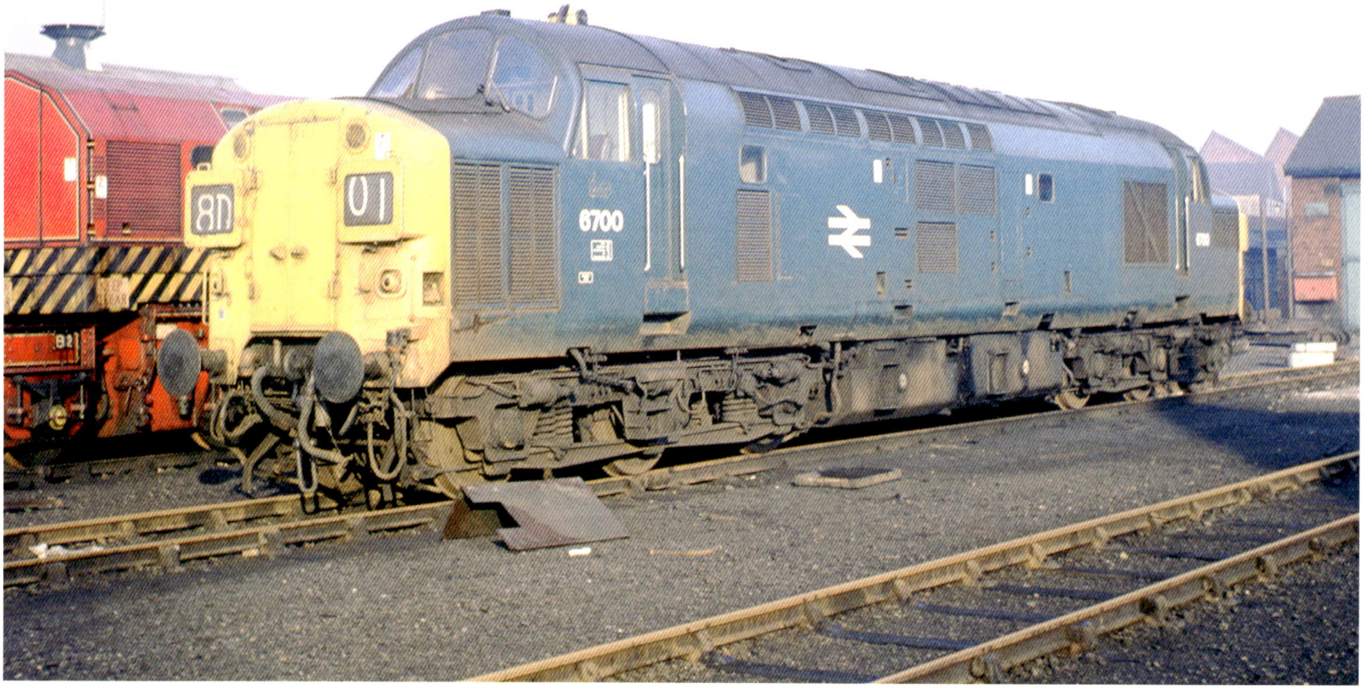

Doncaster Works was more concerned with repairs when visited on 22 November 1970 when 31B March allocated 6700 was in for maintenance. ***Jeffrey Lane***

During a society visit in the spring of 1976 we find Deltic 55021 Argyll & Sutherland Highlander here for a Heavy General Repair which would take until 19 January 1977. This included the plating over of route indicators, sand-box fillers and cab quarter light windows. ***Late John Ferneyhaugh/Strathwood Library Collection***

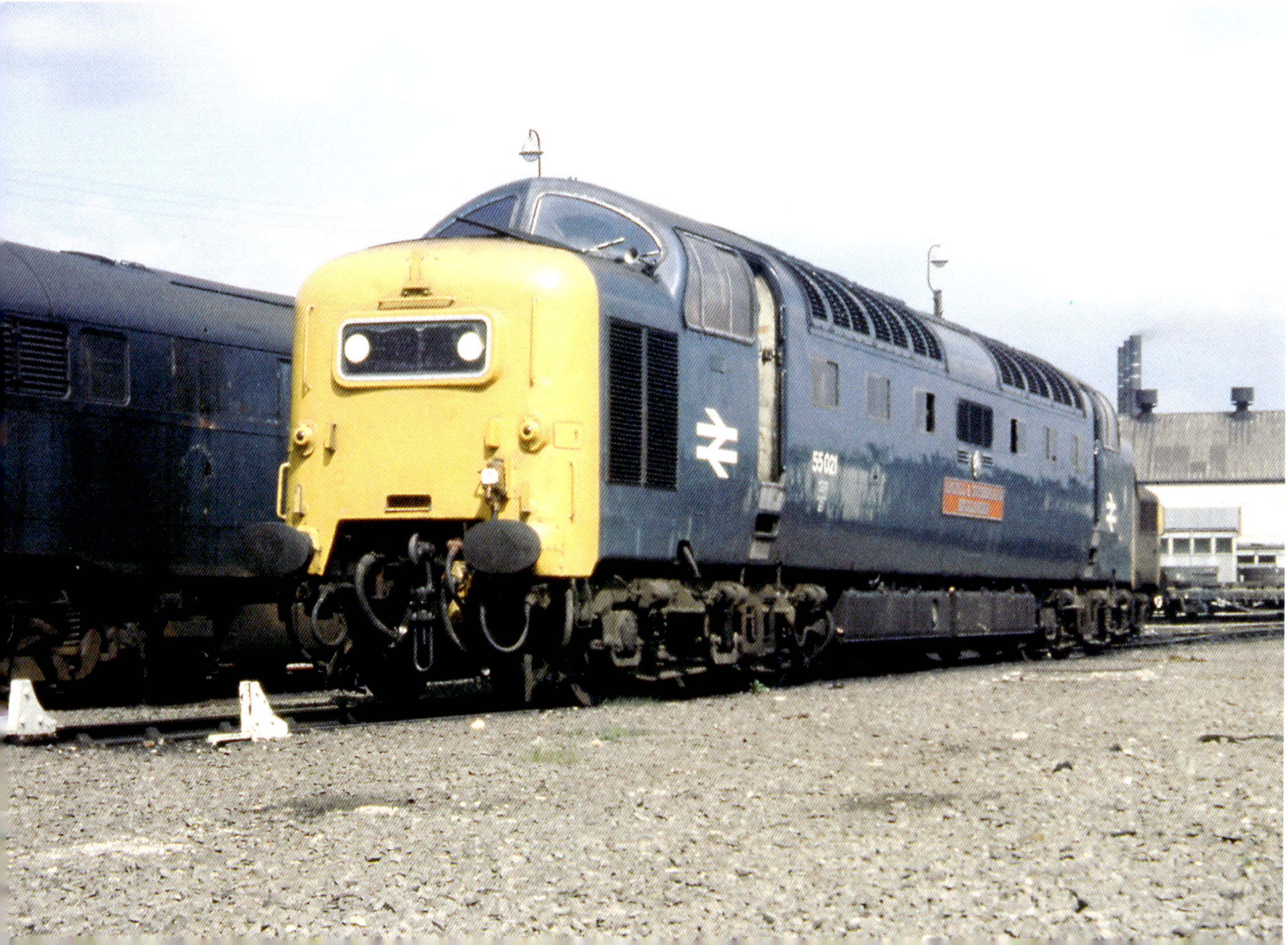

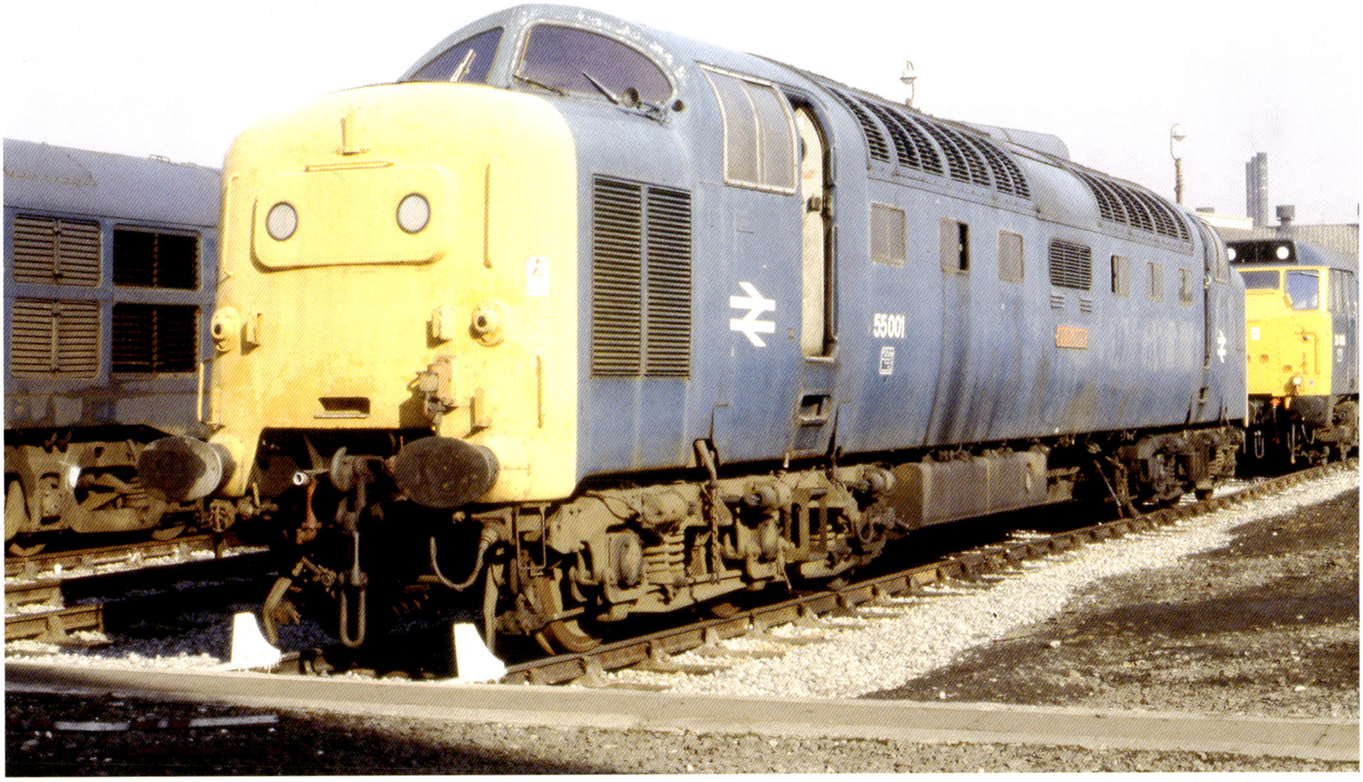

On 24 March 1978 55001 St. Paddy worked the 08:00 King's Cross - Edinburgh as far as Doncaster having suffered an engine failure at Retford. It found its way into the works, however, repairs never took place. ***Stuart Broughton***

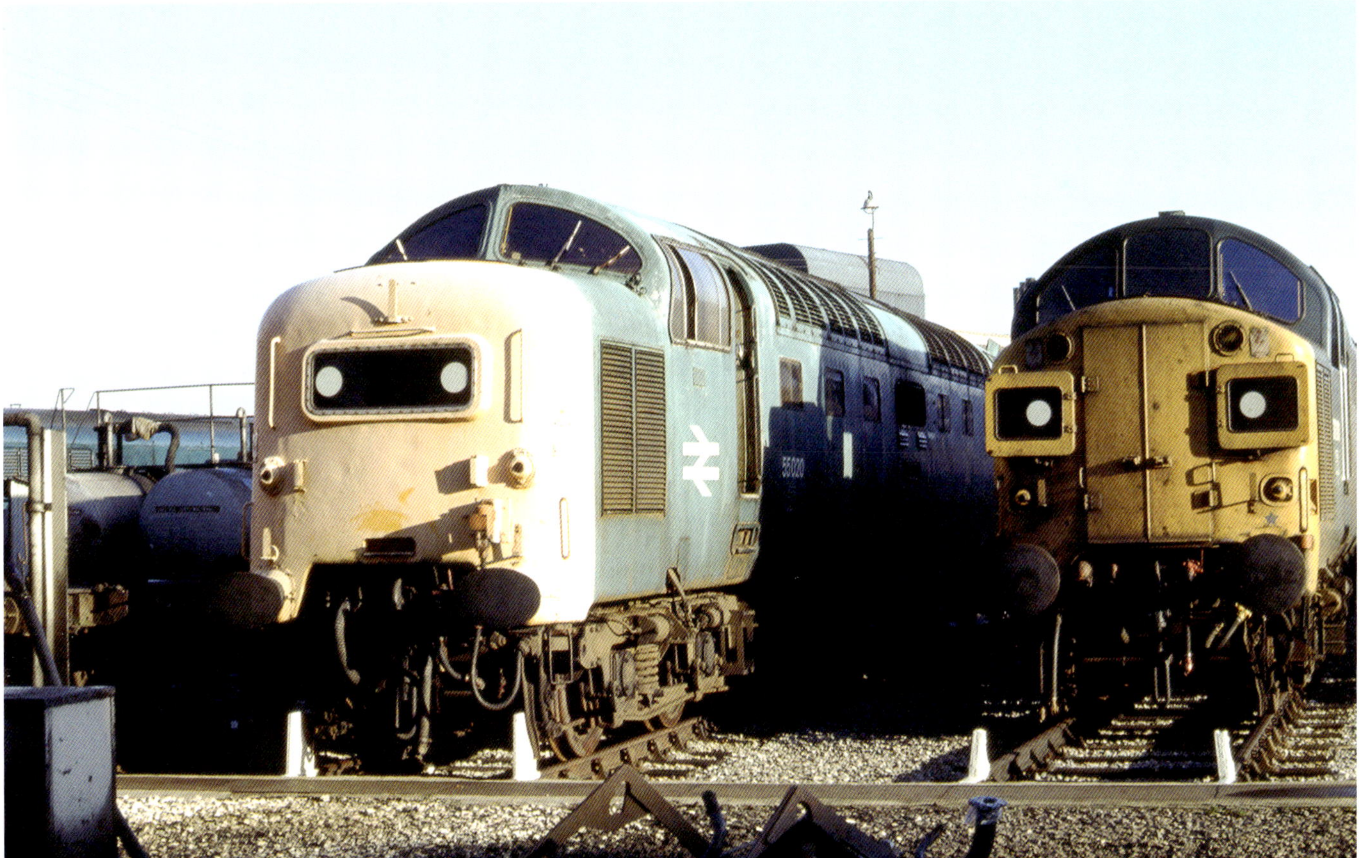

The late Ray Smith, chairman of the Deltic Preservation Society, announced on 27 October 1979 that repairs to 55001, 55004 and 55020 had been sanctioned whilst undertaking the DPS annual general meeting. Repairs were to be given to 55004 first with 55001 and 55020 following in that order. Unfortunately due to the cost of getting 55004 up and running and given the time span the class as a whole had remaining, a decision was taken at the highest level, that both 55001 and 55020 Nimbus seen here would be stripped for spares and cut up. ***Greg Wyett***

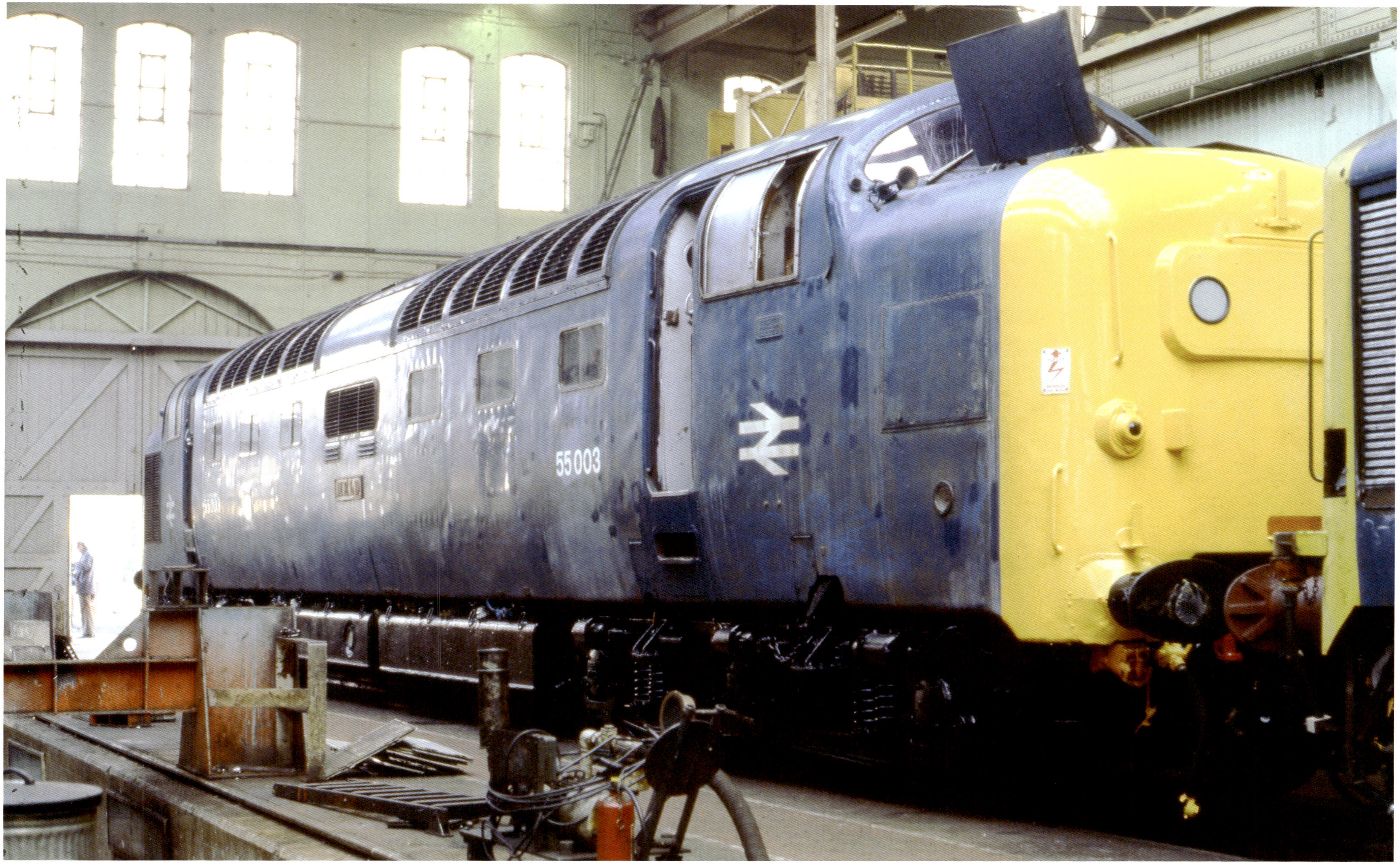

One nameplate from 55003 Meld was removed whilst the locomotive was at Doncaster Works during November 1978. It was sent to Derby where a plastic injection mould was taken from it. the plate was returned to Doncaster by 7 December for refitting. ***Stuart Broughton***

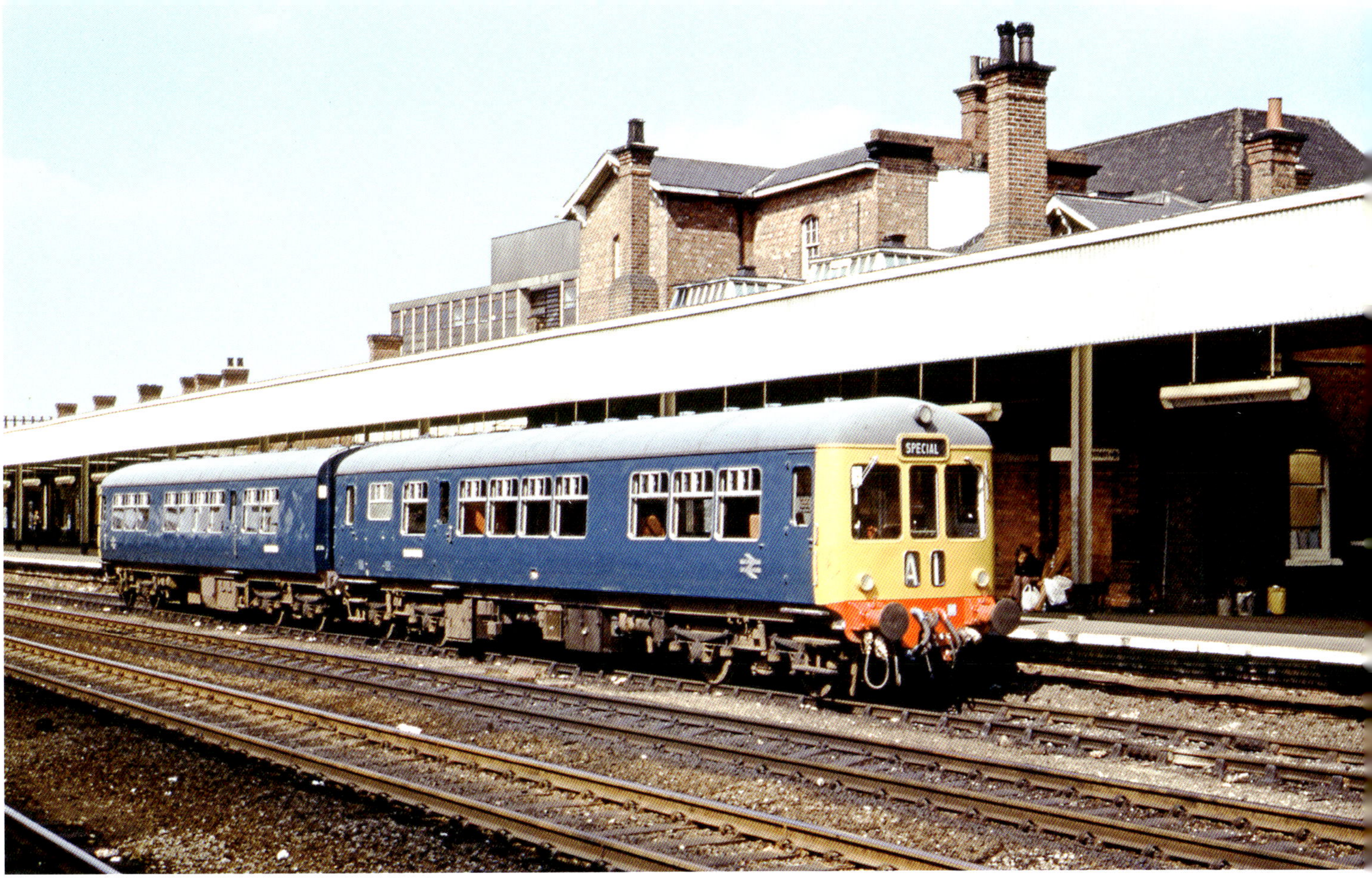

The Eastern Region Doncaster Divisional Manager's saloon was from 1966 a Wickham built two car DMU, numbered DB975005-6. On 3 June 1973 it was stopped in the station for refreshments to be added before heading off for another sortie around the region. ***Late Derek Whitnell/Strathwood Library Collection***

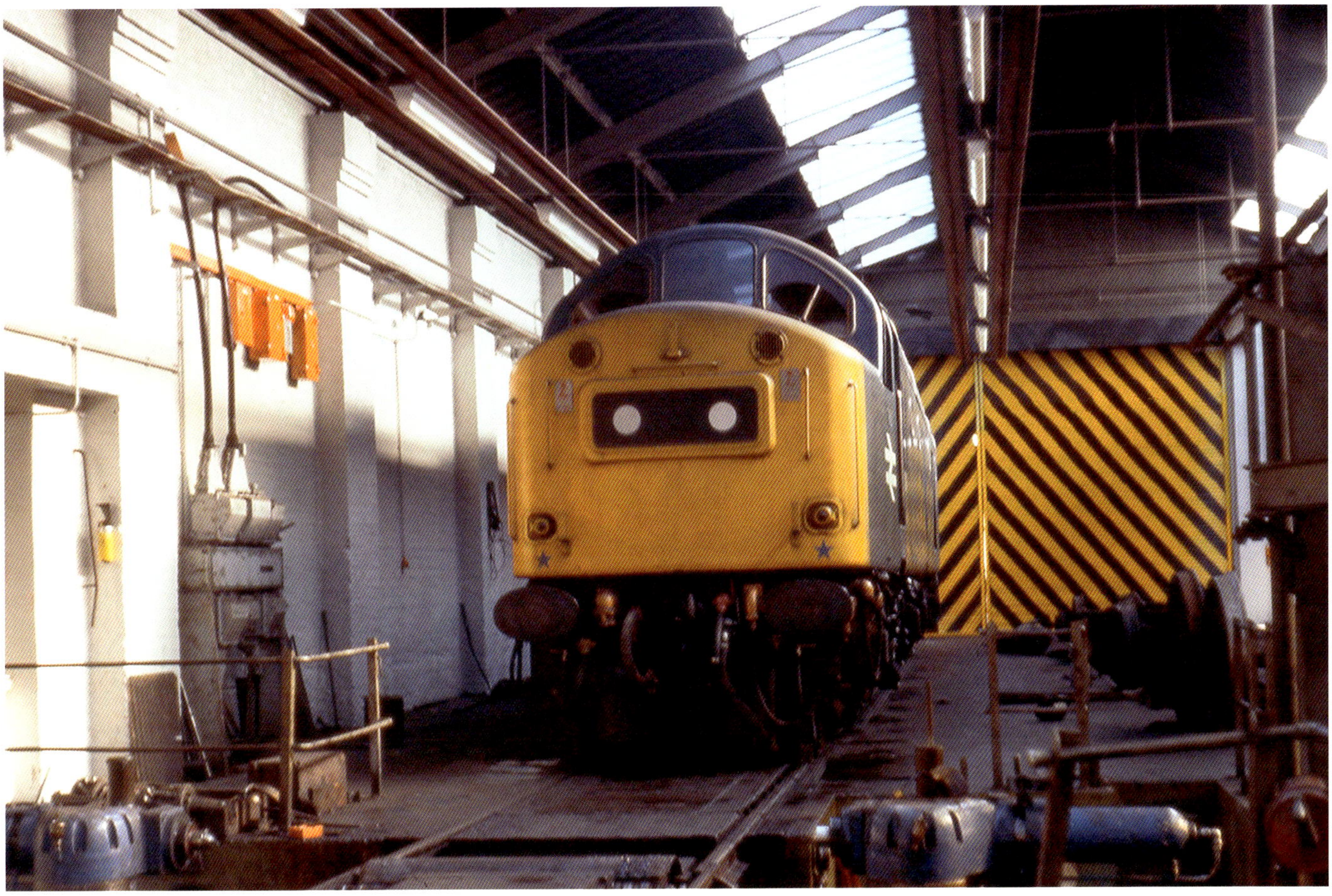

Doncaster's wheel turning lathe would be put to good use shortly on Thornaby allocated 40194 on 4 March 1978. In the late summer the previous year this Class 40 had been based at Hereford on the Western Region for crew training for a few months. ***Brian Daniels***

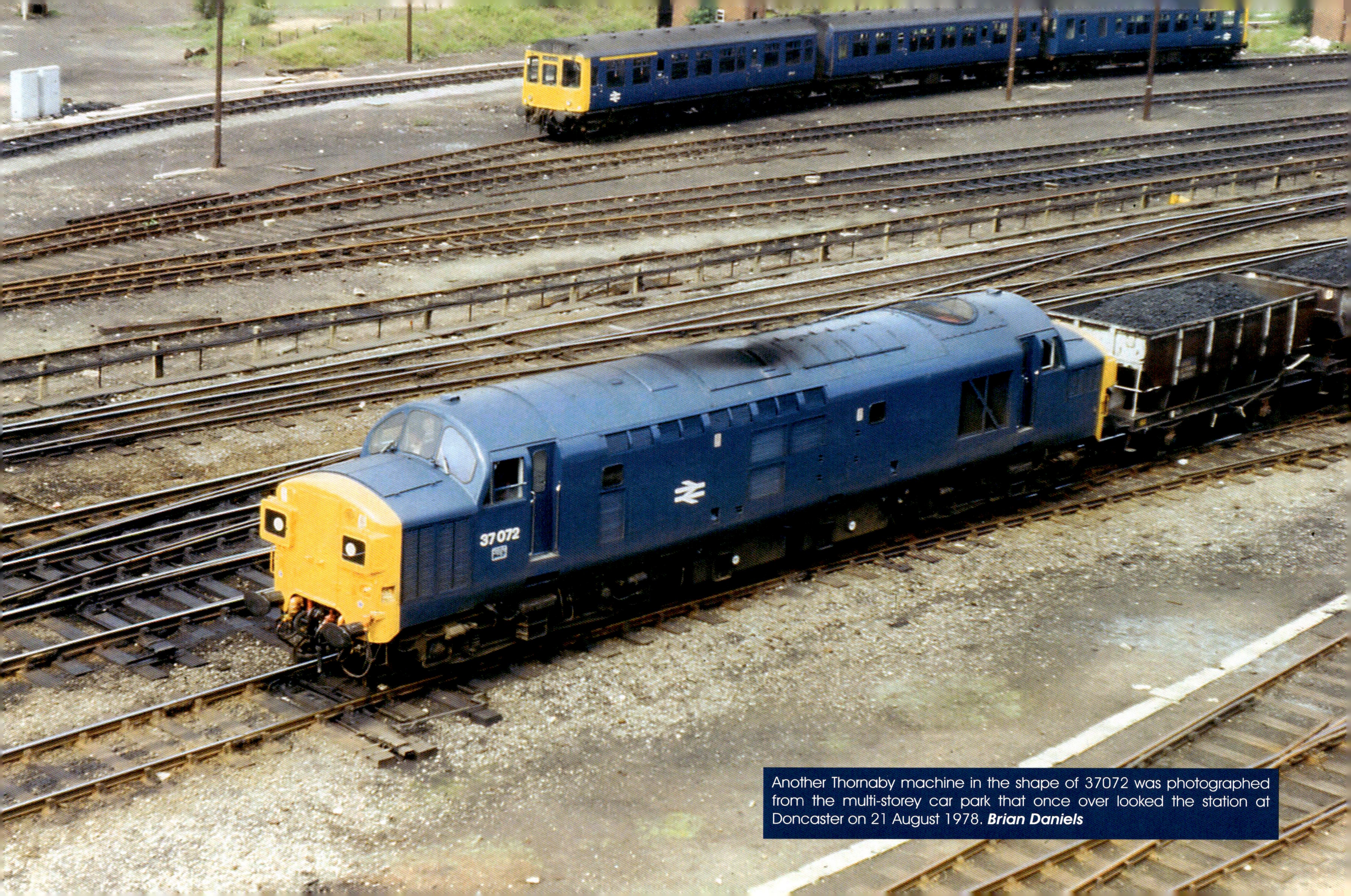

Another Thornaby machine in the shape of 37072 was photographed from the multi-storey car park that once over looked the station at Doncaster on 21 August 1978. ***Brian Daniels***

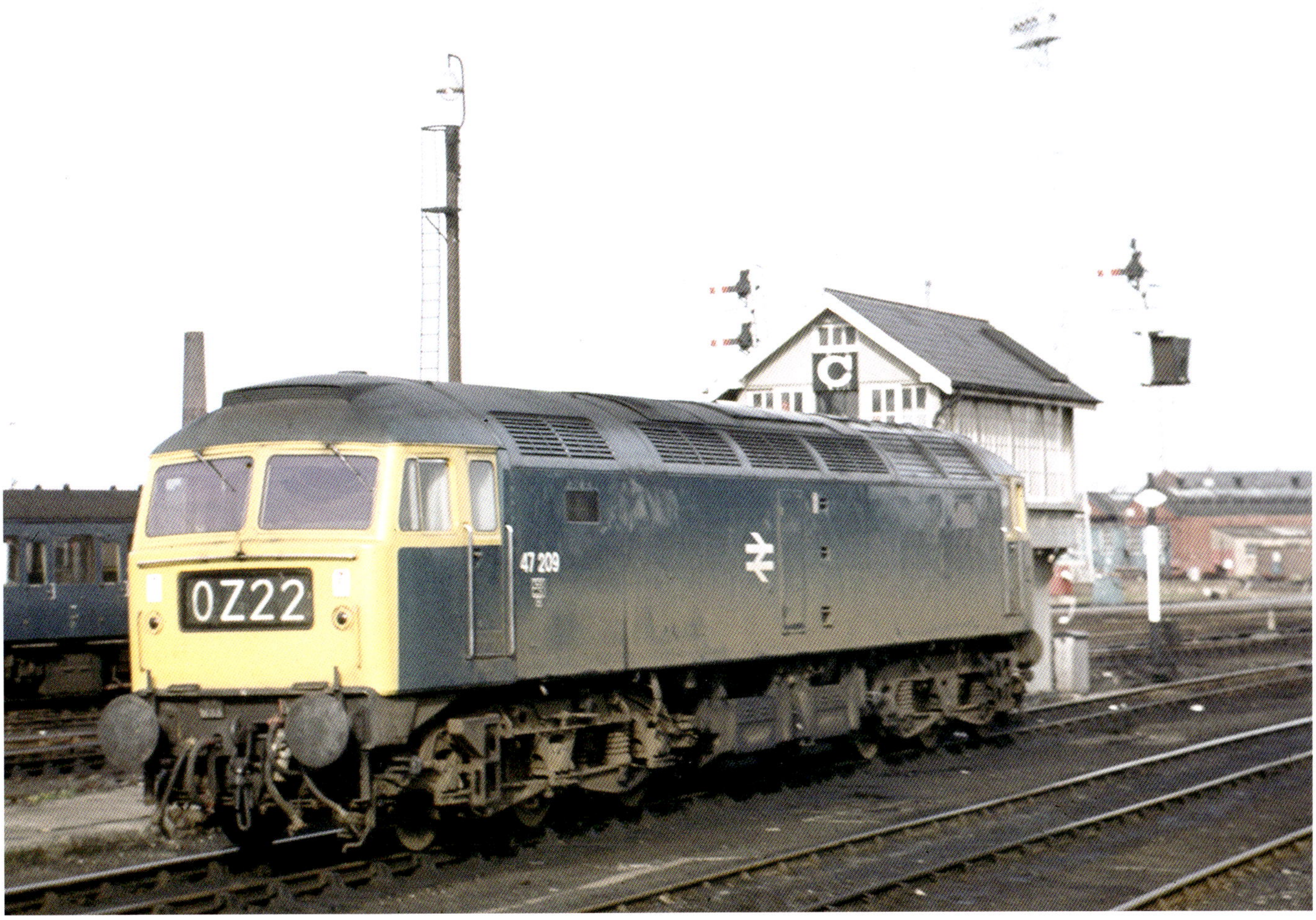

The headcode on 47209 suggests its use on a special when seen in 1974 light engine by Doncaster's C signal box, this Class 47 was to become a long term resident of Immingham until the end of the seventies. ***Dave Southern***

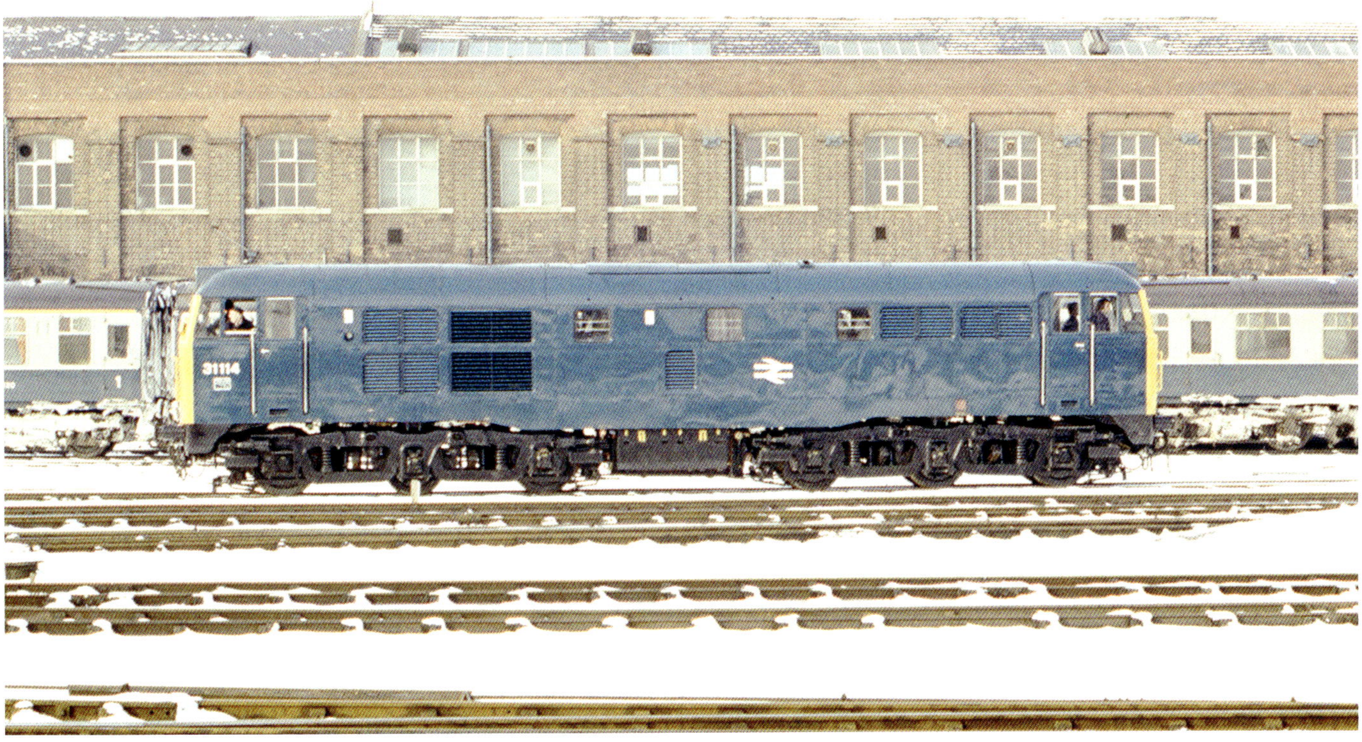

Both cabs of ex-works 31114 are occupied as it goes out on test in the snow on 13 February 1978, once signed off the Class 31 would return to service based at Stratford. A new cult BBC show Blake's 7 was into it's first series with an episode on television that evening. ***Barrie Watkins/Strathwood Library Collection***

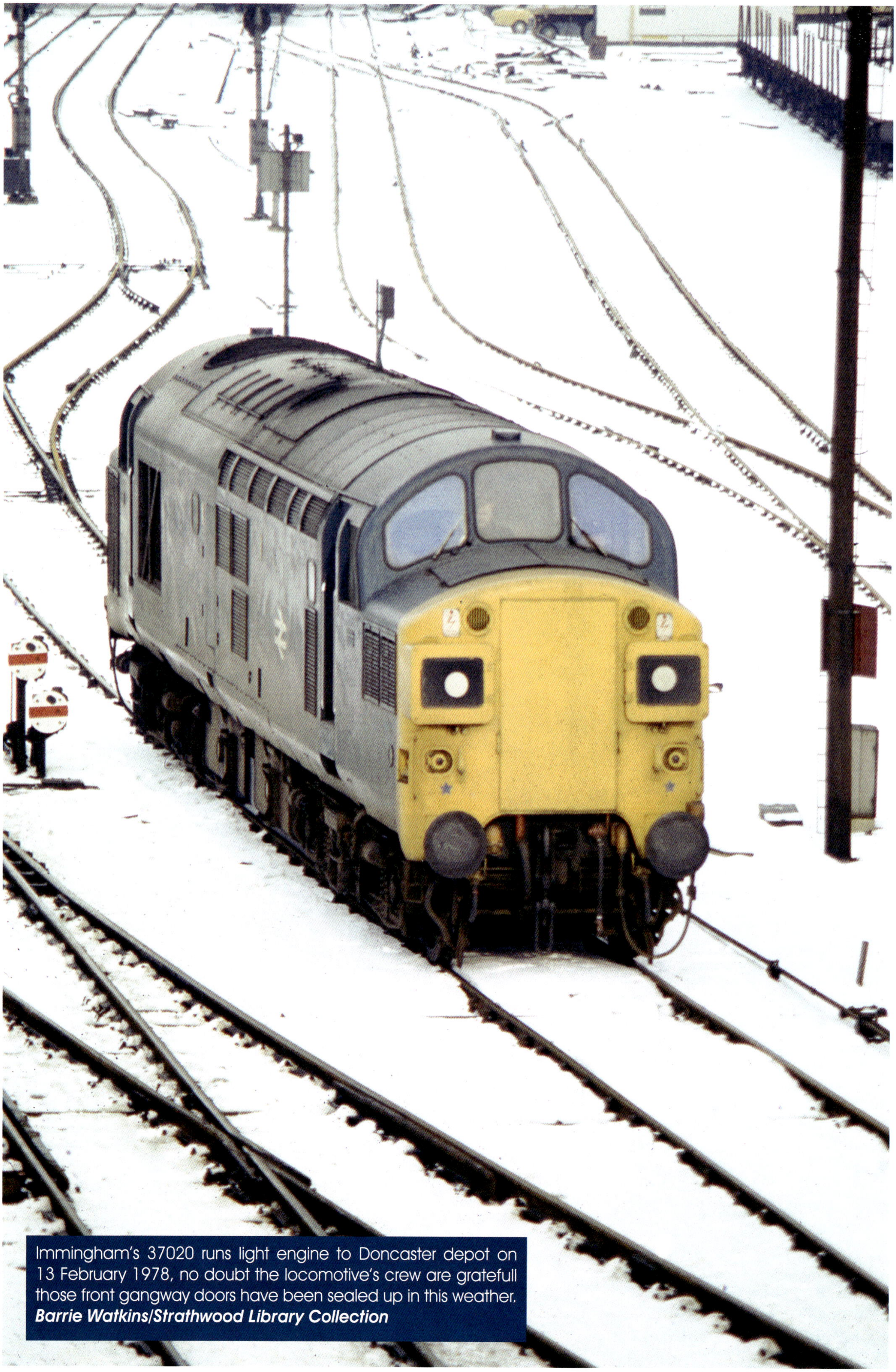

Immingham's 37020 runs light engine to Doncaster depot on 13 February 1978, no doubt the locomotive's crew are gratefull those front gangway doors have been sealed up in this weather. ***Barrie Watkins/Strathwood Library Collection***

North Eastern Reflections

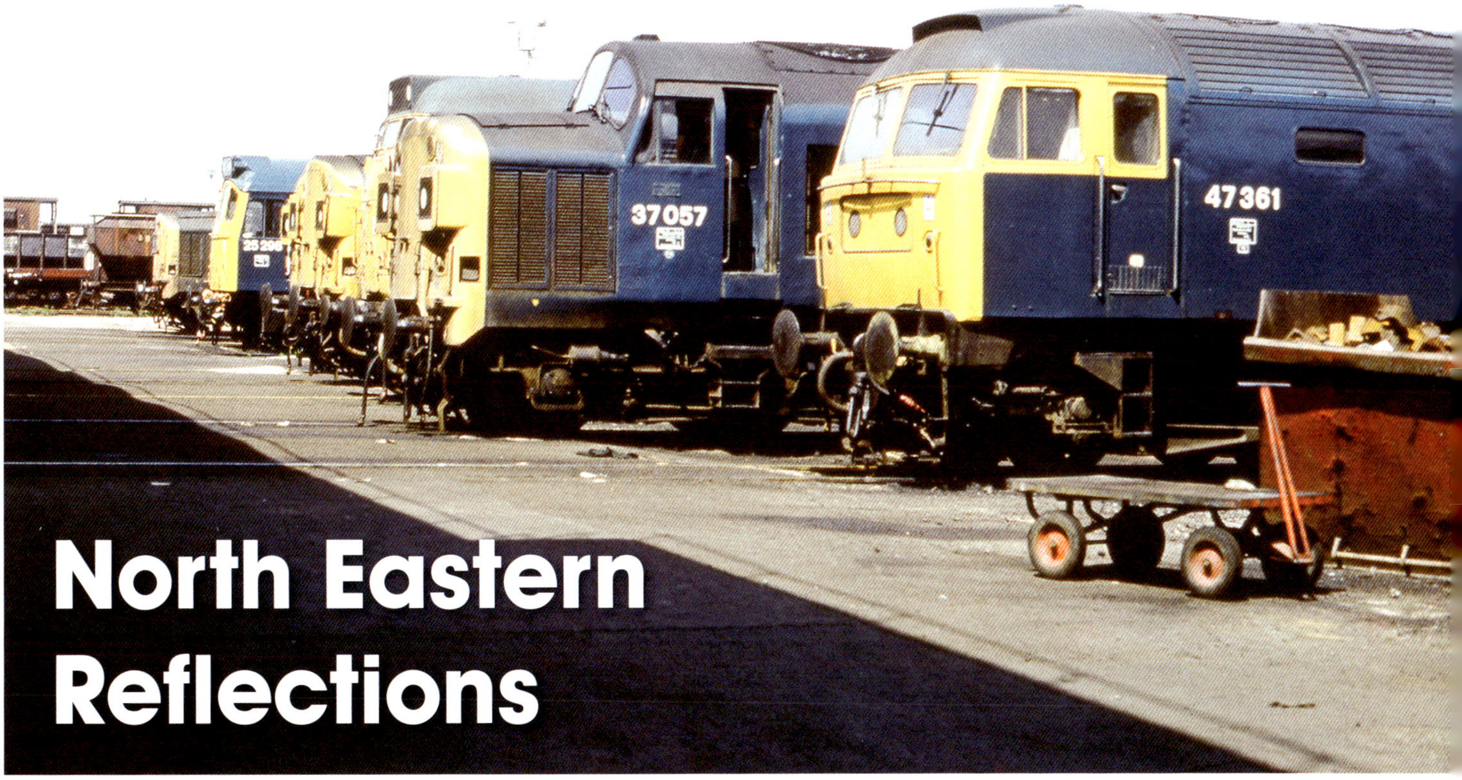

An impressive line up of locomotives outside Thornaby on 24 June 1978 in the sunshine, such was the variety we enjoyed back then at even a depot with so many freight rosters. ***Phil Bidwell***

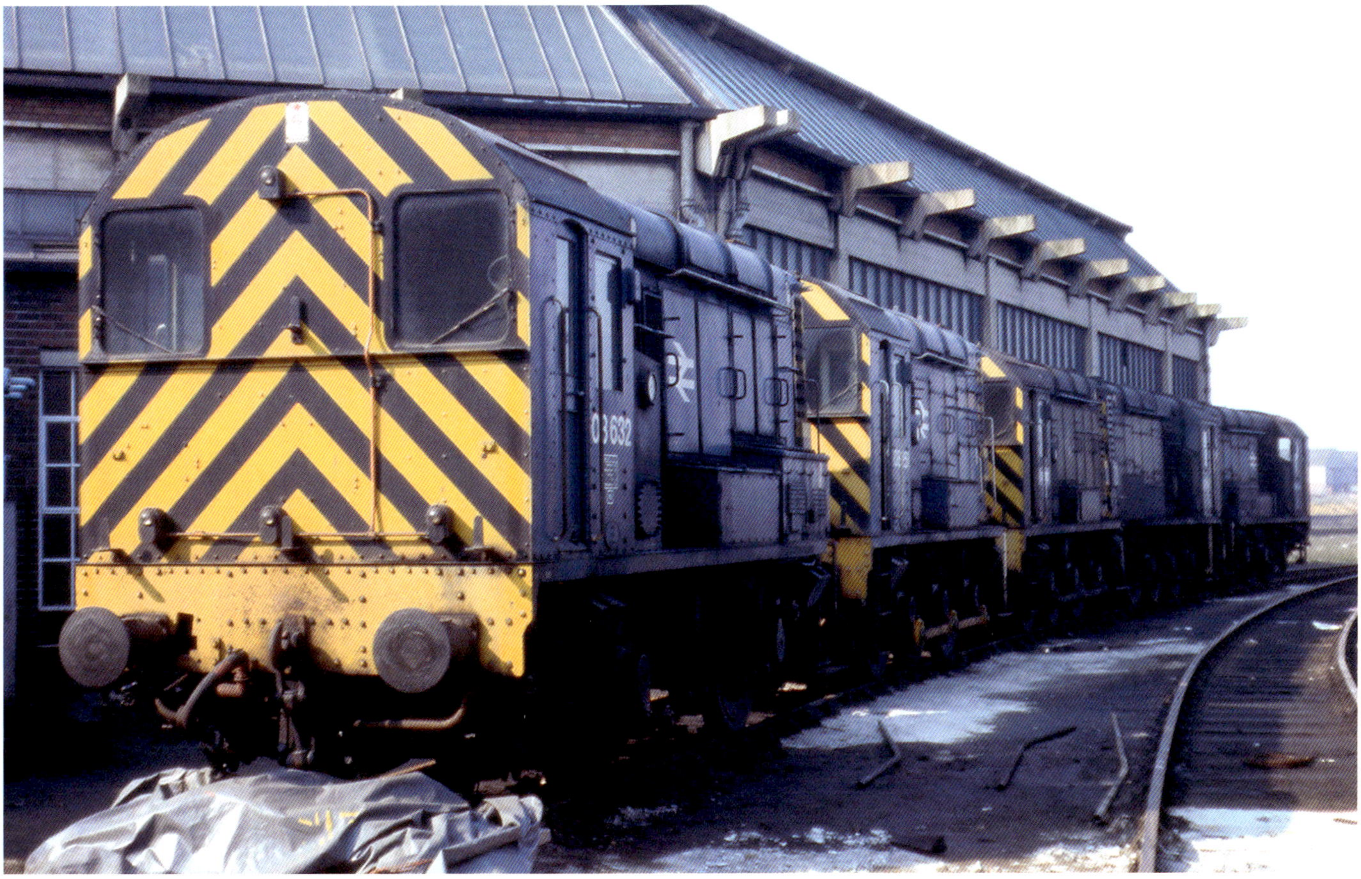

On 19 April 1978 08632 and others from the Thornaby allocation were parked up alongside the concrete roundhouse. The depot opened as a steam shed in June 1958 with the depot code 51L. It took over most of the allocations of the steam sheds at 51B Newport and 51D Middlesbrough. A year later Thornaby also absorbed the bulk of the allocations of close by 51E Stockton and 51G Haverton Hill. ***Brian Daniels***

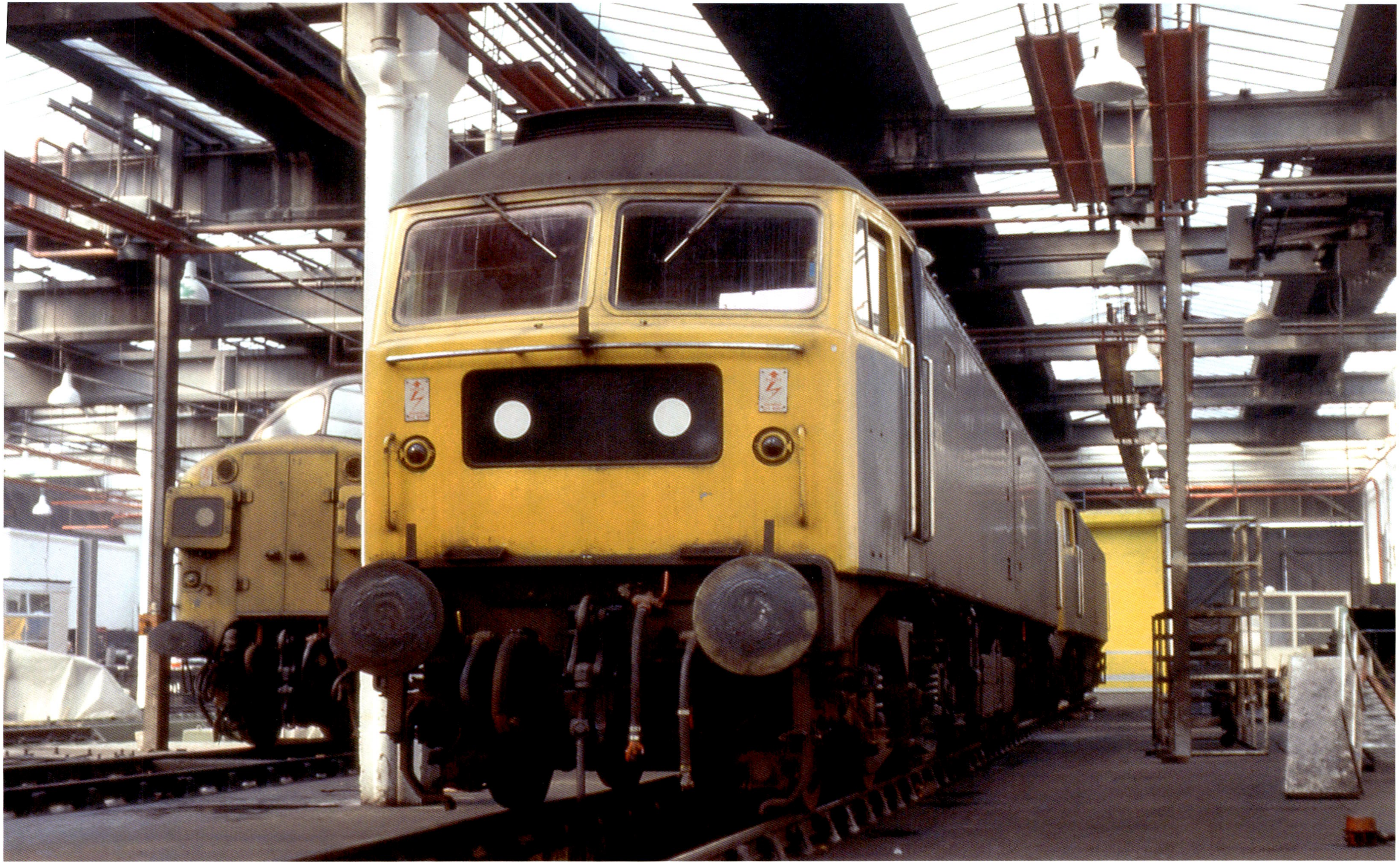

As well as the roundhouse, there was a large and airy straight shed complex where this same visit rewards us with 47363 on its home depot of Thornaby. ***Brian Daniels***

Opposite: Another visit a few months later on 17 July 1978 brings us 37100 also seeking shelter within its home depot. ***Brian Daniels***

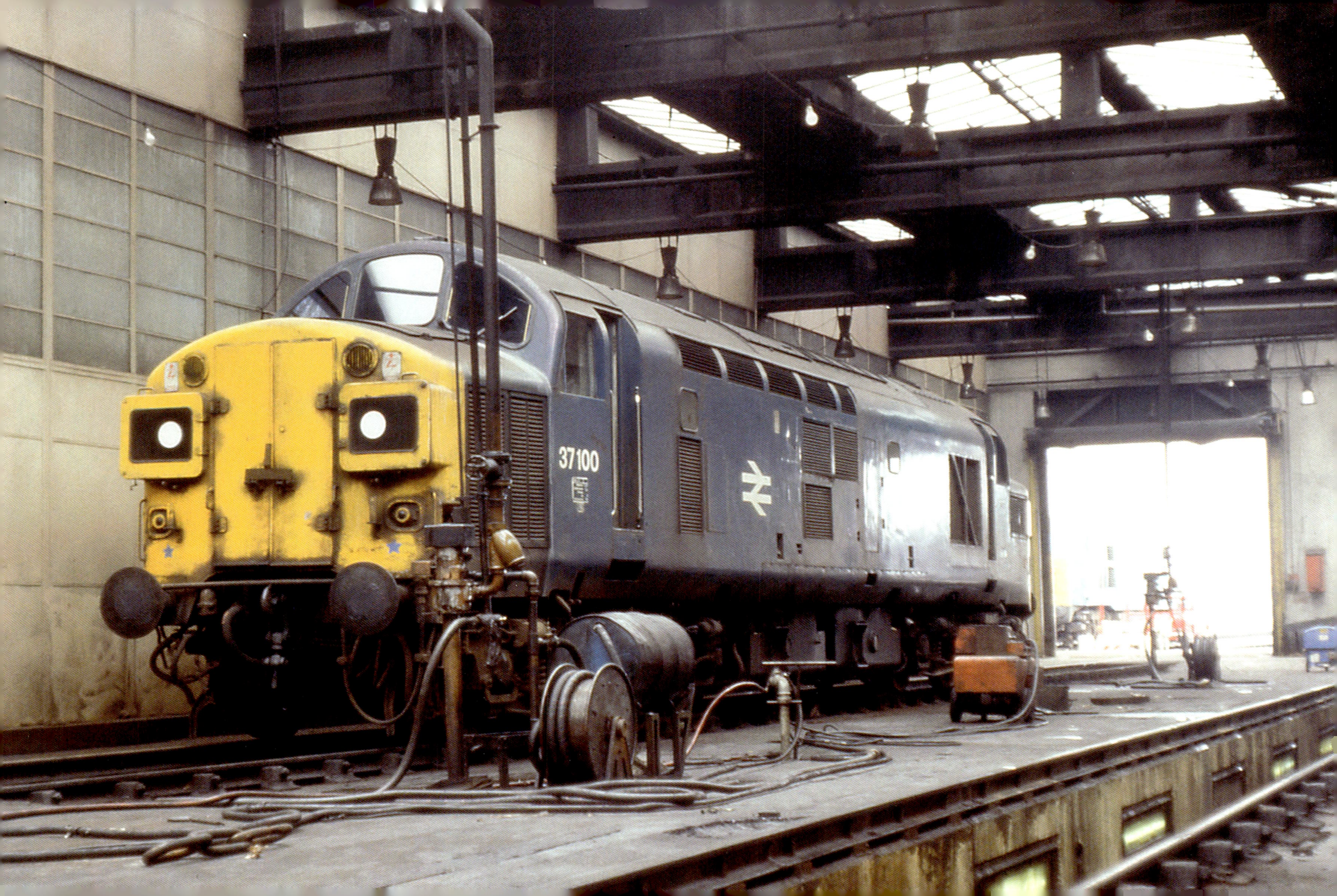
37100

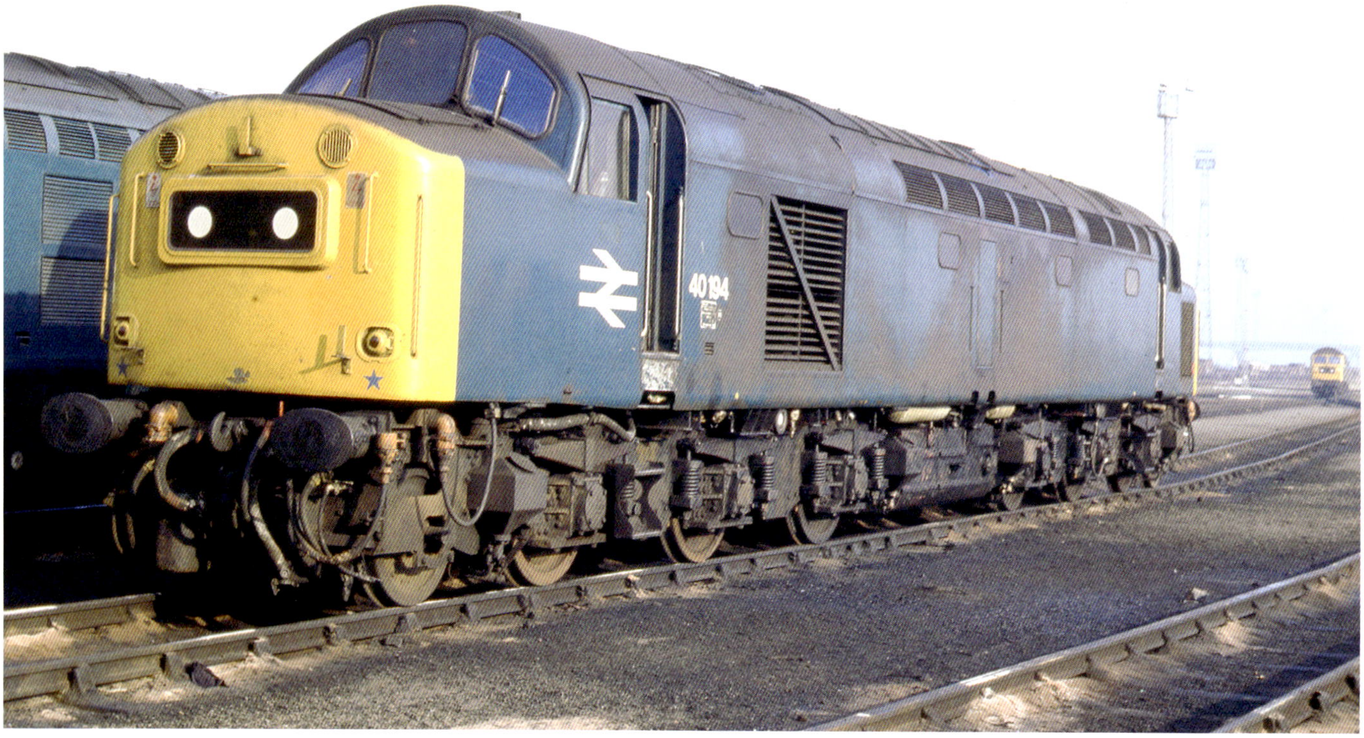

Captured outside Thornaby in the crisp early winter sunshine during a Pennine Railway Society visit on 11 November 1978 was 40194 seen earlier awaiting tyre turning at Doncaster. ***Greg Wyett***

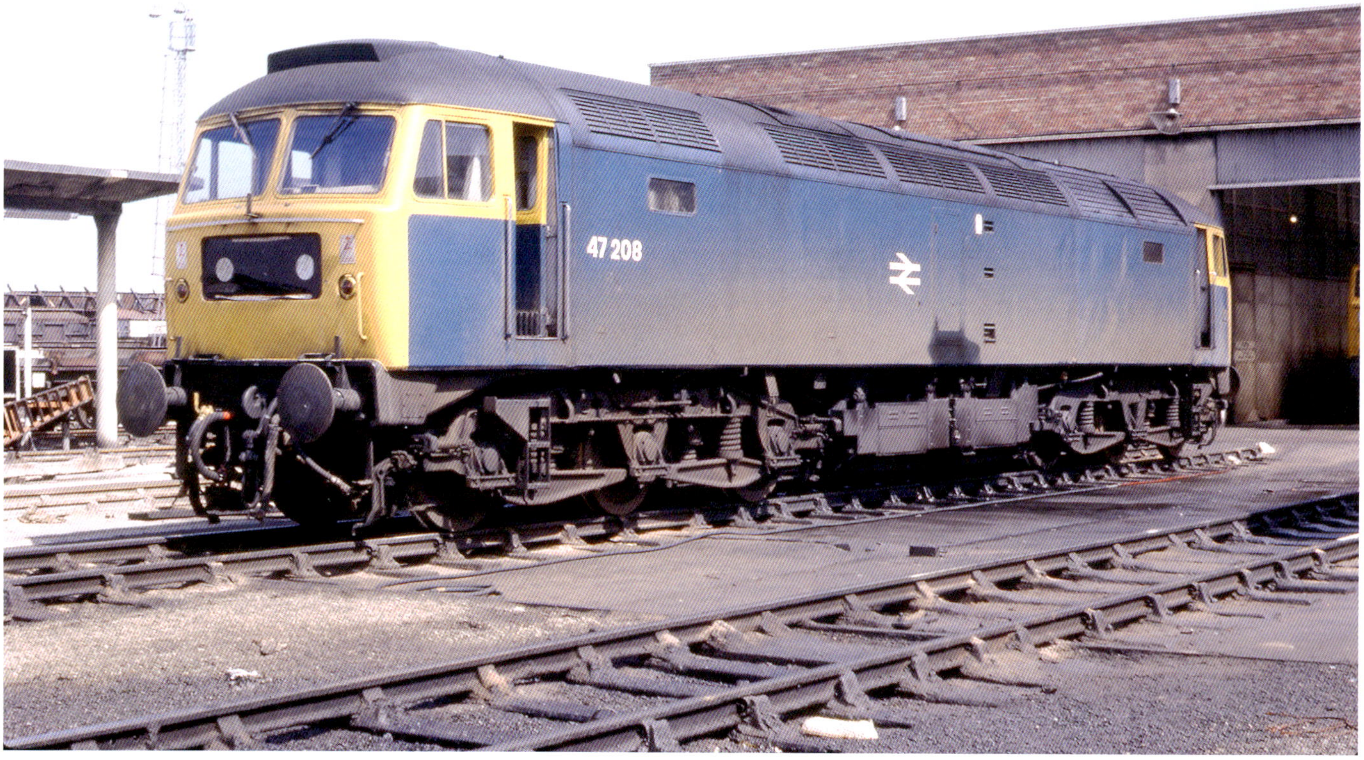

Another sunny day on Teeside in June 1979 delivers Haymarket's 47208. Soon after on 22 October the same year this locomotive ran into the rear of another train at Invergowrie and was severely damaged. The wreck was recovered to Dundee depot after being withdrawn on 27 January 1980, it was cut up in the yard here during March and early April 1980. ***A J Haliwell***

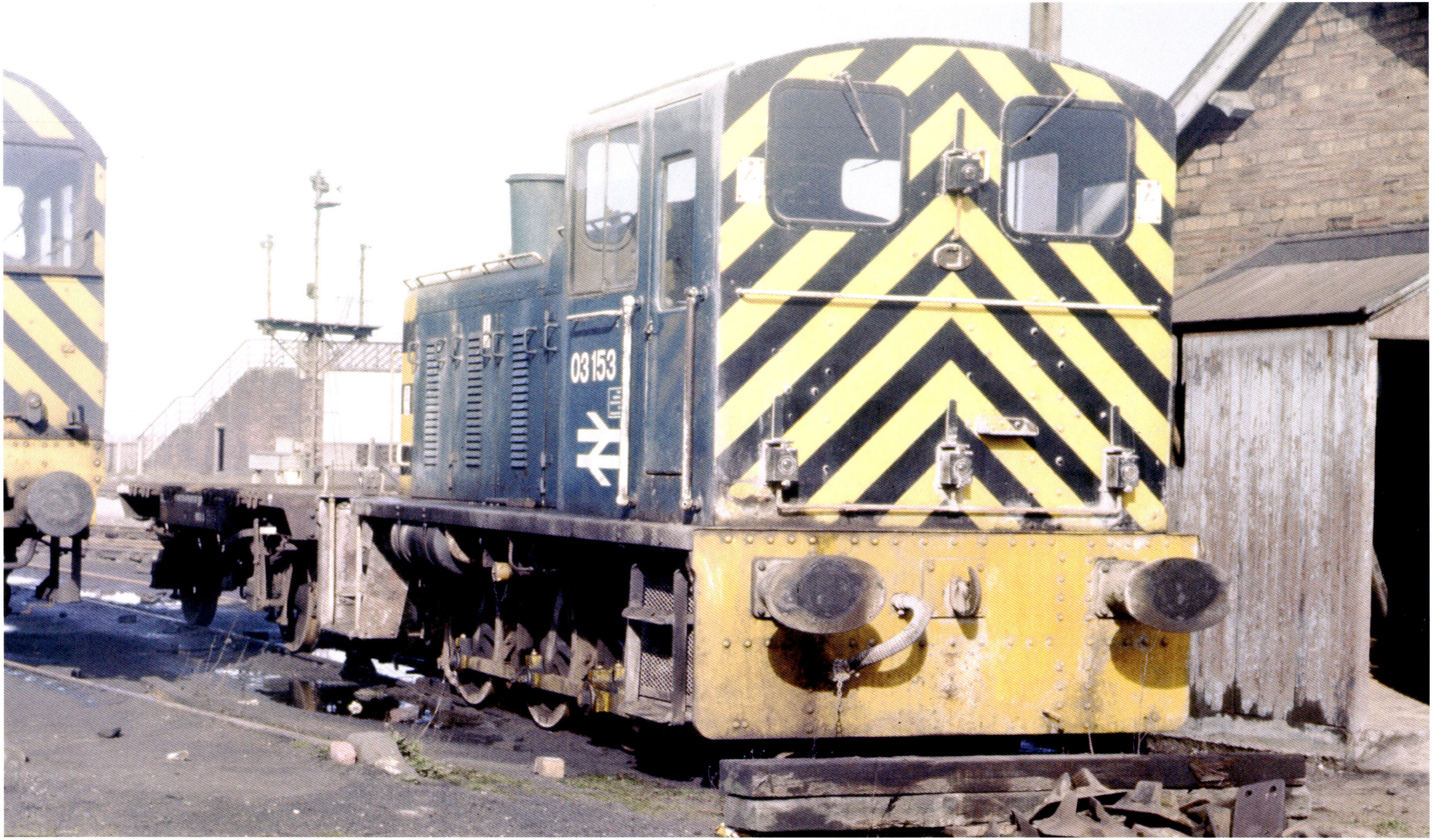

The history of 03153 seen at West Hartlepool on 16 March 1975 is an interesting one. Having been based around the Humber and Tees areas since new in 1960, its next move would be a long one once withdrawn on 11 November a few months after this view was taken when it was sold to P. Wood of Queenborough on the Isle of Sheppey in the Thames estuary. However before it was moved to their premises they had sold it for export to Italy. It would be taken to Stranraer in the far south west of Scotland for shipping in the late spring of 1976. By 1984 it was seen out of use at Trieste. ***Phil Bidwell***

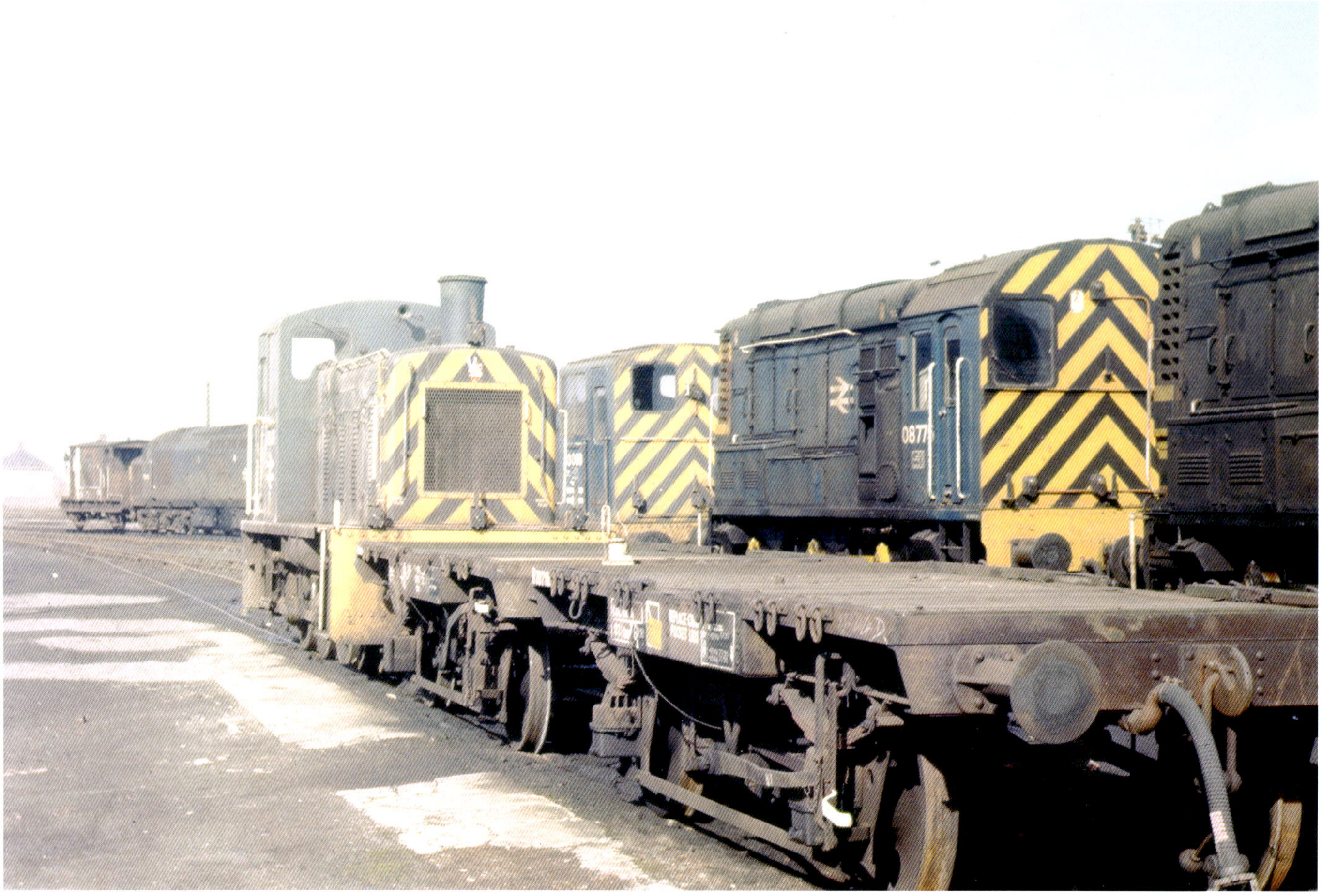

There was still work for a small fleet of shunters around West Hartlepool on 16 March 1975, with 03076, 03099, 08775 and 08310 all duly employed. ***Phil Bidwell***

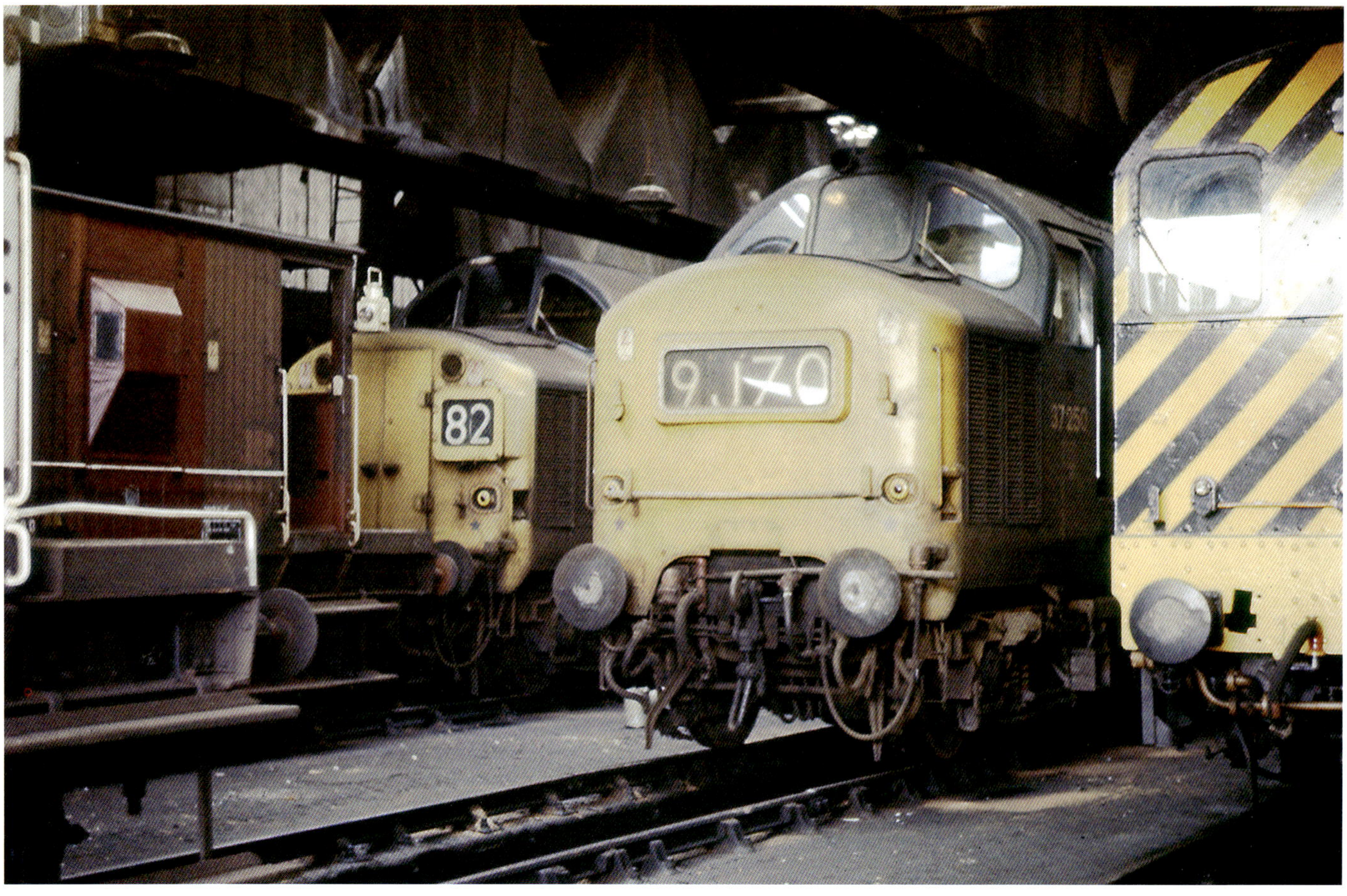

The old steam shed at Sunderland was used to shelter not only 37150, 37082 and 08116 on 13 July 1975 but also many of the Brake Vans used on the local colliery workings. ***Phil Bidwell***

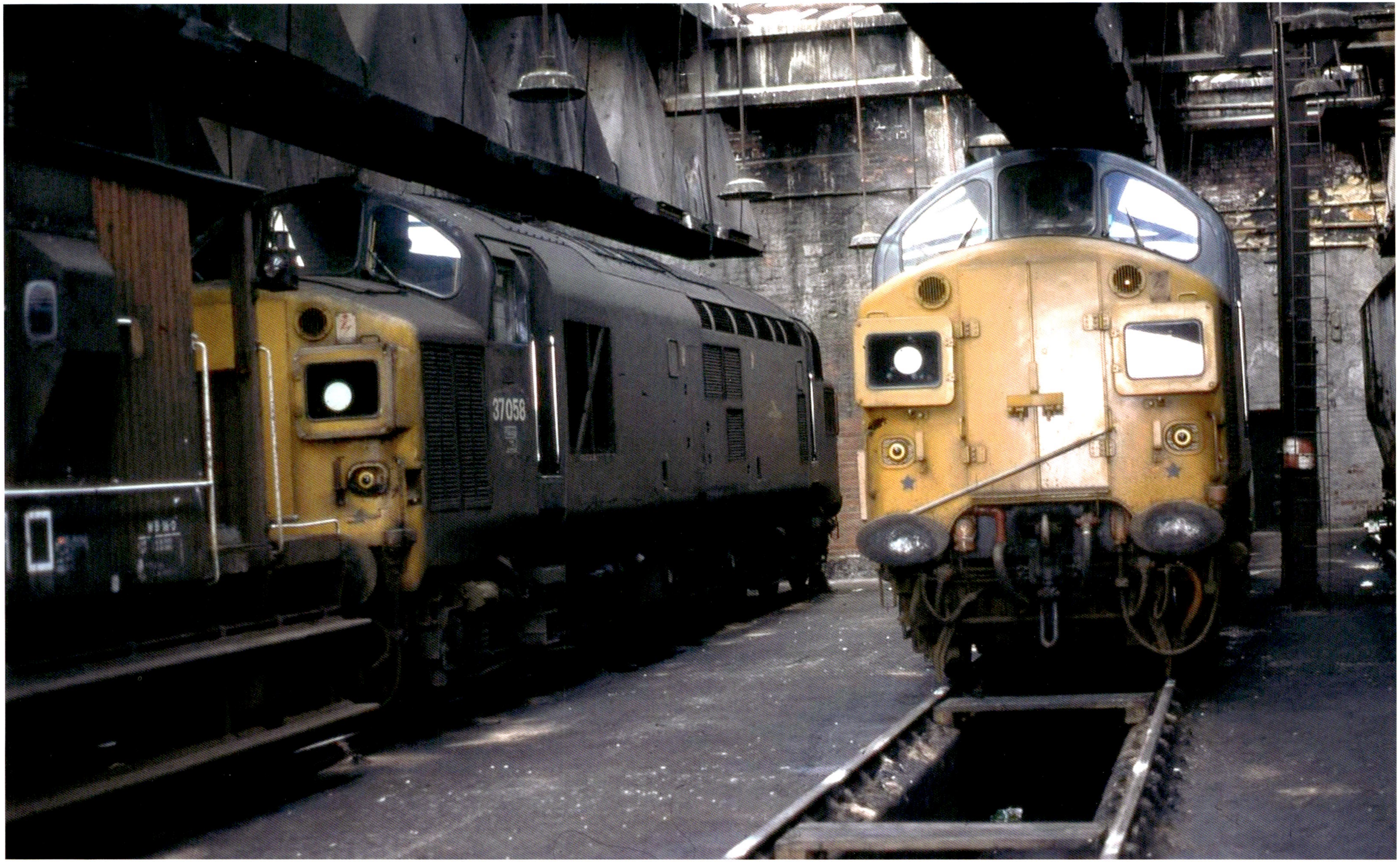

Weekend visits to Sunderland such as this one in April 1978 would always reward the spotter with a collection of locally based Class 37s during the decade, almost all with the depot's trademark shunter's poles worn as an accessory to their buffer beams. ***Steve Burdett***

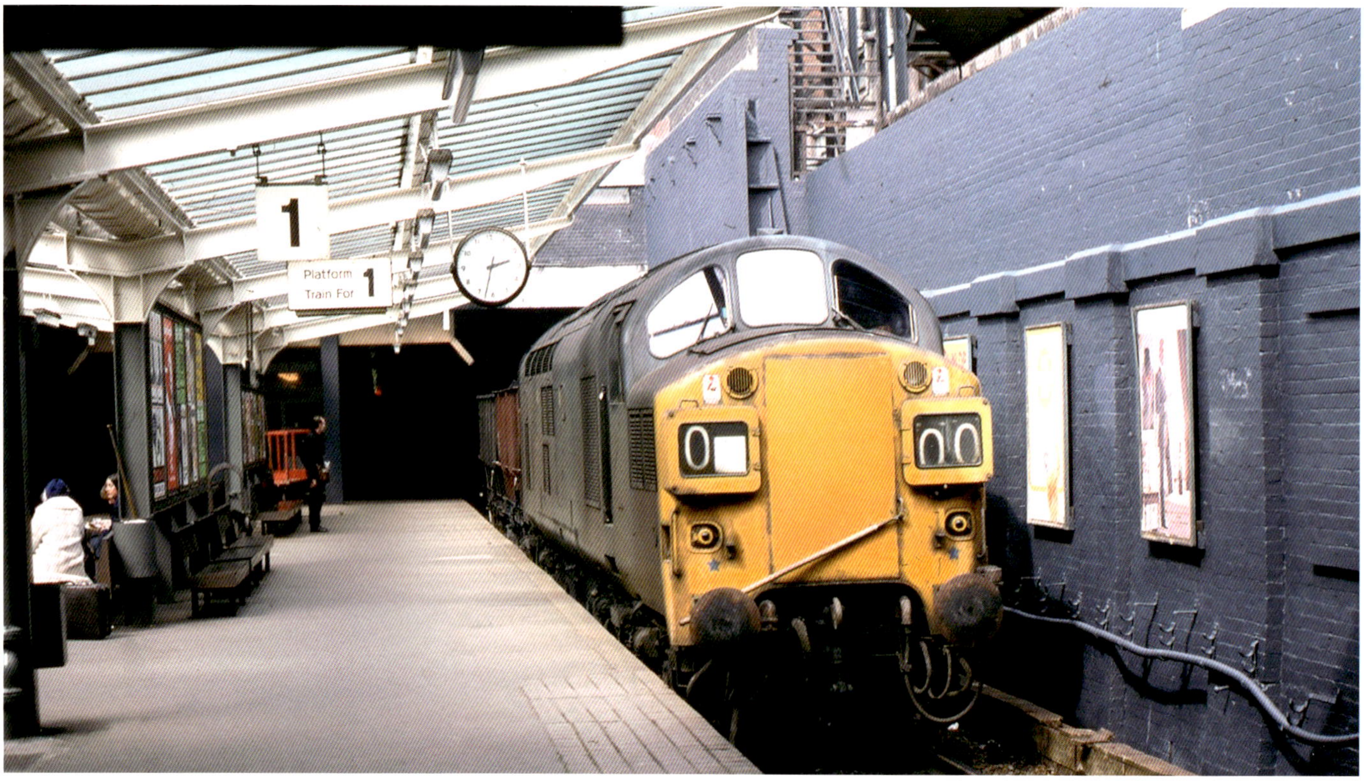

Rolling a rake of clattering coal hoppers through Sunderland station on 10 May 1977 was 37066 again with shunter's pole to the fore. On this same saturday afternoon the Celtic legend Kenny Dalglish played his last game for the Glasgow club. Three days before Kenny lifted the Scottish Cup after a 1-0 win over Rangers when he had strangely refused the chance to score the winning goal from a penalty, Andy Lynch doing the honours. He lost his medal in the celebrations afterwards and only found it after a search aided by policemen. Before the Cup Final he had signed a new contract which misled the supporters as it looked as if he had pledged his future to Celtic but had he not signed he would have been ineligible to play in the final due to the complications of the contract system prior to freedom of contract in 1980. He may have signed but privately he had made it clear to the club that he wished to move on. After scoring Scotland's winner the Home Internationals at Wembley in June and starring in Scotland's South American tour in July against Brazil, Argentina and Chile, The player refused to travel to Celtic's tour of the Far East, citing tiredness as the reason. Rumours abounded about his departure and 9 August Kenny Dalglish signed for Liverpool for a British record fee of £440,000, Liverpool having just cashed a cheque for £500,000 for the transfer of Kevin Keegan to the West German club SV Hamburg and looking for a replacement, how has inflation affected football's fees in the years since? ***Steve Burdett***

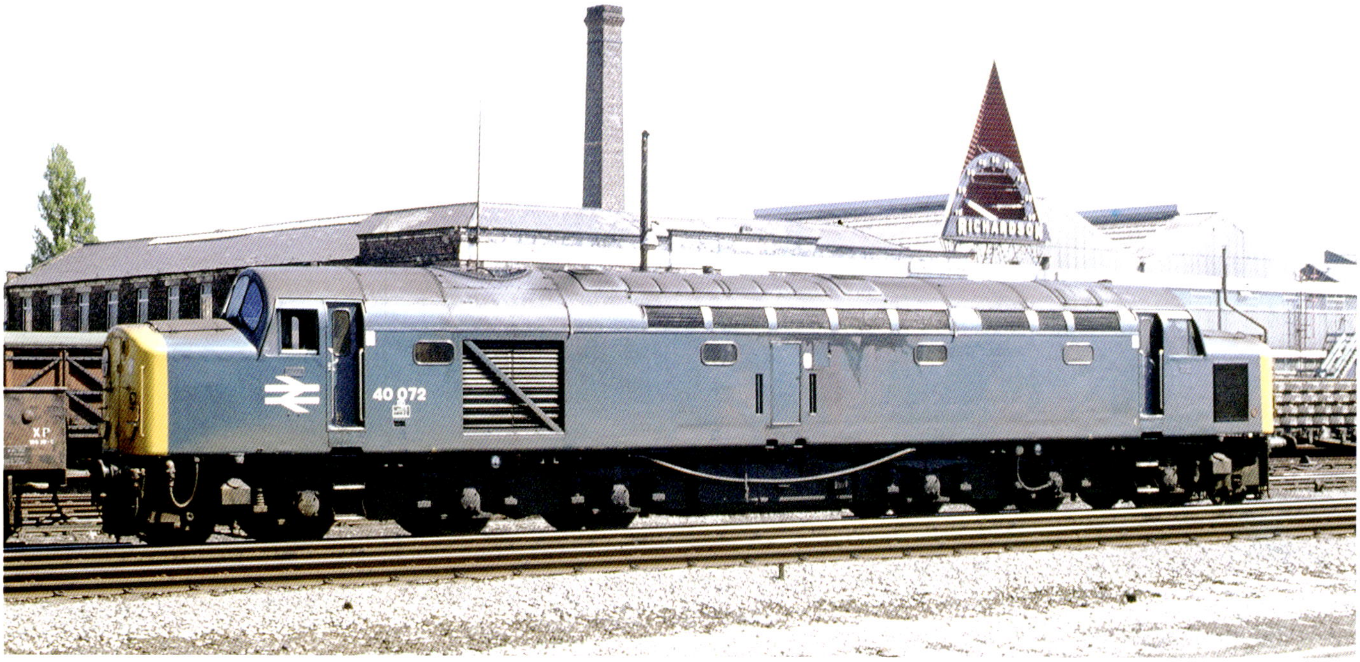

During the same year on 27 May 40072 whistles through Darlington, withdrawn a few months later on 17 August as already Kenny Dalglish had opened his goal account at Liverpool three days beforehand in his first game the season opener at Wembley, in the Charity Shield against Manchester United. The Class 40 above would be cut up at Glasgow's St. Rollox works a few miles from the footballer's birthplace by June 1978. ***Strathwood Library Collection***

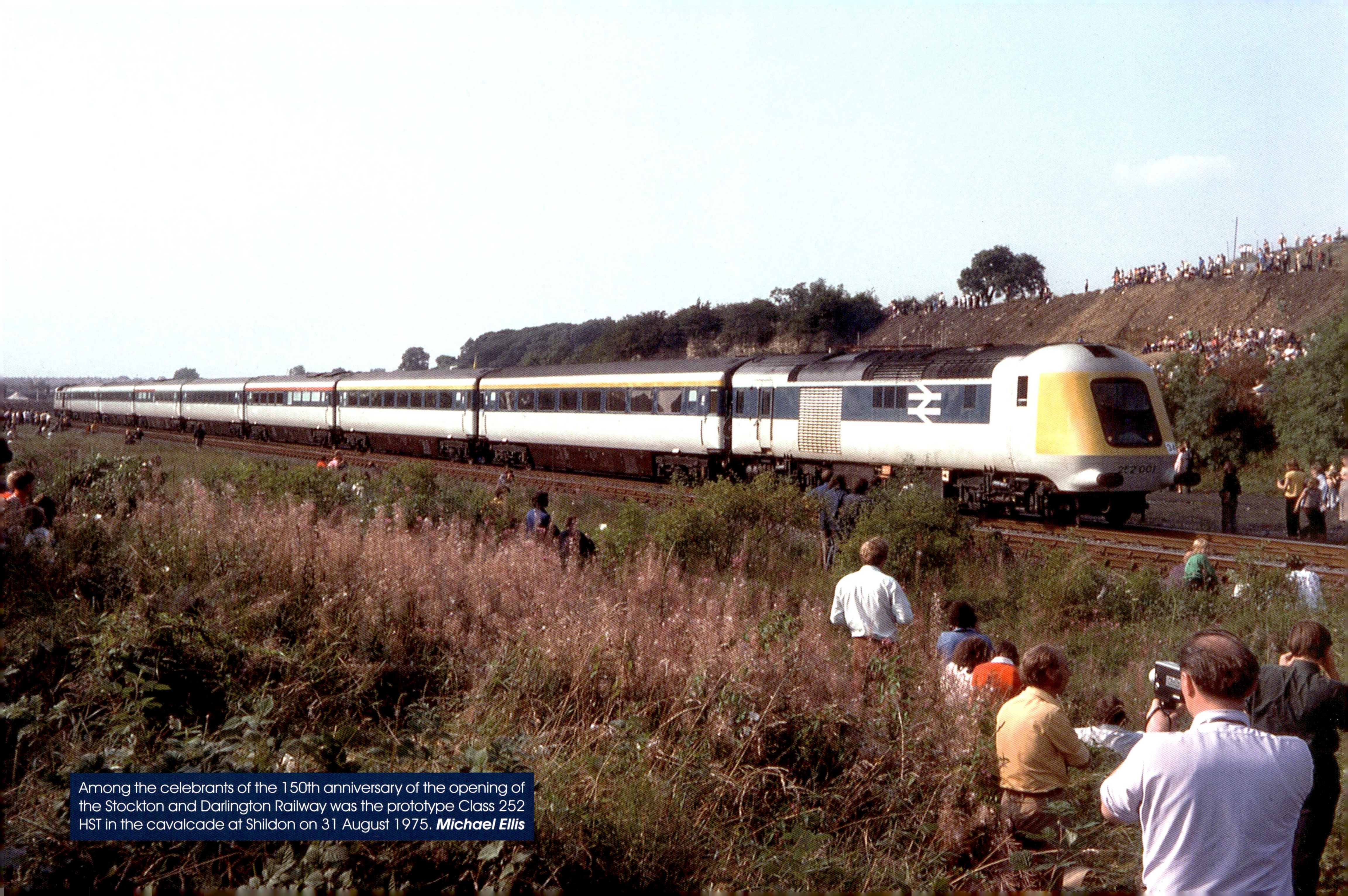

Among the celebrants of the 150th anniversary of the opening of the Stockton and Darlington Railway was the prototype Class 252 HST in the cavalcade at Shildon on 31 August 1975. ***Michael Ellis***

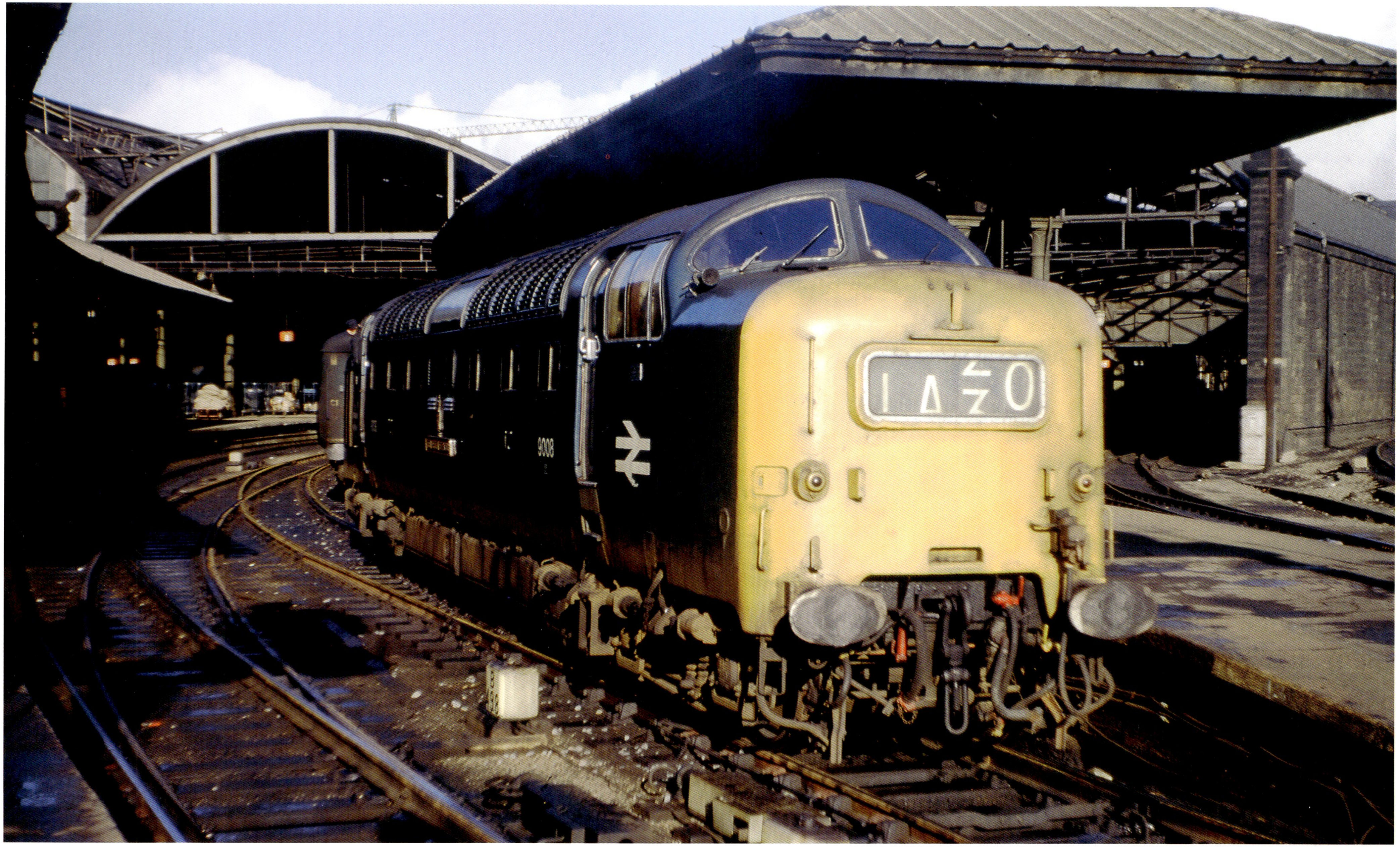

Newcastle Central station reverberates to the twin Napier Deltic engines of 9008 The Green Howards on 24 February 1973. This locomotive was allocated new to Gateshead on 7 July 1961 and was named in a ceremony at Darlington station on 30 September 1963. The career of this Class 55 was almost exclusive to Gateshead as it remained here until May 1979 when transferred to York until the Deltic's demise on 31 December 1981. ***Don Brooks/Richard Derry Collection***

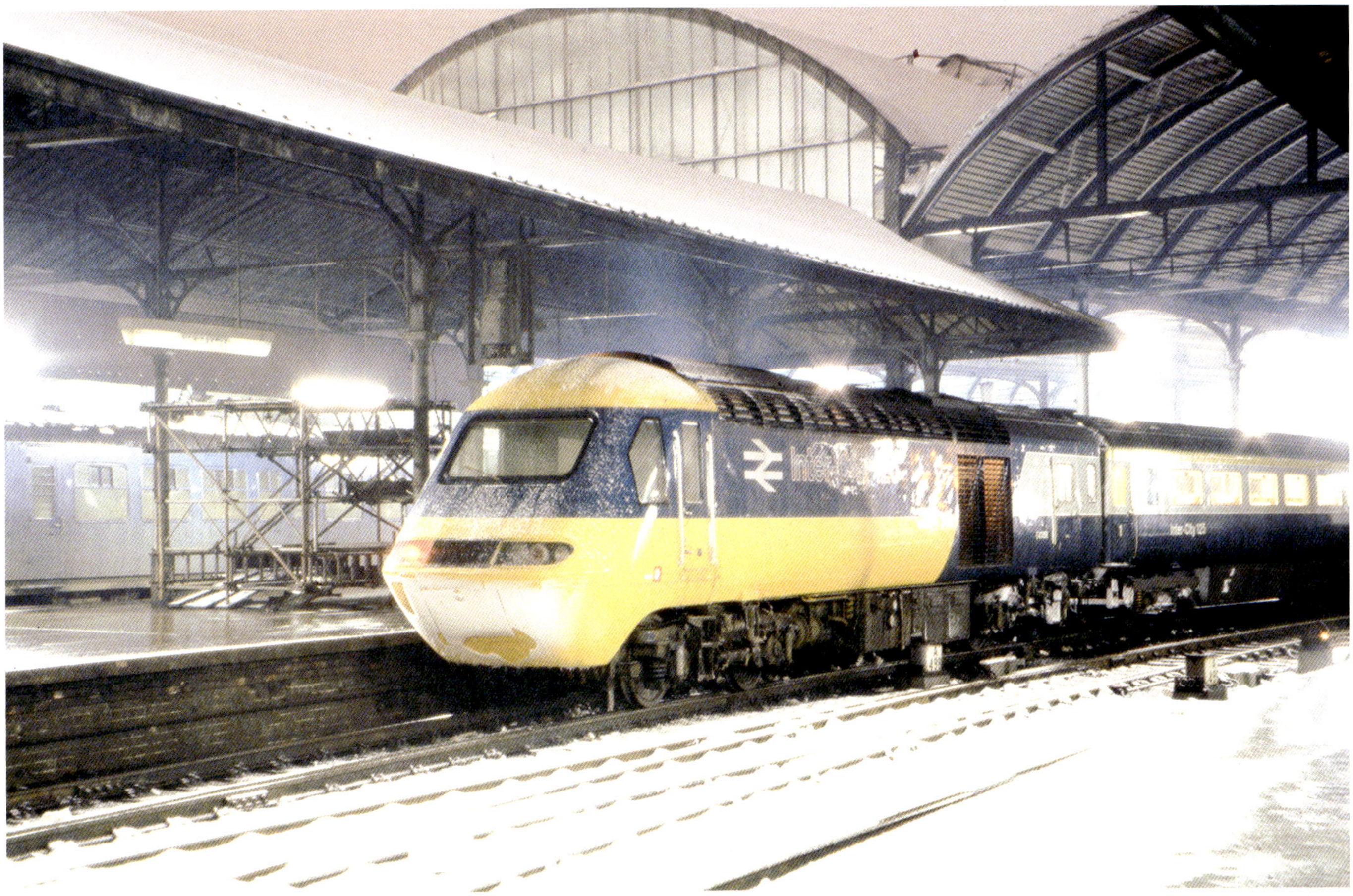

The replacements on the East Coast Main Line for the Deltics on the expresses were to be the HST fleet until the electrification of the route was completed in late 1990. It would be a snowy journey for the passengers of this HST service from Newcastle Central on 17 March 1979. ***Nev Sloper***

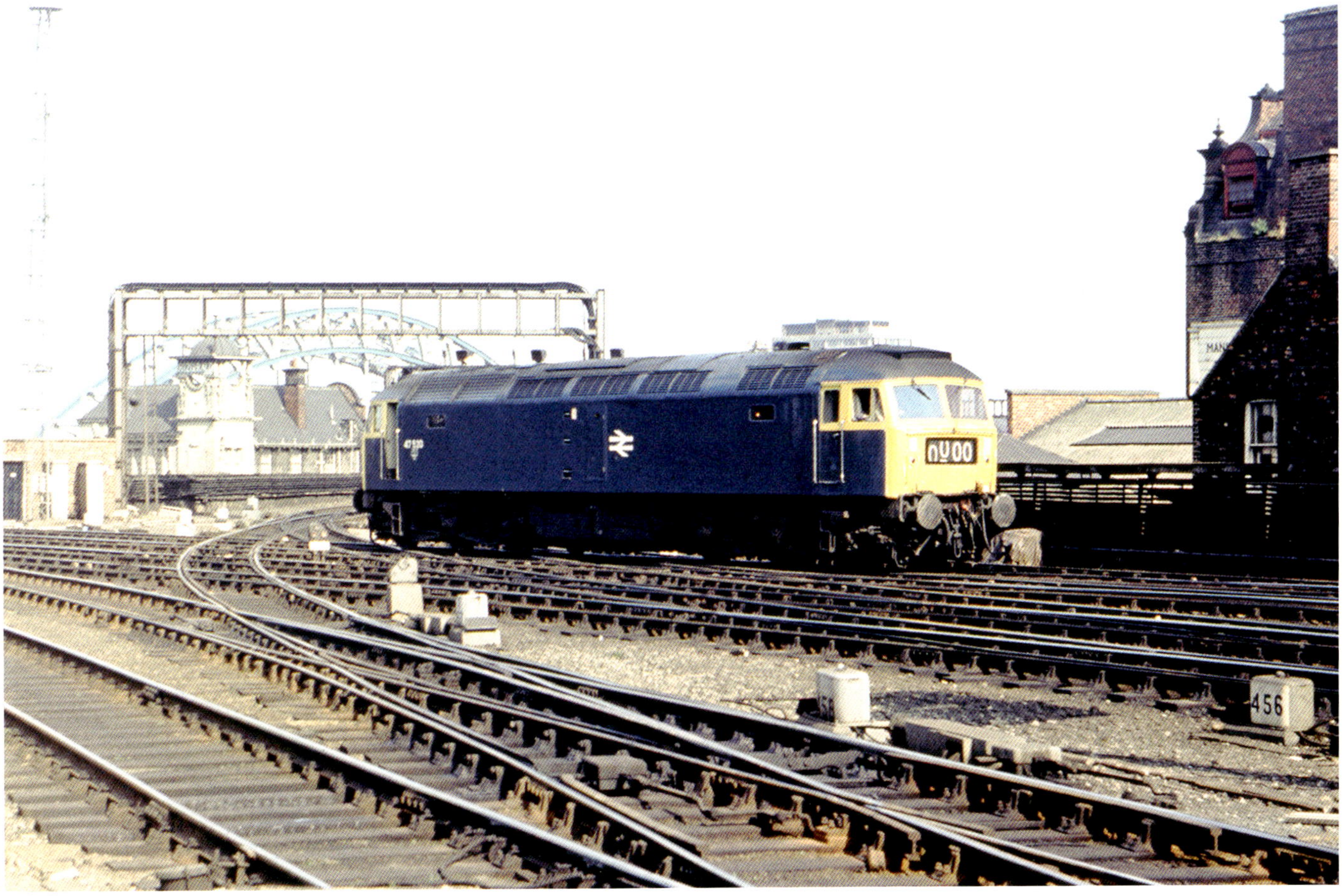

Its sunshine across the River Tyne as 47520 moves light engine into Newcastle Central on 25 June 1976. One of the most notable Albums of the early Seventies was to be Fog on the Tyne from Lindisfarne released in October 1971. ***Phil Bidwell***

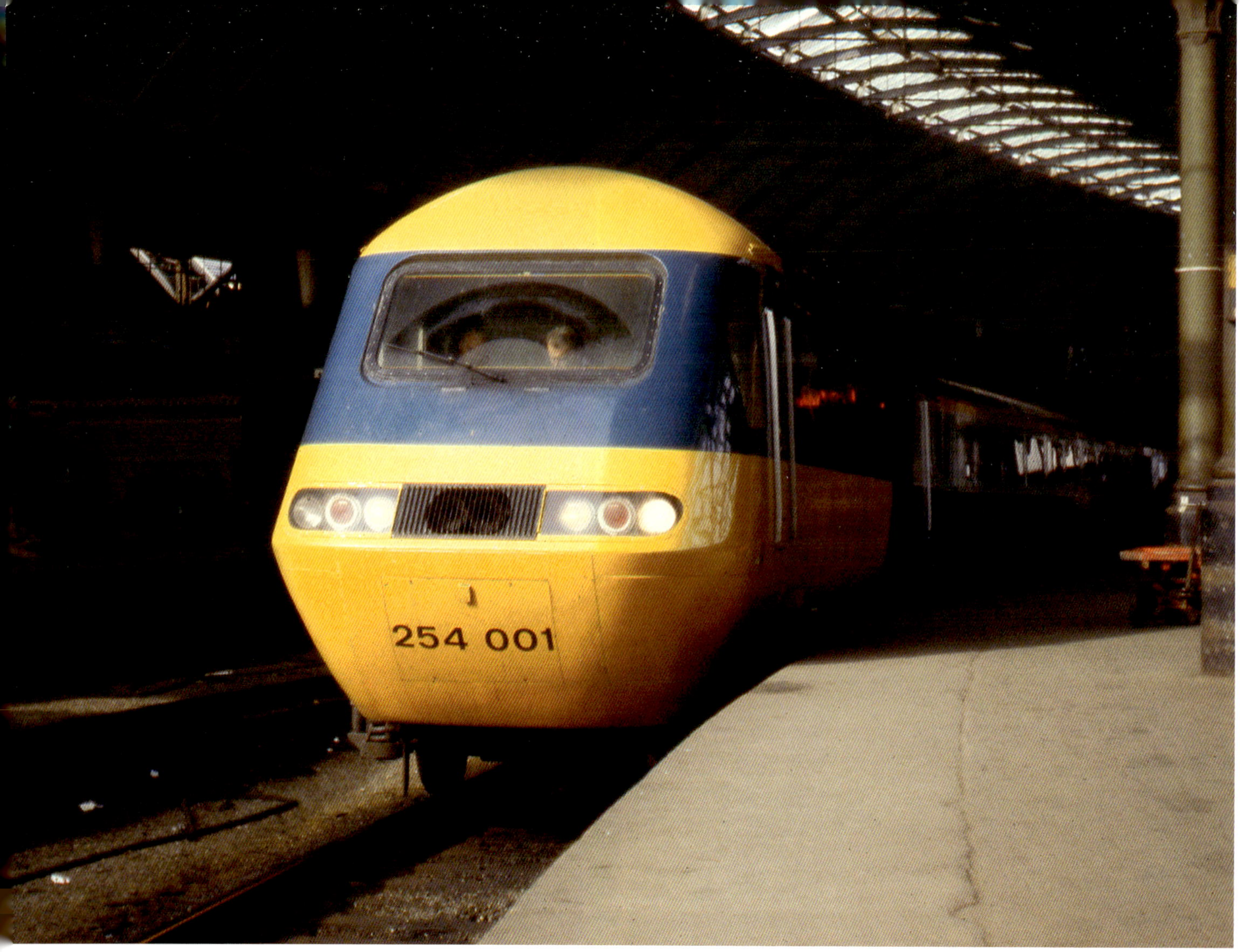

The first of the Class 254 HST sets with power car 43056 at its head stands at Newcastle Central on 17 July 1978 as Jimmy Saville was extolling this was the Age of the Train. ***Brian Daniels***

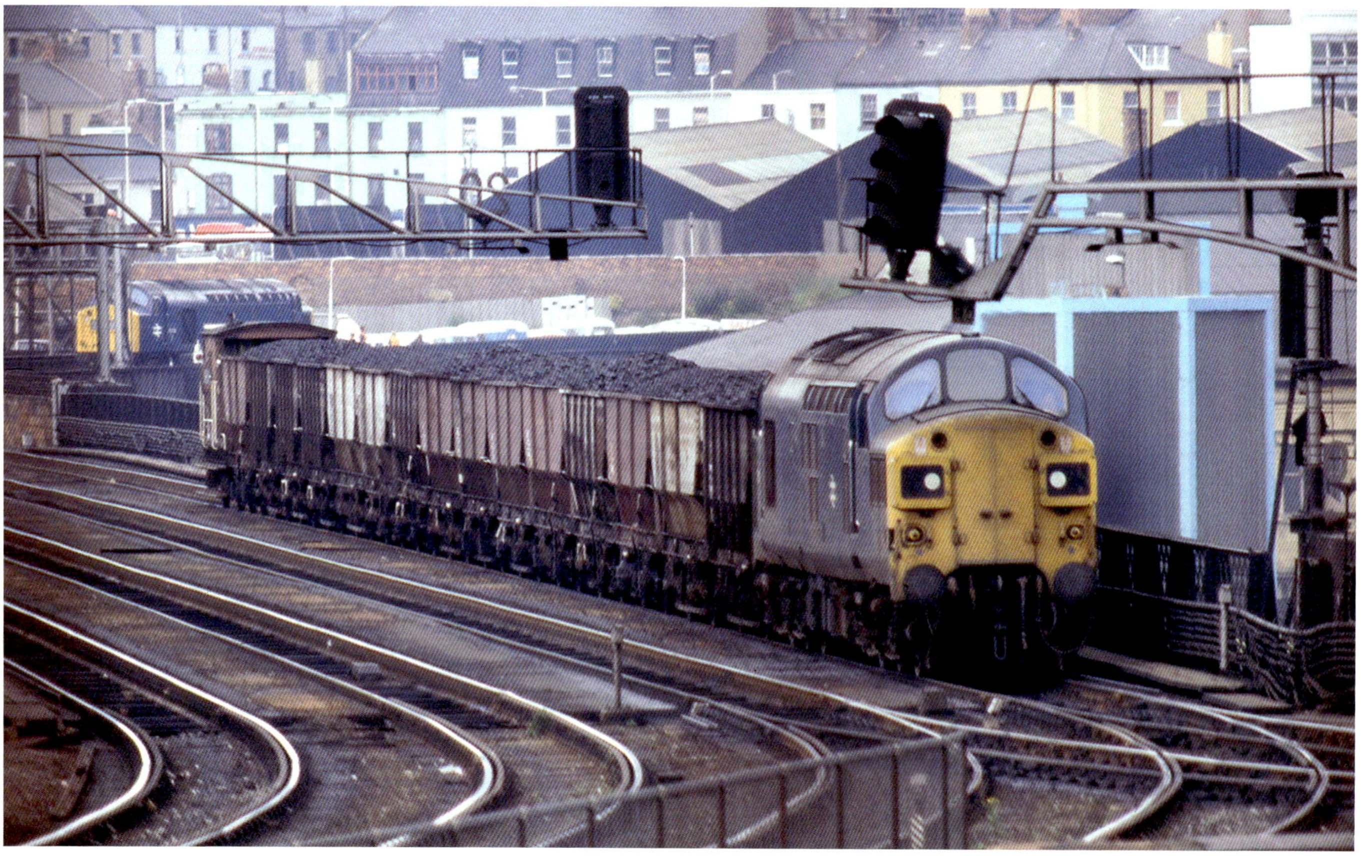

In this view a Class 40 lurks in the background as we see 37008 making its way across the River Tyne onto the King Edward Bridge the following day. ***Brian Daniels***

The traditional vantage point overlooking the station throat on 18 July 1978 sees 55015 Tulyar making it's way away from Newcastle Central. ***Brian Daniels***

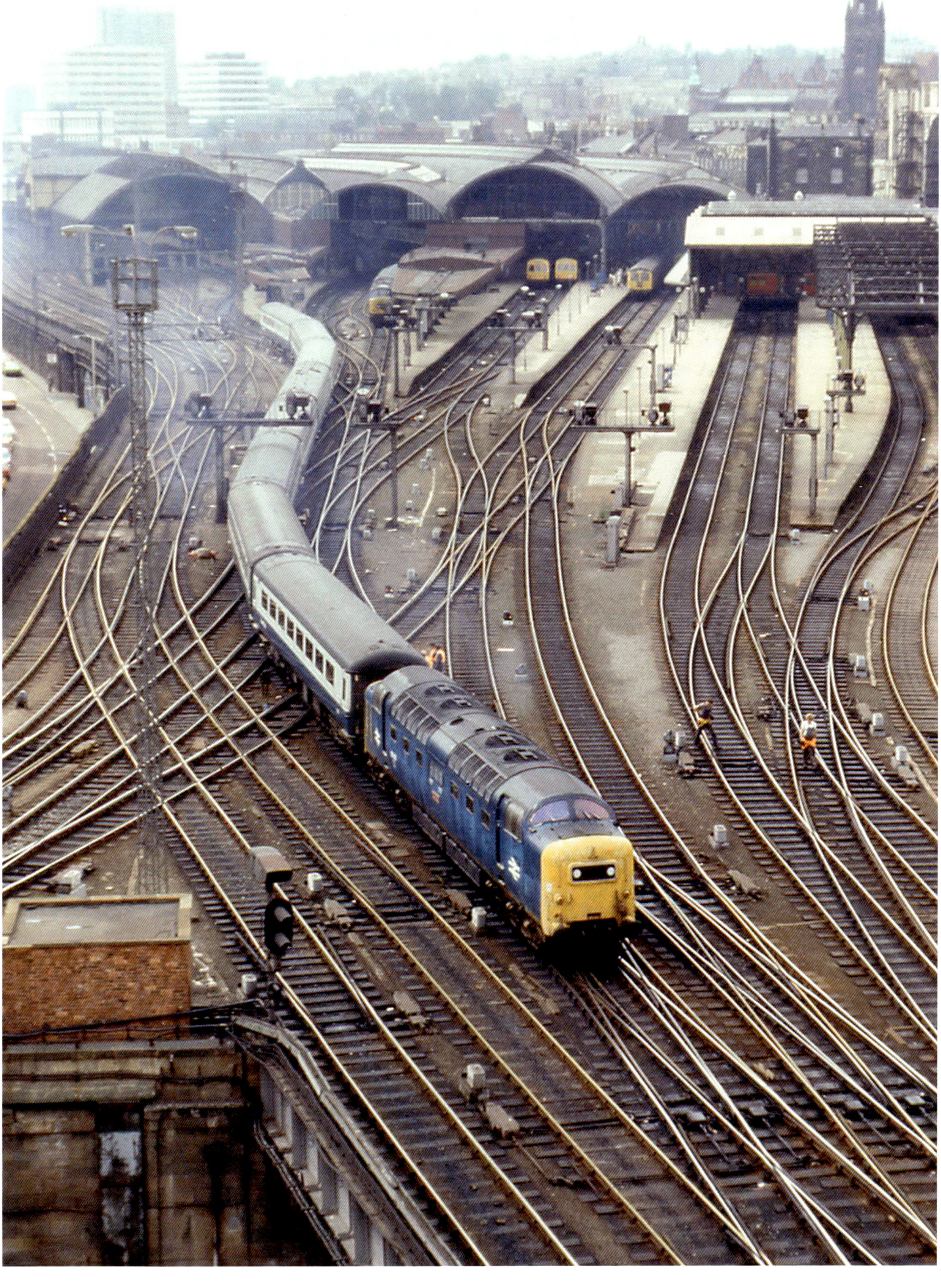

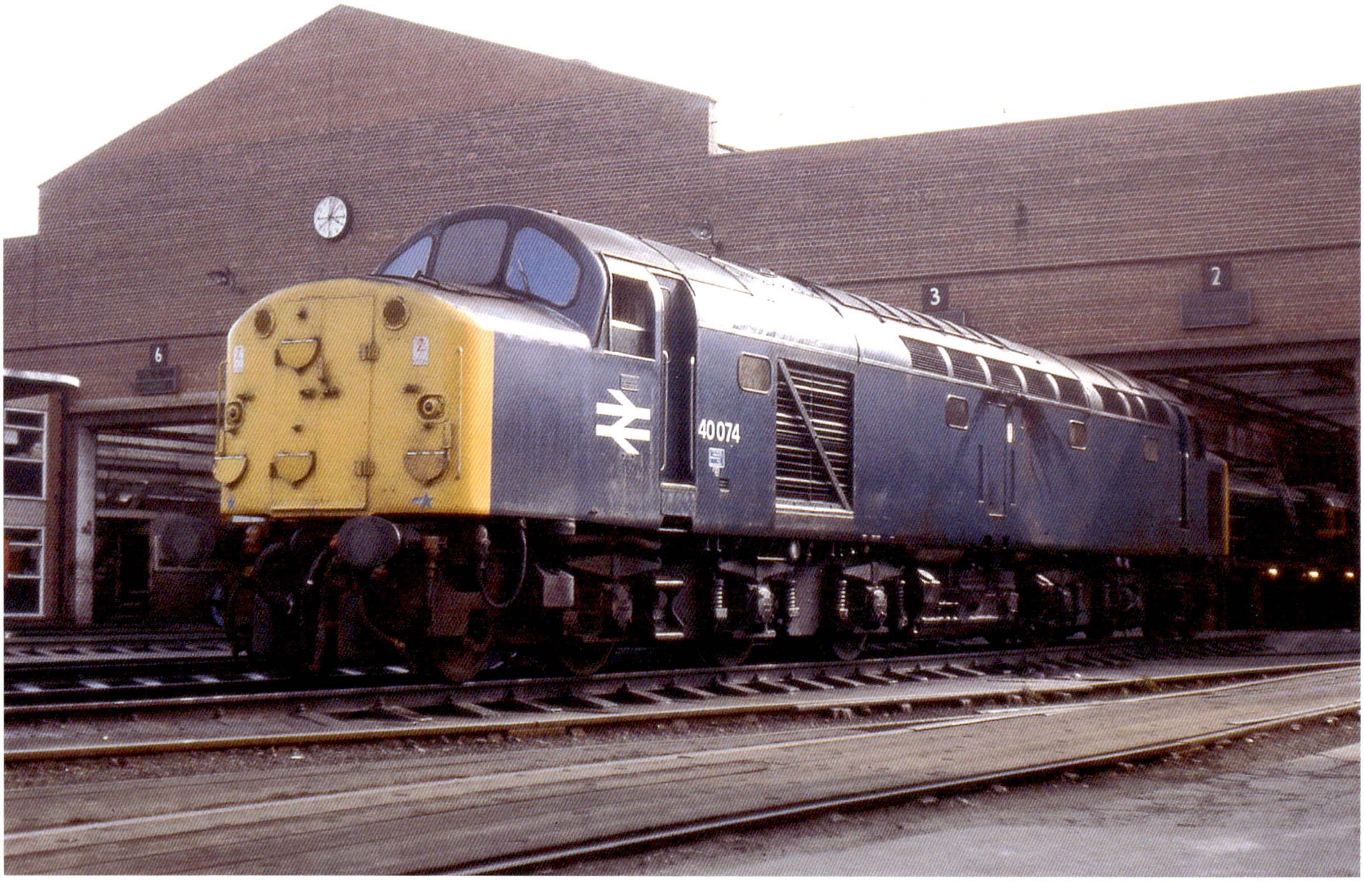

Standing proud outside its home depot Gateshead on 17 July 1978 was 40074. The shed in the background was the result of rebuilding in the 1950s and later modified for diesels after the steam allocation left in October 1965. ***Brian Daniels***

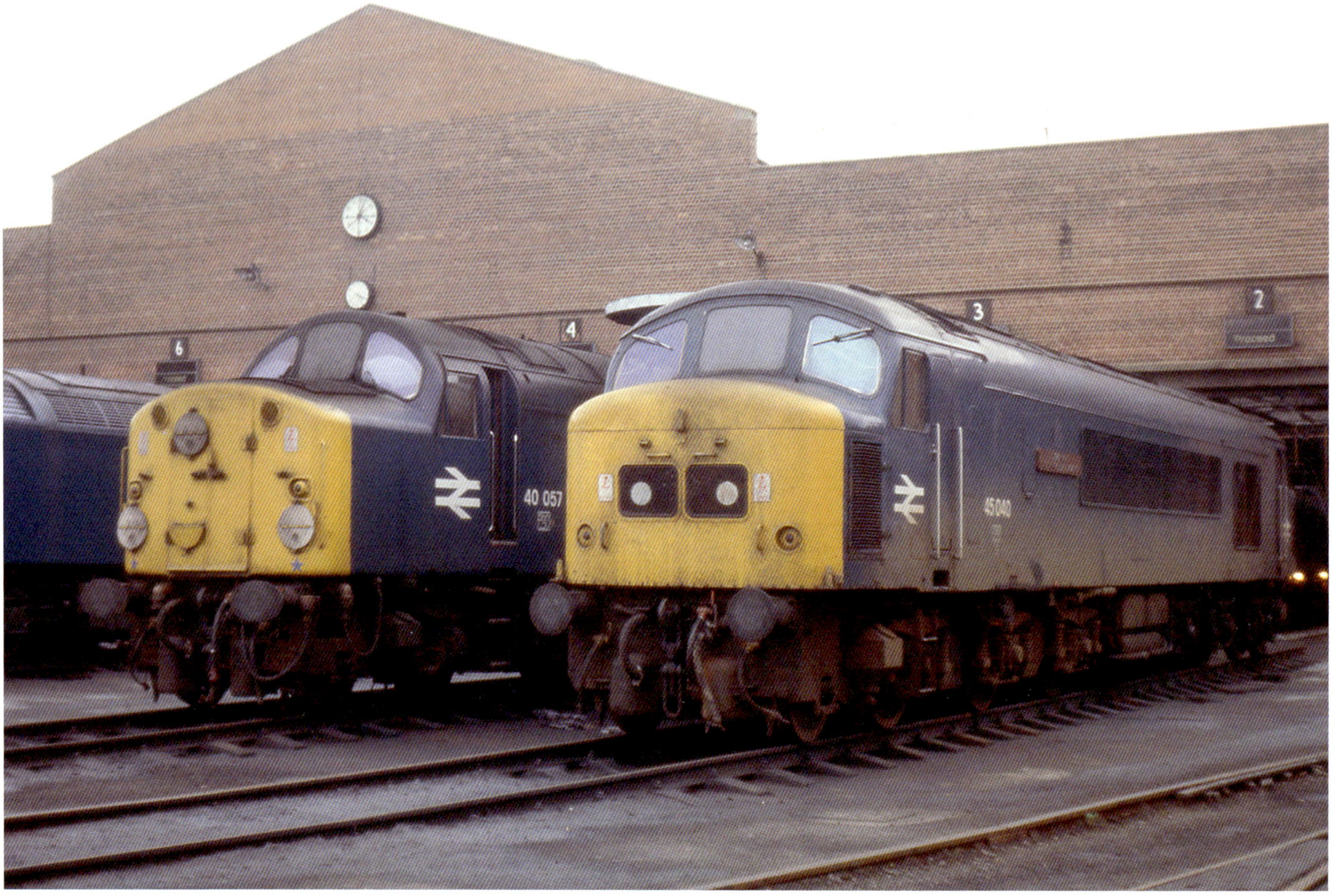

Another visit on 10 September 1978 yields Tinsley's 45040 The King's Shropshire Light Infantry alongside another of Gateshead's Class 40s in the shape of 40057. ***Brian Daniels***

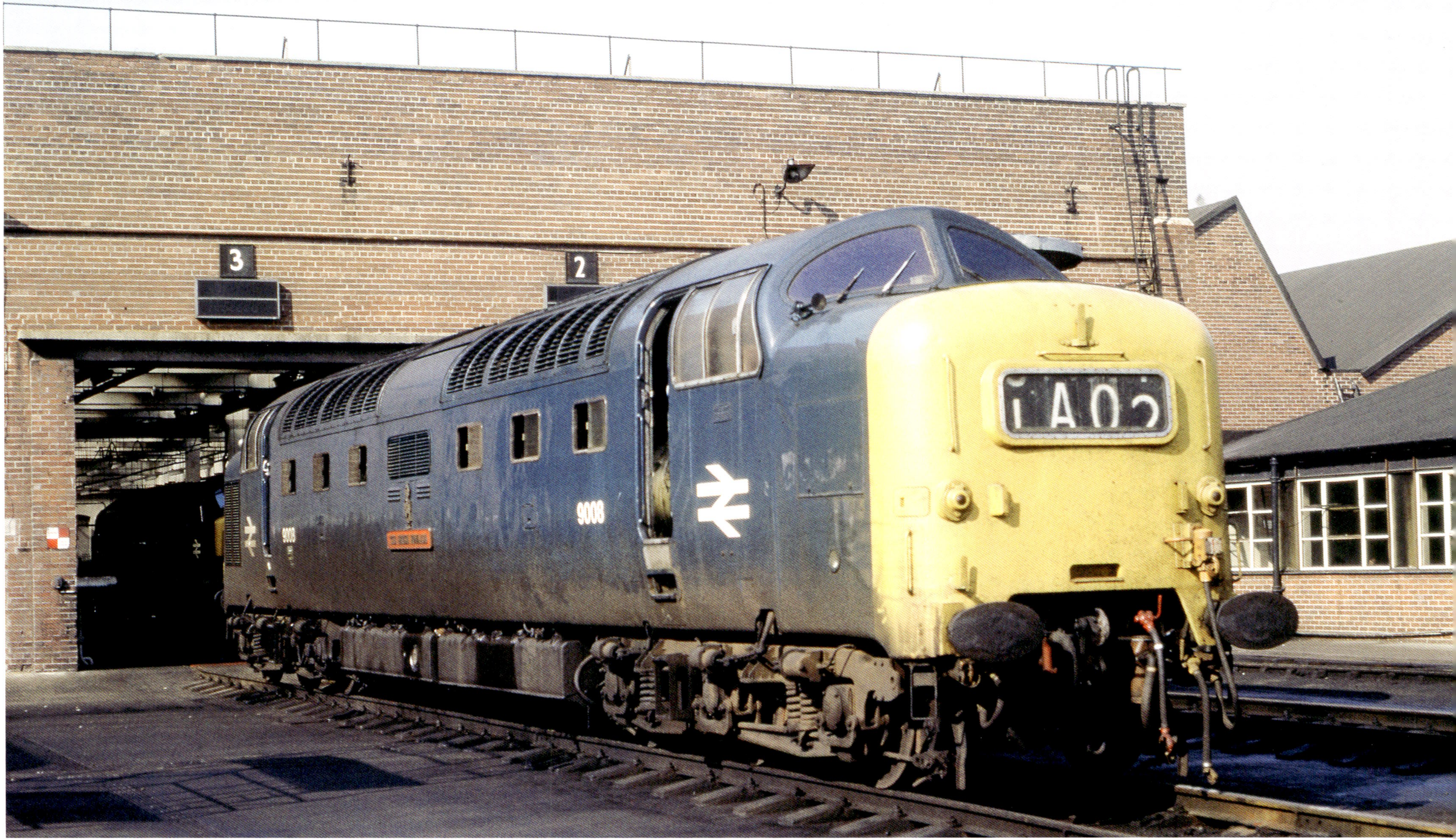

Once again we catch Gateshead's 9008 The Green Howards in its home city during September 1973. This area of the city was the setting for the classic sitcom Whatever Happened to the Likely Lads? broadcast between 9 January 1973 and 9 April 1974 on BBC1. It was the colour sequel to the mid-1960s hit The Likely Lads. It was created and written, as was its predecessor, by Dick Clement and Ian La Frenais. In all there were twenty six television episodes over two series; and a subsequent 45-minute Christmas special was aired on 24 December 1974.In 1976 a feature film spin-off was made. Around the time of its release, however, Rodney Bewes and James Bolam fell out over a misunderstanding involving the press and have allegedly not spoken since. ***Ian King***

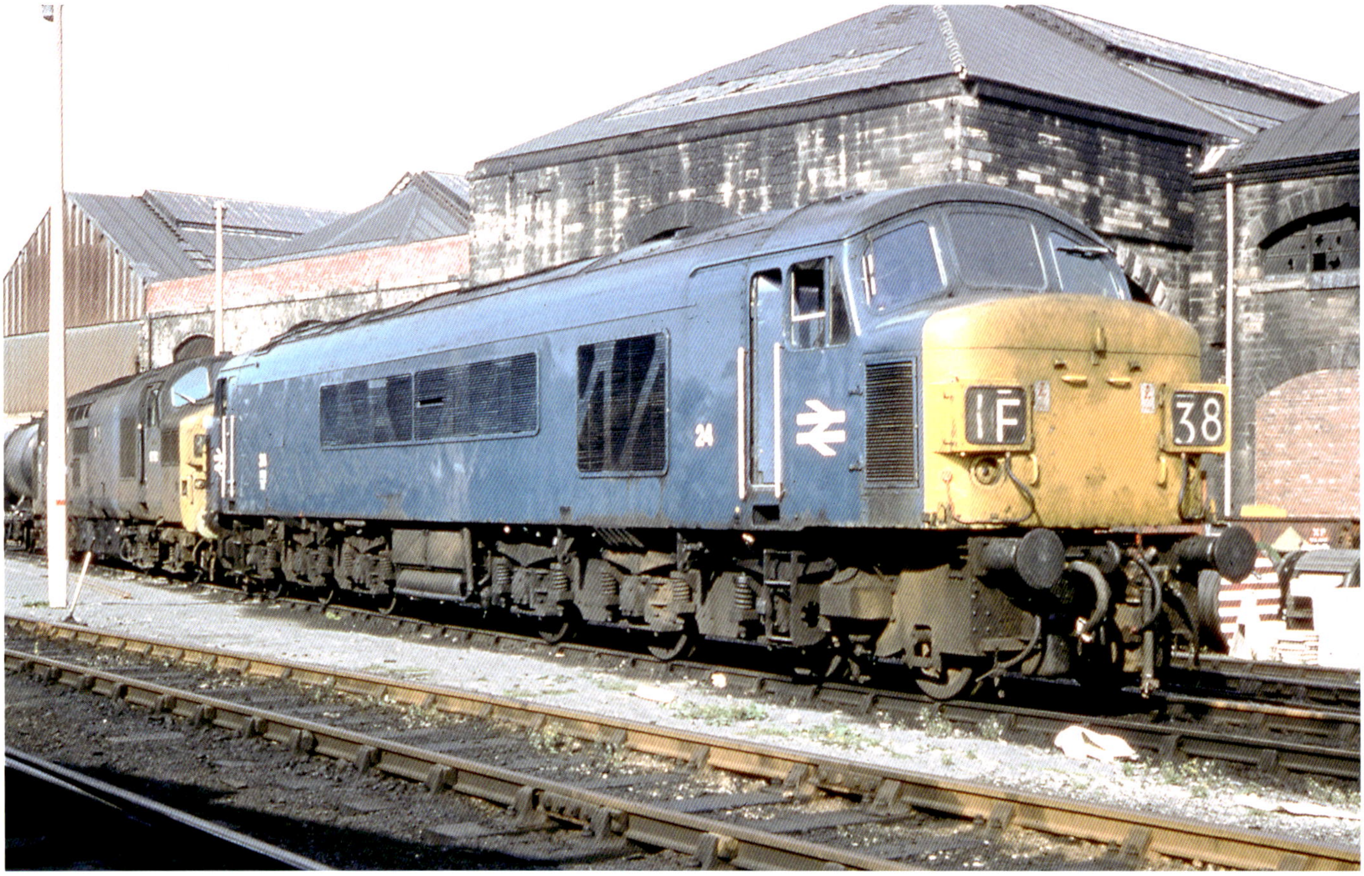

The buildings of the former North Eastern Railway's locomotive works at Gateshead form the backdrop to this Class 45 Peak from Holbeck having worked into Newcastle during 1972. ***Strathwood Library Collection***

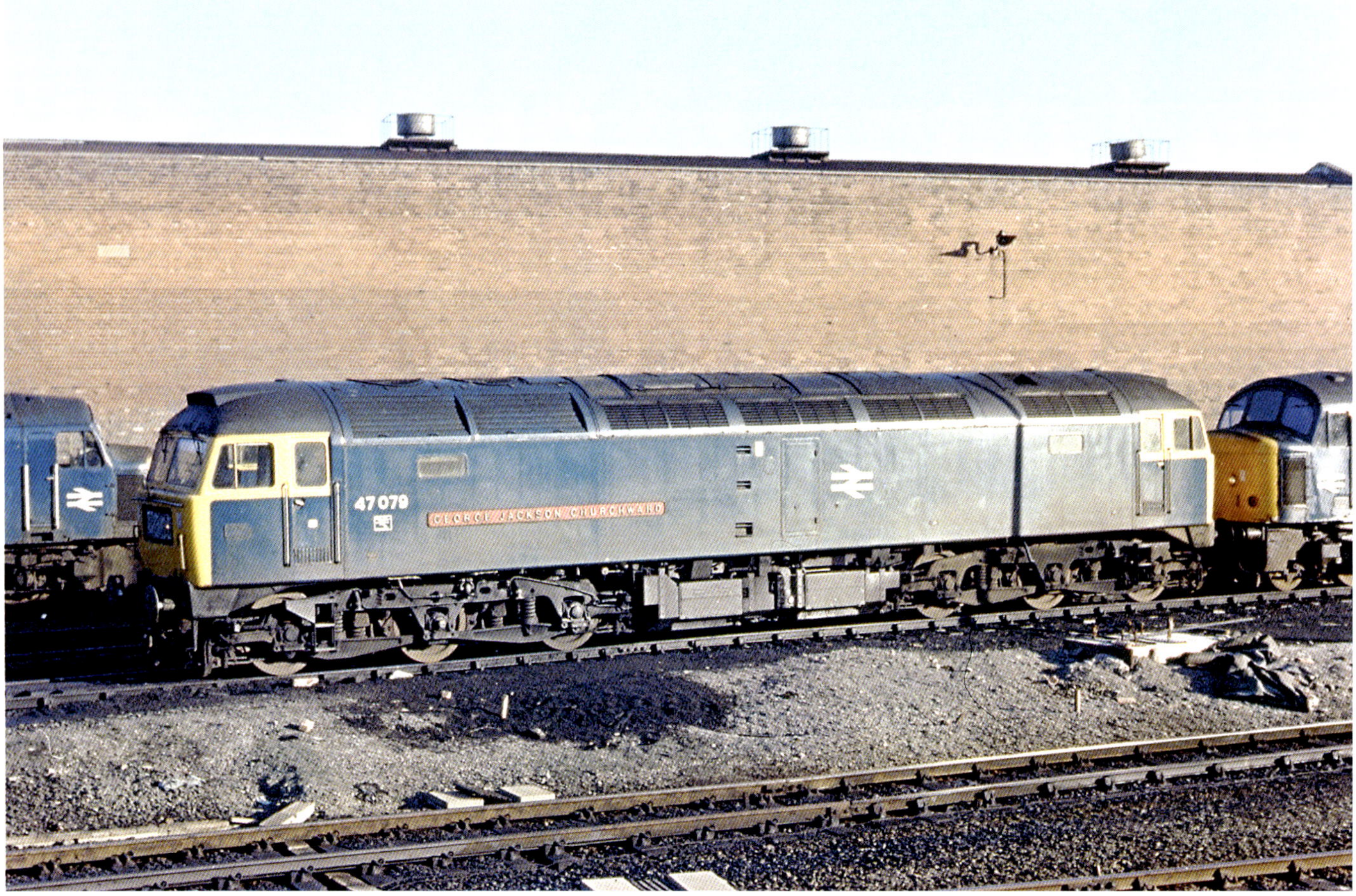

With a background of the red brickwork of the 1950s built shed building at Gateshead was Old Oak Common's visiting 47079 George Jackson Churchwood on 8 March 1976. ***Strathwood Library Collection***

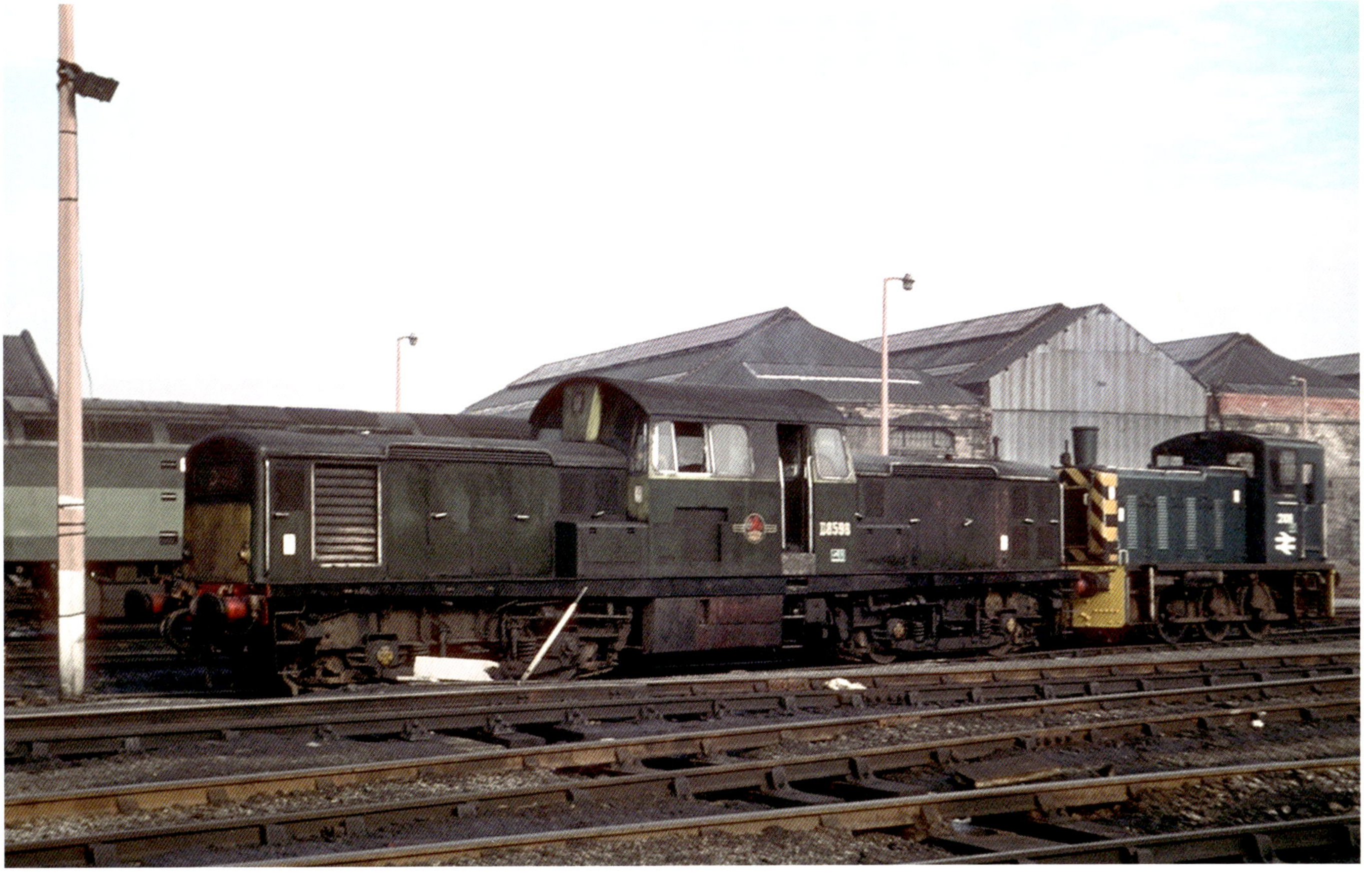

As the sixties became the seventies Gateshead still enjoyed an allocation of Type1s including Class 20s and a small number of Class 17 Claytons including D8598 seen here in the company of one of the depot's many Class 03s. ***Strathwood Library Collection***

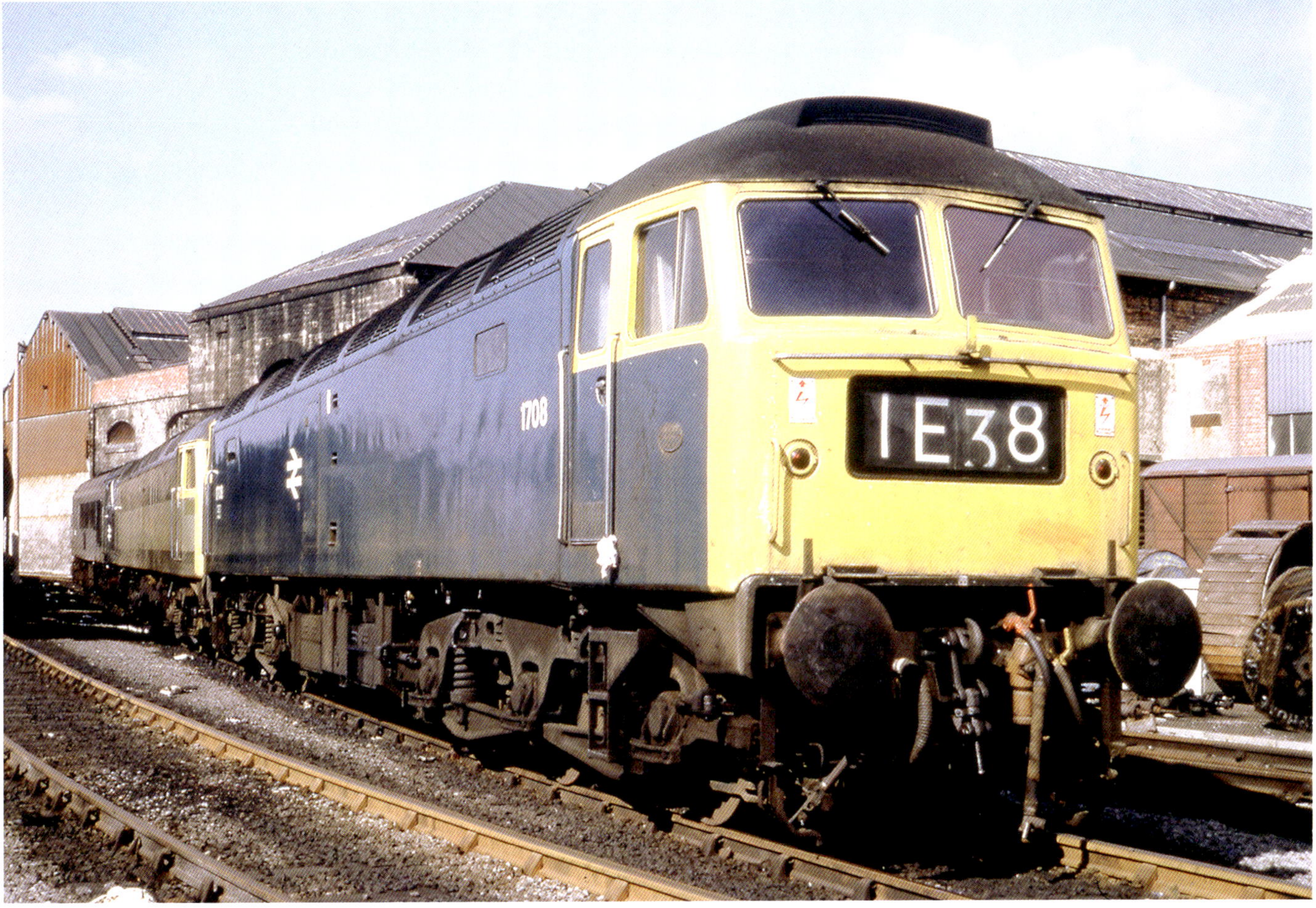

Another view from the early 1970s shows 1708 then allocated to D02 Birmingham Division stabled with a two tone green classmate along with a Peak out in the depot yard. ***Strathwood Library collection***

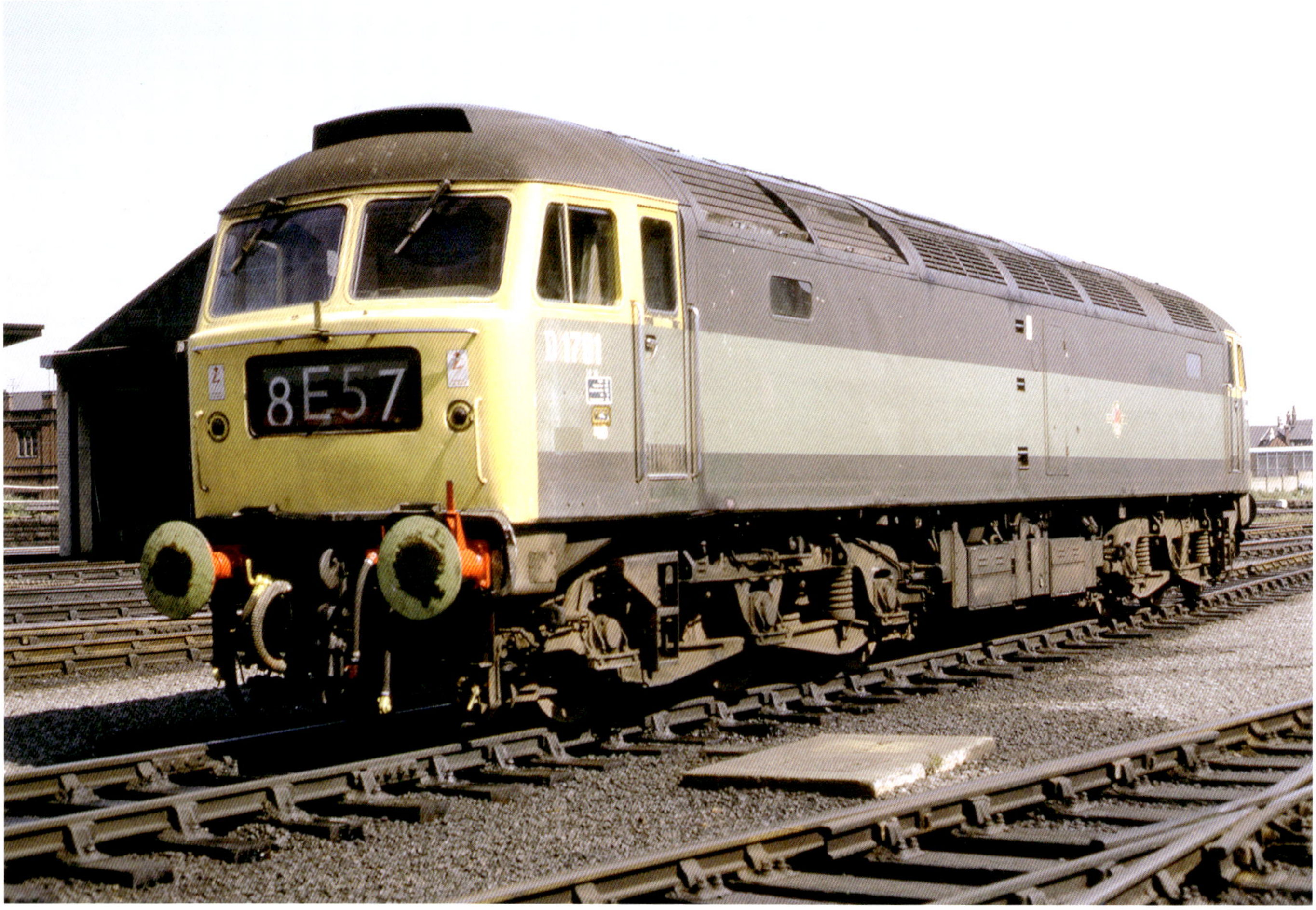

As late as January 1974 D1791 was still carrying the D prefix to its number as it was renumbered into TOPS as 47310 the following month it is unlikely the D was painted out as on so many of the other Class 47s. ***Ian King***

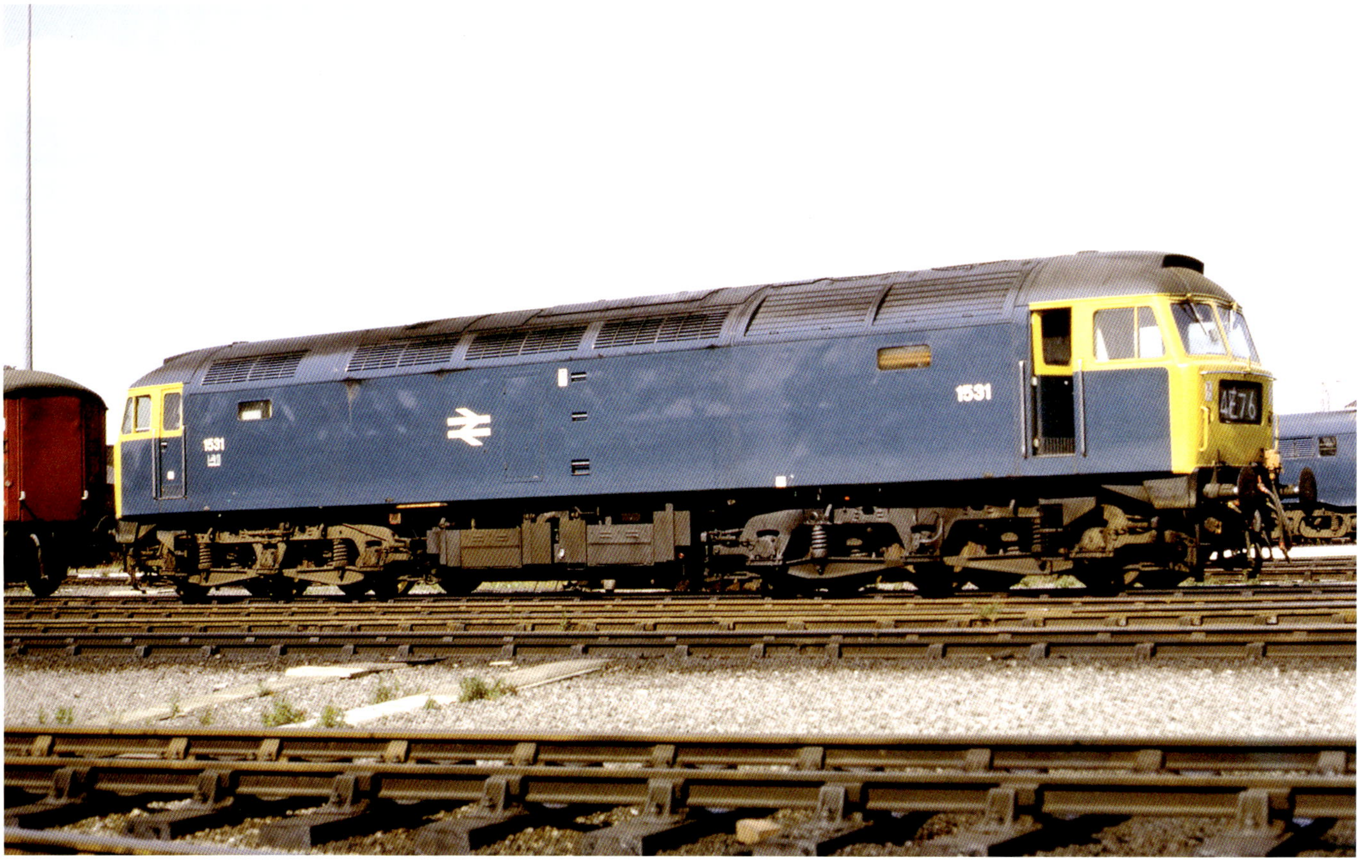

This view of 1531 visiting from Tinsley on the same day at Gateshead shows the moving of the numbers away from the cabsides as applied to many blue repaints of the class, this example becoming 47424 in May 1974. ***Ian king***

Opposite: A view towards Manors across the city of Newcastle as 47527 is seen arriving with with the 12.40 Edinburgh to Kings Cross on 31 March 1976 as a coal working drifts off northbound into the distance. ***Barrie Watkins/Strathwood Library Collection***

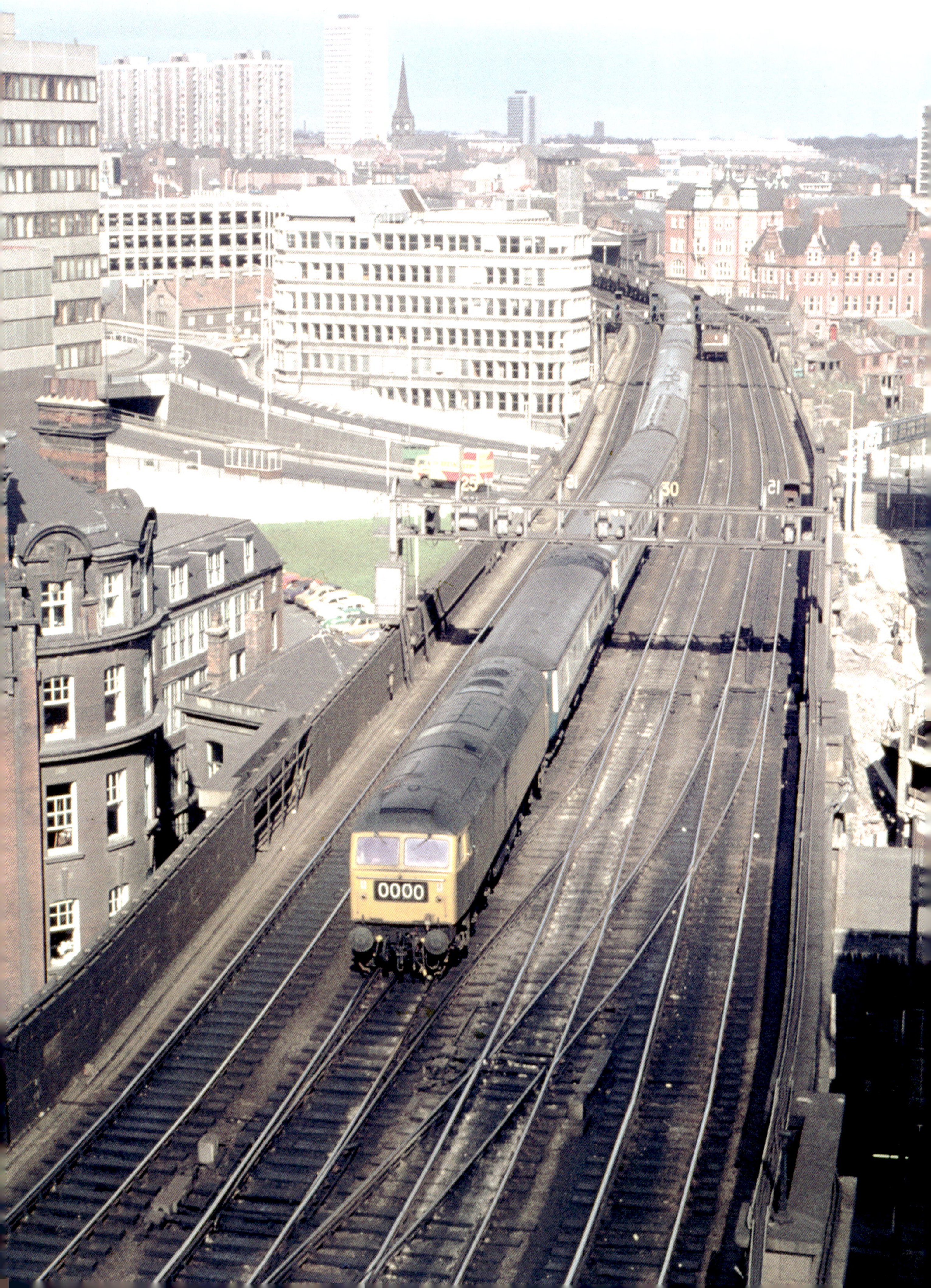
0000
25
30
15

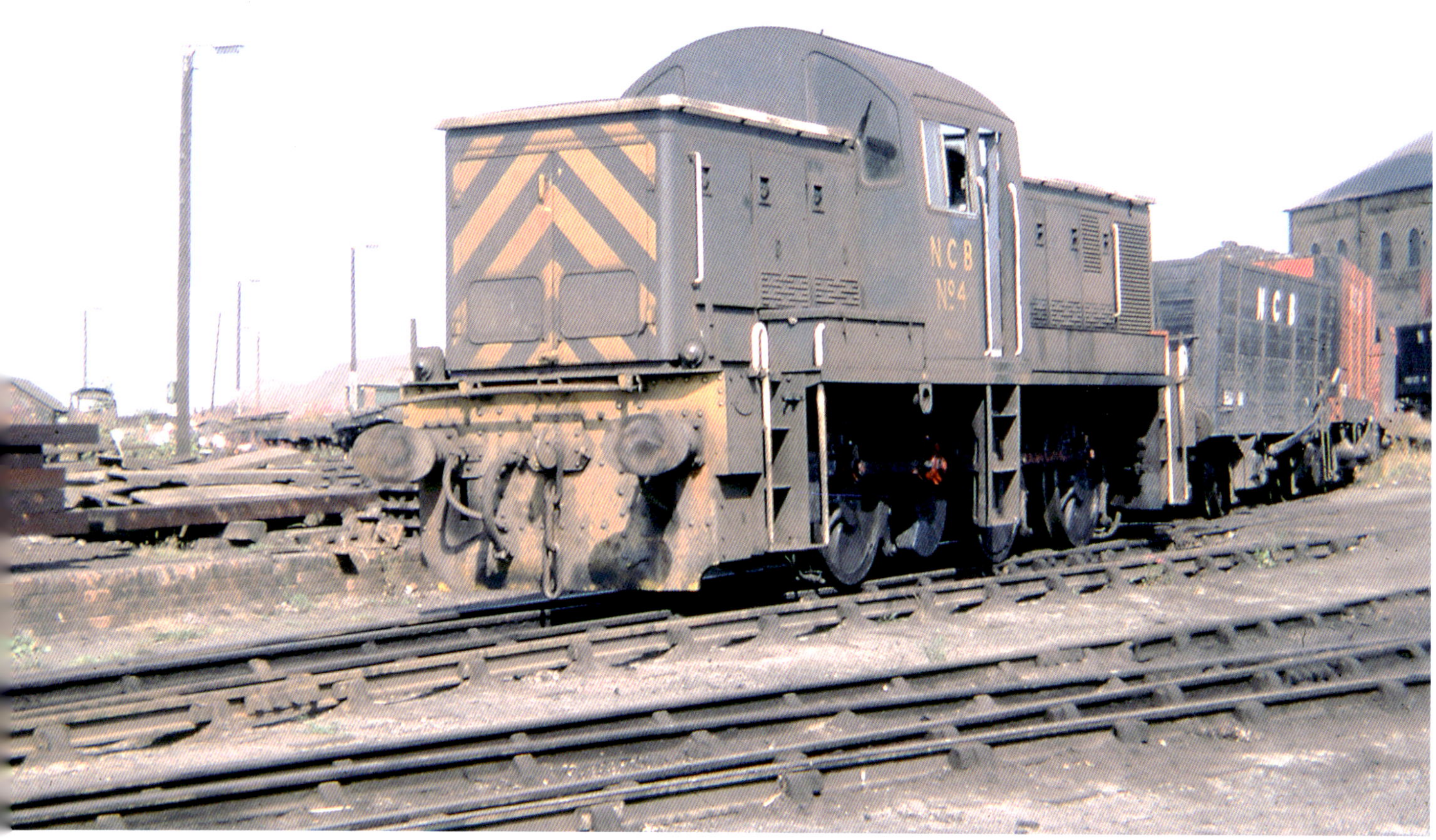

One of the attractions of the complex railway system at Ashington, which linked it to a number of other collieries nearby was the fleet of ex British Rail Class 14 Type 1s. This is the ex D9514 now numbered No.4 in September 1976, whilst below is No.9 which was D9508 taken the same day. ***Both: Alan Rintoul***

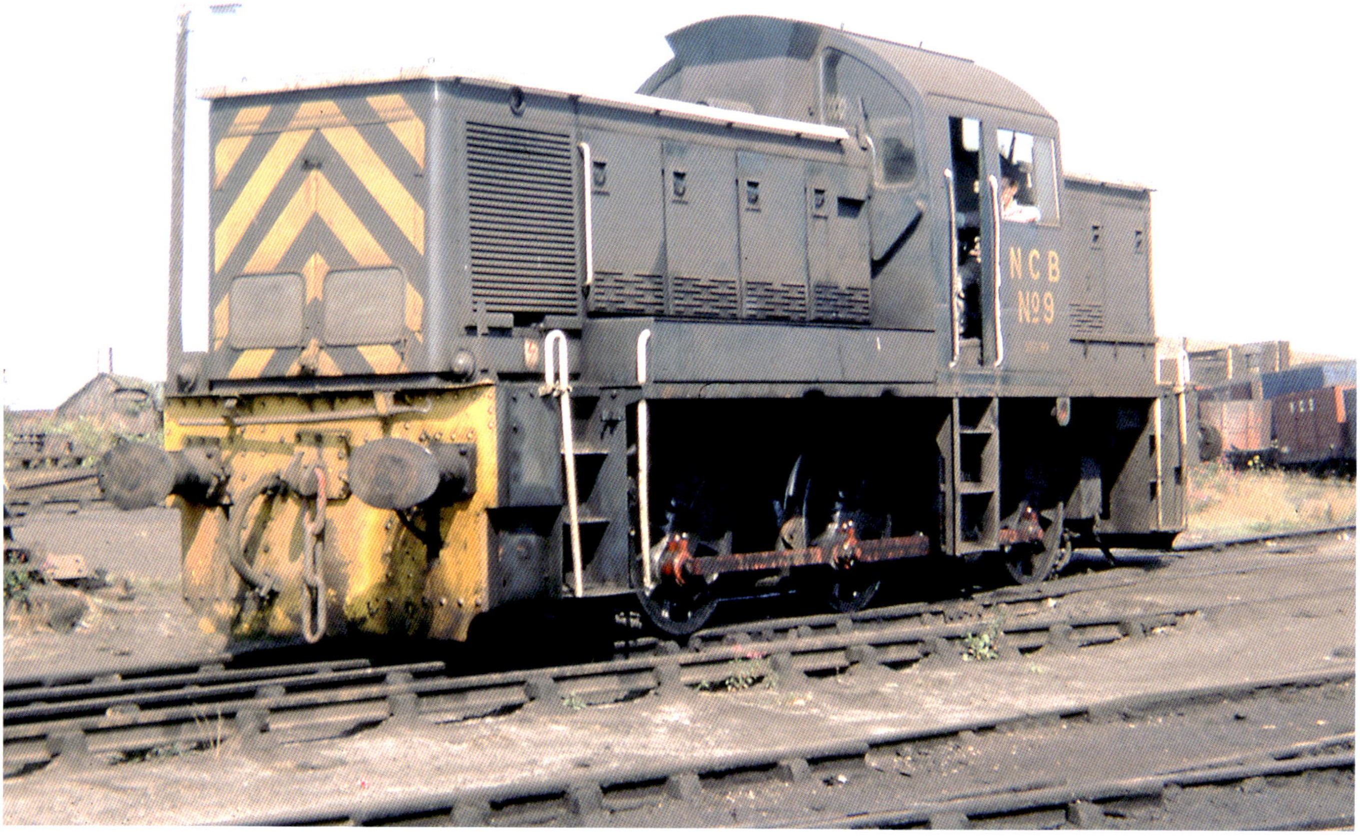

Opposite: A visit on 20 May 1972 sees the ex D9527 now running as 9312/93 in the shed yard at Ashington, eighteen of the class would find their way here, allowing many to be purchased after closure of the system for preservation. ***Frank Hornby***

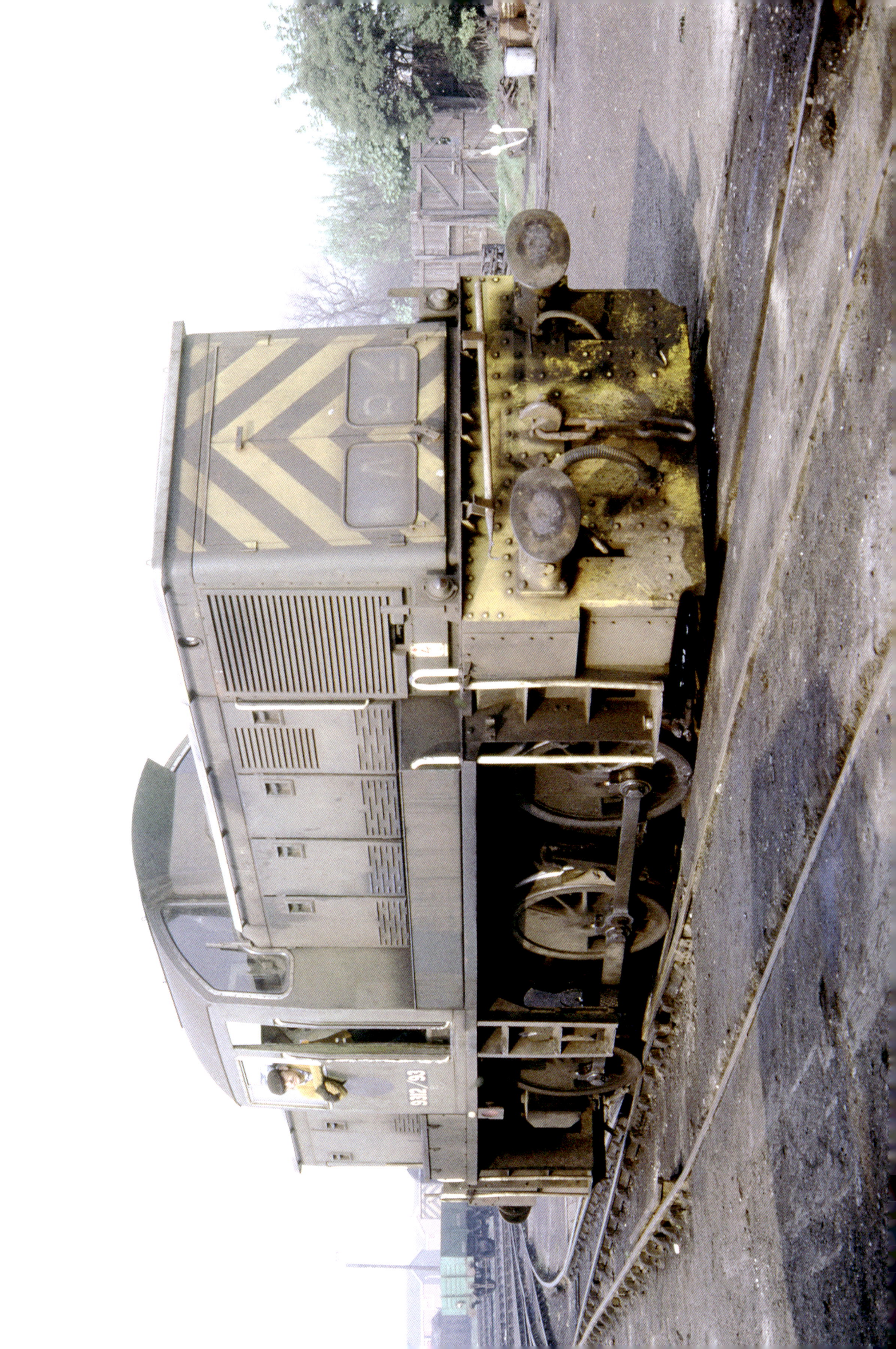

Help To Preserve Our Railway Heritage

Strathwood not only publish books on our railway heritage but have also set up the Railway Photographic Preservation Association as a Charitable Trust to house an archive of images comprising over 200,000 photographic negatives and slides.

The archive was established to not only preserve the collections of over one hundred photographers both living and deceased, but to also make their work available to a younger audience for the future. To achieve this aim, we have begun an energetic programme to publish a considerable number of books. Allied to this we are making as many as possible of the photographs and slides we hold, available as copies to interested enthusiasts, individuals, societies and other publishers.

Many photographers have chosen Strathwood to care for their collections and to publish the best examples of their work for posterity.

If you have negatives or colour slides of transport subjects then we would like to hear from you. We purchase, accept on loan, or welcome donations of material to the archive. Photographers always receive recognition for their work when it is used by publishers (A N Other/Strathwood Library). To answer why so many images are just credited as Strathwood Library Collection in this volume, the reason is we do not know who the original photographer was. This is usually because their collection gets split up via auctions or collectors upon their death with no record of the late photographer for us to credit. Please do not let this happen to your collection. Make contact with us today to discuss what can be done to ensure your work is fully credited and recognised for both today and the future.

Please call us today if you would like to see your work in print, perhaps in a similar fashion to this publication. We also undertake publications to benefit charities and societies on behalf of our contributors. In addition we can store, and catalogue collections on behalf of clubs and societies by way of loan, thereby releasing such groups to concentrate on other aspects of their activities.

Strathwood Ltd,
Glenavon House,
Kinchurdy Road,
Boat of Garten,
Inverness-shire,
PH24 3BP.

Telephone 01479 831139

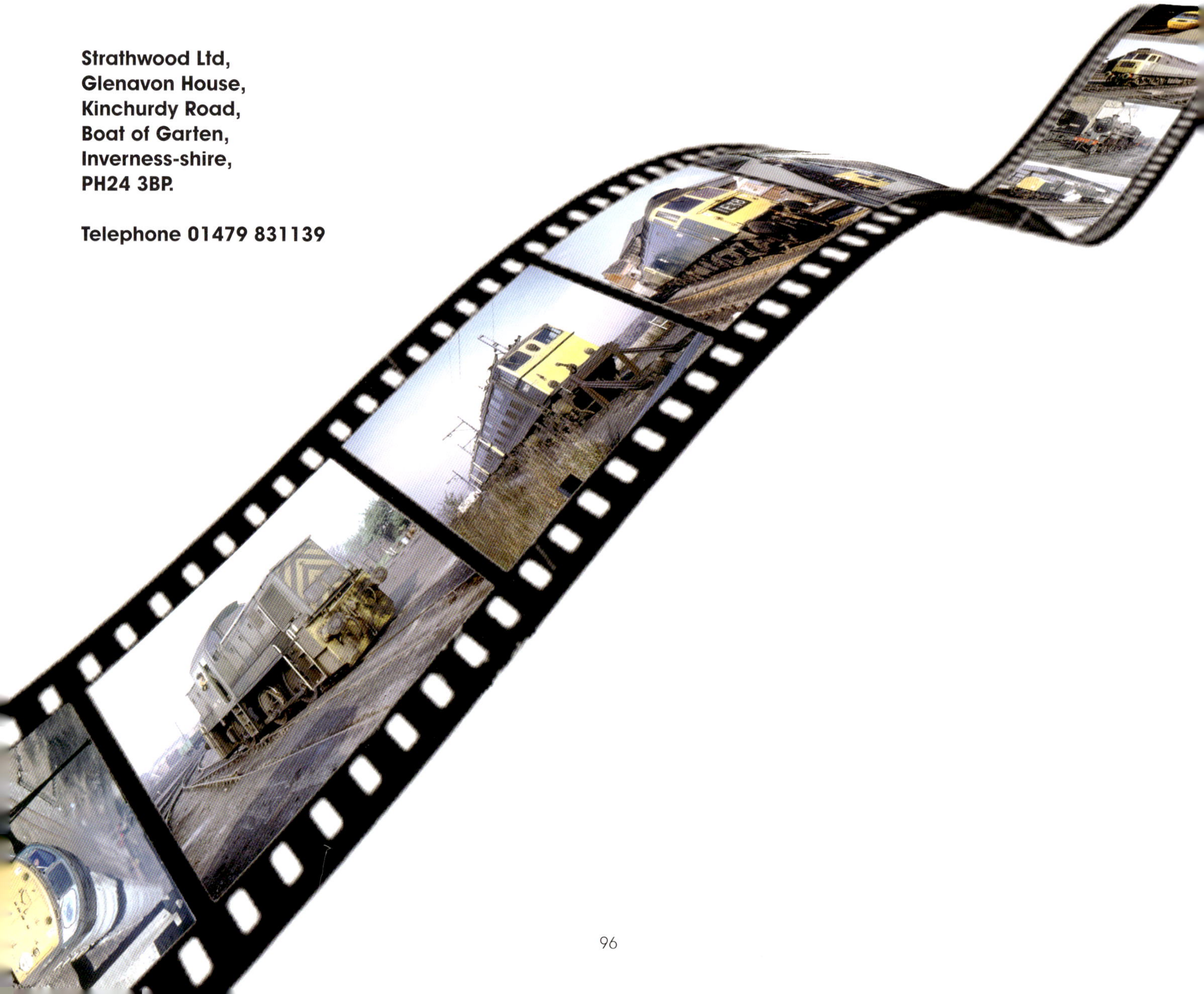